China
in
Disintegration

The Transformation of Modern China Series
James E. Sheridan, General Editor

The Fall of Imperial China
Frederic Wakeman, Jr.

China in Disintegration
The Republican Era in Chinese History, 1912-1949
James E. Sheridan

China at the Center
300 Years of Foreign Policy
Mark Mancall

Intellectuals and the State in Modern China
A Narrative History
Jerome B. Grieder

Mao's China and After
A History of the People's Republic
Maurice Meisner

China
in
Disintegration

China in 1930

China
in
Disintegration

The Republican Era in
Chinese History, 1912–1949

James E. Sheridan

THE FREE PRESS
A Division of Macmillan Publishing Co., Inc.
NEW YORK

Copyright © 1975 by The Free Press
A Division of Macmillan Publishing Co., Inc.

The Free Press
A Division of Macmillan Publishing Co., Inc.
866 Third Avenue, New York, N.Y. 10022

First Free Press Paperback Edition 1977

Library of Congress Catalog Card Number: 74-28940

Printed in the United States of America

printing number
        8   9   10

Library of Congress Cataloging in Publication Data

Sheridan, James E
    China in disintegration.

    (The Transformation of modern China series)
    Bibliography: p.
    Includes index.
    1. China—History—Republic, 1912-1949.
I. Title.
DS744.S54   951.04   74-28940
ISBN 0-02-928610-7
ISBN 0-02-928650-6 pbk.

Contents

List of Maps

Acknowledgments

OF THE DEBTS I have incurred in preparing this book, I am particularly sensible of those to the many writers whose published studies form the basis for so much that I have said in these pages, in most instances without specific acknowledgment. I also have a special feeling of gratitude to those friends who showed me portions of their own unpublished studies relating to the republican era; I have tried to cite every instance in which I have used material from these sources, but I want to acknowledge here the generosity of the scholars who wrote them. Chi Hsi-sheng allowed me to read two chapters of a book-length study of warlordism he is preparing. Diana Lary sent me her dissertation on the Kwangsi Clique. Odoric Wou let me read his expanded dissertation on Wu P'ei-fu. Lloyd Eastman loaned me a draft of his latest book, a study of the Nanking Decade, 1927–1937. At a recent meeting, Eastman and I discovered that each of us had been thinking of national integration as a unifying concept in republican history; these were independent developments, and there was no discussion of the concept in the draft he had earlier loaned to me.

C. Martin Wilbur was extremely kind and helpful in making available materials from the Chinese Oral History Project of Columbia University's East Asian Institute, particularly the reminiscences of Chang Fa-k'uei, which were developed with the aid of questioning by Julie Lien-ying How, and the autobiography of Li Tsung-jen, developed with the assistance of T. K. Tong.

I was fortunate to have Robert H. Wiebe vigorously criticize an early draft of this book. George Dalton gave me splendid editorial advice on one chapter before his departure for research in Europe deprived me of his counsel.

Portions of this book are based on work done while holding a fellowship from the Joint Committee on Contemporary China of the Social Science Research Council and the American Council of Learned Societies; I am very grateful to the Joint Committee and its sponsoring agencies. I am also indebted to Northwestern University for its generous support. However, none of the individuals or organizations mentioned above is in any way responsible for the errors, inadequacies, or general content of this work.

JES
January, 1975

China
in
Disintegration

Introduction

IN THE MIDDLE of the nineteenth century, Western trading nations discovered that the ancient Chinese monarchy was virtually impotent in terms of modern international power. Through the decades that followed, and into the early twentieth century, these nations and Japan forced a host of territorial, economic, and political concessions from China, and ultimately threatened the nation's very existence. China's desperate efforts to meet that threat, combined with the effects of dissident movements and foreign cultural influences, produced a fundamental breakdown in a social system that had existed for centuries. The old order finally disintegrated in the twentieth century in a welter of internal violence, war, and general confusion of personal, social, and cultural values.

In the midst of the wreckage, the compelling necessity to preserve the nation fostered reintegrative movements. Social classes, political groups, and individuals fought savagely to decide who would determine the new political framework and the new social philosophy within which national reintegration could take place. The Chinese Communists won the struggle because they successfully mobilized millions of peasants to defeat their enemies. That mobilization itself constituted an important step toward reintegration, and the Communist-led government established in 1949 created political institutions and launched economic programs designed to create a cohesive and powerful nation. In that fashion, over the course of many decades, an agrarian, traditionalistic, family-centered society of hundreds of millions of illiterate peasants has come to form a dynamic, forward-looking, swiftly industrializing, socialist nation. After years of humiliated helplessness before the armed might of imperialism, China has again claimed the status of great power in world affairs, and has reasserted the ancient dignity of the Chinese people.

This protracted revolutionary transformation occupied more than a century, but in many ways the critical period was the 37 years, 1912–1949, from the fall of the monarchy and founding of a republic to the establishment of the People's Republic of China by the Communists. During this republican period, disintegration and disorder were at their maximum. These were the uncertain years when China was at a turning point in its history and nobody could guess what the future would bring. Indeed, China was so mired in domestic troubles and beset by foreign invaders that there was some doubt that the nation had any future at all as an independent political entity. With the advantages of hindsight, we can now see that the republican era was a transitional period, an historical interregnum between traditional and modern China. It saw the death of one sociopolitical system and the birth of another; emperors and mandarins disappeared in the confusion of the republic, and Communist cadres emerged from it. It is therefore a period of special interest, importance, and complexity. An understanding of its history will cast light on both the traditional agrarian empire it succeeded and the new Communist state that followed.

This book will attempt to analyze the history of the republican era at some length. But it will be useful to begin with a quick overview, a survey in broad and general terms of the entire revolutionary transformation of modern China. This brief analysis will not only serve to introduce events and ideas that later will be treated in more detail, but also will allow for discussion of the concept that gives meaning to those details—the concept of national integration.

National Integration and the Chinese Revolution

THE CONCEPT of national integration has been a central concern of scholars writing about new nations emerging from the tribalism and cultural plurality of colonial Africa, and they have analyzed its meaning in detail.[1] An occasional specialist on China has referred to that country as integrated or disintegrated, but without attempting to show precisely what that means. This oversight is surprising, for the notions of national disintegration and reintegration clarify the central processes of modern Chinese history.

National Integration

National integration refers to the degree of cohesiveness of a nation, the extent to which its various elements interconnect to form a consolidated national unit. One aspect of national integration is territorial—how closely regions and localities are linked together by economic and political transactions and by psychological and cultural similarities. Another is social, which refers to the extent to which the various strata of society—from the ruling elite to the masses—are bound together by a common culture, by national loyalties, by functional specialization and interdependence, and by participation in national movements and undertakings. Although it is useful to distinguish between these two aspects, they are interrelated and overlap in many ways. An examination of the various elements of national integration will show that most of them relate to both aspects, though usually much more to one than the other. Either can provide the primary basis for a degree of national political integration, but the strongest political integration is produced when there exists a high level of both.

The quality and extent of national communication and transport facilities are particularly important for territorial integration. Well-developed networks of roads, railways, navigable waterways, and airlines, together with the necessary vehicles to travel them, all foster the growth of a national market, and population mobility. Movement of a large number of people provides them with familiarity with their nation as a whole, creates a multitude of business and social contacts in various regions and social strata, and cultivates interest in national affairs, all of which strengthen national integration in both of its aspects. Other communications facilities—telegraph, radio, movies, television, newspapers, periodicals, the post office, and books—also influence integration. Where these are well advanced, national consciousness will normally be keener than where they are not.

Government authority is another significant aspect of territorial integration. In a highly integrated nation, the judicial and fiscal power of the government, and the services it offers, can effectively reach to the farthest point and the lowest societal level. Where there is only weak integration, regions and localities may be semi-autonomous, or virtually free from central control.

Interdependence is also an aspect of integration. A nation is integrated to the extent that people in its different sectors and in all social classes and groups are dependent upon one another. Interdependence takes many forms, but the most common is economic. A nation in which people rely upon others throughout the country to fulfill a large portion of their economic needs is more integrated than one in which many areas and groups are largely self-sufficient, which is tantamount to saying that economic modernization fosters territorial integration. In highly industrialized nations, each area's resources and products are widely diffused, and each person, firm, and region is a specialist producer. In the United States, for example, people in, say, southern California are linked with many other parts of the nation through a need for products (cars from Detroit, wheat from Kansas) and markets (for their fruits and movies), and through federal agencies (Interstate Commerce Commission), financial institutions (national insurance companies), transportation facilities (cross-country railways), and the myriad other facilities and institutions not limited to California but necessary for California to function. Moreover, industrialization strengthens many other integrative elements. For instance, an industrialized society has effective communications and transport, facilitating population mobility and fostering the expansion of a shared culture. The same communications network that promotes cultural uniformity allows the government to indoctrinate and control people in all parts of the nation. It is economic modernization, however, with all its diverse effects and influences, that can be the most effective and viable basis for territorial integration.

Territorial integration is strengthened when people in all parts of a nation share the same values and have the same historical heritage, though these are elements that are even more critical in social integration. Generally speaking, the greater the cultural differences between the elite and the masses, the more difficult it is to achieve social integration. Such a culture gap may come about in numerous ways, but the most relevant to note here occurs when an elite adopts the life-style, values, and aspirations associated with "modernization" while the masses continue to live more or less in the traditional fashion. In such circumstances, the elite may become alienated from the population as a whole and define national problems and policies in terms that are either foreign to the actual circumstances or do not appear to the masses to meet their real needs. Social integration is even further weakened when the elite is also internally divided.

Mass participation in the political process provides one possible way of bridging such a gap between elite and masses. Social integration may be strengthened if the population at large participates in elections, decisions about the common defense, and many other public activities. Political participation brings the masses and the elite into contact, informing each about the other, and it can foster a feeling of common endeavor and commitment, a feeling of community.

Ideology can be a powerful integrative force, too, by giving to all individuals not only the same view of themselves and of the rest of the world, but a sense of common purpose as well; it fosters a sense of national unity and identity. Ideology also gives legitimacy to the political system; it supports authority and lends it a moral dimension that enhances its capacity to command the energies and loyalty of the entire people.

Finally, nationalism is a prime component of both aspects of integration, territorial and social. There are many definitions of nationalism. Hans Kohn says that nationalism "is a state of mind, in which the supreme loyalty of the individual is felt to be due the nation-state." Carleton J. H. Hayes sees nationalism as "a fusion of patriotism with a consciousness of nationality." Boyd Shafer defines it as "that sentiment unifying a group of people who have a real or imagined common historical experience and a common aspiration to live together as a separate group in the future."[2] There are many other definitions of nationalism, but nobody has successfully formulated a brief statement that covers all the diverse phenomena incorporated in the term "nationalism" in one or another specific historical context. For present purposes, we may say simply that nationalism is the state of mind of people who feel themselves to be members of a nation, and who give to the nation their primary political loyalty. When that feeling is widely shared, it becomes an important element of national integration.

The meaning of nationalism—the scope of the nationalist state of mind—has changed as the number of people involved in and conscious of national affairs has expanded. When the nation-state first emerged from the dissolution of medieval empires in Europe, the nation was identified with the person of the sovereign. His rights and powers came from God, and nobody else counted in the conception of the nation. Even international law "was primarily a set of rules governing the mutual relations of individuals in their capacity as rulers."[3] After the Napoleonic Wars, the nation came to be identified, for practical purposes, not with the sovereign but with the middle class, and the peasants and workers remained powerless and uninvolved. In the late nineteenth century, this condition too began to change:

The rise of new social strata to full membership of the nation marked the last three decades of the 19th century throughout western and central Europe. Its landmarks were the development of industry and industrial skills; the rapid expansion in numbers and importance of urban populations; the growth of workers' organizations and of the political consciousness of the workers; the introduction of universal compulsory education; and the extension of the franchise. These changes, while they seemed logical steps in a process inaugurated long before, quickly began to affect the content of national policy in a revolutionary way. . . . Henceforth the political power of the masses was directed to improving their own social and economic lot. The primary aim of national policy was no longer merely to maintain order and conduct what was narrowly defined as public business, but to minister to the welfare of members of the nation and to enable them to earn their living. The democratization of the nation . . . had meant the assertion of the political claims of the dominant middle class. The socialization of the nation for the first time brings the economic claims of the masses into the forefront of the picture.[4]

By the early twentieth century, mass participation was the rule in Western nations. Nationalism, the state of mind of those who constitute a nation, became, necessarily, a mass phenomenon in the West. And through Western imperialism, the peoples in Asia and Africa, who had not experienced the same historical development, were brought forcibly into sustained contact with nationalistic attitudes. Ultimately, in self-defense, the Asians and Africans sought to create modern nations of their own. Their view of nationhood also involved the development of industry, the spread of education, and all the other characteristics of the nationalist European states that had created the modern phase of nationalism—these traits had come to define modernization, modern power, the modern nation. Mass participation itself had become an element of modernization.

Nationalism can relate to national integration in two ways. People that are increasingly integrated by the creation of a nation-state, with its unified laws, a common currency, countrywide economic interdependence, widely shared technological growth, and extended communications and educational facilities, will come to think of themselves as forming a nation. They will develop a national state of mind as a consequence of forming a national community of interests and transactions. This process underlay the historical development of Western nation-states

However, it is possible for a national state of mind to exist where economic and technological modernization have not yet happened, or are only beginning. Anti-imperialist resentments, for example, can cultivate a feeling of nationalism that can then be directed to the task of intensive economic modernization. During the past two centuries or so, just such a process has converted a portion of the intellectual elite to nationalism in various colonial, or semi-colonial, traditionalistic agrarian countries, including China. But the elite can achieve little without mass support; the creation of a modern nation requires, as we have noted, mass involvement. Yet nationalistic ideas are not inherently persuasive, particularly to peasant masses whose experiences and needs have always been local. Nationalistic indoctrination of the masses is most rapid and effective where it is linked closely with the satisfaction of strongly felt local needs. When such indoctrination is achieved, a mass nationalism can be generated even where economic modernization and territorial integration are extremely undeveloped.

With some oversimplification, we can say, then, that nationalism can be both an effect and a cause. In the first instance the feeling of nationalism is an outgrowth of national integration, particularly in its territorial aspects, produced by economic modernization. In the second case, the feeling of nationalism comes first, fostering social integration, and setting up a complex of goals that includes economic modernization and a high degree of national integration. The first, which has been the normal pattern in the long-established states of the West, requires an extended period of time, as economic and technological changes gradually alter the living patterns, values, and expectations of the population. The second, which with some variation has been the' more recent pattern in a number of economically underdeveloped colonial countries, requires the forcible and swift alteration of values and expectations, and tries to bring economic and technological conditions into line with both as quickly as possible.

Many of the factors that determine the extent of national integration also operate on small as well as large scales. We can speak of the integration of villages, or other local communities, and also of international integration. But whatever the scale, it is apparent that integrative forces can be joined in a great variety of combinations and intensities. Although we can speak of disintegrated or malintegrated communities, just as we can of integrated communities, we cannot define precisely the point at which one becomes the other, the point two writers call the "threshold of integration."[5] This problem highlights the fallacy of the view that the phrase "national integration" is a tautology because the concept of nation necessarily implies integration.[6] Despite a kernel of truth in this view, it obscures the fact that integration is relative. Some communities, including some nations, are "loosely" or "weakly" integrated, whereas others are "tightly" or "strongly" integrated.

The process by which weakly integrated, traditionalistic peoples have in modern times become more integrated through nationalist movements has been called "social mobilization." Karl Deutsch has explored the ramifications of this concept, and Chalmers Johnson has applied it to China for the period of the anti-Japanese war (1937–1945). The image conveyed by the phrase social mobilization is one of recruiting and welding together small groups to create larger, more cohesive units for special purposes. It is nation building. But as Deutsch has pointed out, the process involves two stages: "The . . . uprooting or breaking away from old settings, habits, and commitments; and . . . the induction of the mobilized persons into some relatively stable new patterns of group membership, organization and commitment."[7] Where elements of a national community exist—but where there is a "weak" national integration—the first stage of "breaking away from old settings, habits, and commitments" may produce a weaker national integration, or disintegration, a changing condition that lasts until stable new patterns of organization and commitment are created. This process has occurred in China during the past century and a half. China has gone from a condition of weak integration under the Manchu Dynasty, to extreme disintegration during the republican period, to a condition of reintegration that is being increasingly consolidated by modernization under the Communists.

Integration in Traditional China

Traditional China was strongly integrated on the local level and somewhat less tightly integrated on the provincial level. On the national level, however, territorial integration was weak even though social integration was strong.

From time immemorial, China has been an agricultural country of peasant masses living in villages where their affections focused. Nonetheless, the peasants did have needs outside the village; they sought to sell some of their agricultural and handicraft products to people from neighboring villages in order to obtain some of their neighbors' produce, local commercial goods, or an occasional item from far away. To meet these needs, market towns developed to serve a cluster of villages; anthropologist William Skinner, who has analyzed their structure, has designated these towns as a "standard market area."

The density of villages in each cluster depended upon geographical, economic, and other local conditions, but 19 or 20 villages in a cluster was about average. Although economic needs led to their formation, these village clusters also served as the framework for the peasants' recreational and social life. They provided marriage partners, friends, and constituted the unit for control and guidance by the local gentry. Rural organizations, such as secret societies, lineage groups, and occupational associations, all took the standard marketing area as their unit of organization and activity. Weights and measures were standardized and closely regulated throughout each area, varying from one standard marketing area to another. Each adult knew virtually every other inhabitant in his cluster of villages, which fostered common speech patterns along with a kind of parochial patriotism. All these traits reflect a high degree of integration on the village-cluster level. "Insofar as the Chinese peasant can be said to live in a self-contained world," says Skinner, "that world is not the village but the standard marketing community."[8]

These clusters of rural communities, however, were only loosely bound to the larger national entity. Some long-distance trade occurred in luxury items, but not a great deal. Transportation facilities were primitive in many regions. Most goods were shipped by human power, an expensive mode of transport that sharply limited the range within which exchange could take place. Most agricultural activities required little or no labor or resources from people or agencies outside of the community, including the central government. Each peasant family tended its own land, although at harvest time neighbors and relatives helped. Those rich enough to own draft animals rented them to the poor, and the poor rented their muscles to the rich. These transactions, however, seldom extended beyond the basic market area. One economic historian reports that:

> An appraisal of the actual performance of the Ming and Ch'ing governments and the effect of that performance on farm output . . . [shows] that Chinese farmers did sometimes benefit from official activities, but that the actions that benefited them most tended to be those carried out by local authorities. Only rarely did the rural Chinese economy require much that the central government in Peking was able to give.[9]

Despite one prominent scholar's insistence that flood and irrigation facilities required centralized control, it was the villages themselves or district government agencies that managed water control, at least after the fourteenth century. One dramatic indication of the economic self-containment of localities and regions is that there were so many local and regional famines, and so little effective aid from nearby localities and regions.

Ties other than economic were similarly weak beyond the basic rural community. Associations such as secret societies operated within the standard market area. Trade and merchant guilds were local in character. Even kinship ties diminished with distance. There was little geographical or occupational mobility, partly because of poverty and the dearth of travel facilities and partly because of the powerful ethnocentric affection Chinese had for their home localities. Traditional Chinese would have understood perfectly the Boston matron who sympathized with the man who traveled four days by train from the West Coast to Boston saying: "I have never traveled that far. But then, I am already here."

Language played an ambivalent role. The Chinese written language, stable and changing little over the centuries, and with only negligible regional variation, exercised a powerful integrative influence in the country as a whole. Yet only a minority of Chinese were literate. The vast majority knew only spoken Chinese, and variations in the spoken tongue were great. Several mutually unintelligible dialects divided China into major linguistic regions; local differences in spoken Chinese were also common within linguistic areas, emphasizing the isolation and specific identity of each local community.

Local integration was so strong, and national integration so feeble, that one scholar has found it "surprising . . . that China held together at all."[10] What were the national integrative bonds? What did hold China together? The most important forces of national integration were the monarchy, the state bureaucracy, a general uniformity of culture with the Confucian value system at its core, and, perhaps surprisingly, the local gentry.

There is no reason to believe that the mass of the Chinese people had intense feelings of loyalty to the Chinese emperor. Even so, they accepted him, tacitly acknowledging the legitimacy of his rule, and were vaguely aware that large numbers of other peasants, as well as town dwellers, similarly acquiesced in his suzerainty. They knew that his mere existence and the ritual functions he exercised as emperor somehow symbolized the unity of all Chinese. The emperor, moreover, had power to appoint and remove provincial and local officials, to punish criminals, and to issue decrees that affected the lives of the people. The emperor's nationwide power had a crucial influence on national integration.

The national bureaucracy was a powerful integrative force. As an agency of the court, its functions were to carry the authority of the monarchy to all parts of the country. Bureaucrats were selected by examinations, which fostered the development of an educational system throughout the country that used identical texts and spread the same values and world view. The ideals of public service it taught were not qualified by regional considerations. Moreover, the national character of the bureaucracy was reflected in the recruiting system, which was both nationwide and uniform and used quotas to ensure that every region was represented. The national quality of the bureaucracy was particularly symbolized by the law of avoidance, which forbade an official to hold office in his home province, where local obligations might interfere with his national duties and loyalties. Because the bureaucracy was the chief source of wealth and power in the nation, it was the natural career goal for all ambitious and able men, including peasants. Thus the aspirations and dreams of those in all localities and in all social strata were focused on a national institution.

Such aspirations helped make the local gentry one element of national integration. This gentry consisted of the local political and economic elite, including the Confucian literati who had studied for the examinations. It was especially composed, however, of those who had passed one or more of the civil-service examinations and had not attained office. When officials retired from the bureaucracy, they often returned to their rural homes and became part of the local gentry, which had two characteristics, local and national. Its members had superior local roles as landlords, businessmen, and spokesmen for their localities. In that capacity, they represented their localities and defended local interests against the national. But the gentry also functioned as a kind of unofficial lowest echelon of the central bureaucracy. National officials treated the local gentry with special courtesy, and normally dealt with localities through it. The local gentry thus constituted the administrative connection between the localities and the national bureaucracy, and in that fashion served, like the bureaucracy itself, as a component of territorial integration.

Because of its dual aspect, too, the local gentry fostered national social integration. It was a class of people that functioned within, and contributed to local communities, and it was accepted as such by the peasantry, with whom the gentry had constant and close contact. But the gentry also represented the Confucian literati that ruled the nation at all levels. By exemplifying and preaching values accepted by the masses, the gentry was living evidence that Chinese society was operating in accordance with sound principles.

These principles were expressed by Confucian orthodoxy, the major element in integrating traditional China. The precise denotation of "Confucianism" has changed through history; Han Confucianism differed from Chou Confucianism, and Sung Confucianism —the official orthodoxy until the twentieth century—was not the same as that of the Han. Moreover, within each of these variants were intellectual currents that though purporting to be Confucian differed from the mainstream of Confucianism. Without attempting to define comprehensively Confucianism as it existed in the Ch'ing Dynasty, it is worth noting some of its most salient features, features that were so thoroughly accepted by all Chinese as to have a powerful integrative force.

Central to Confucianism was a patriarchal family system in which status was determined by age, sex, and generation; elders dominated younger, and male dominated female. Filial piety was the chief virtue, but all other obligations of superiority and subordination inherent in the family hierarchy—such as those between older and younger brothers and between generations—were also strictly observed. Confucian values spread far beyond the family to permeate all of Chinese life and institutions. Chinese law, for example, enforced the Confucian tenets of family relationships and discriminated according to Confucian notions of age, generation, and sex. Familial values acquired religious force through the practice of ancestor worship.

Confucian economic thought emphasized the basic importance of agriculture. Commerce was nonproductive, parasitic by nature, and engaged in only by little men preoccupied with selfish motives of profit. This fundamental Confucian value was a potent force in traditional and modern China, but it does not follow that commerce was unimportant in traditional China nor that Confucianists were invariably hostile to it. In certain periods, such as the Han and the Sung, commerce flourished, and created great fortunes. However, merchants never acquired political power. And though at all times some Confucian families were drawn by the lure of wealth to dip into commercial activities, they were invariably careful not to endanger their positions as Confucian scholars or bureaucrats.

Confucianism also stressed the unity of the empire under a monarchical, centralized government. The monarch and his officials were supposed to rule through moral force. Not only was moral rule—rule in accord with Confucian prescriptions—held to be the most effective way to gain obedience and social harmony, but a monarch who departed from that rule would lose the Mandate of Heaven, the supernatural sanction of his authority. According to the Confucianists, the chief exemplars of moral rule were the ancient sage kings, and the entire educational system was devoted to studying their achievements and the principles that presumably inspired them. Confucianism, then, was profoundly traditionalistic; it aimed not at a great future, but at the recreation of a golden past.

These Confucian values and assumptions were thoroughly drilled into all educated Chinese, and in large measure they filtered down through the centuries to become part of the value system of the mass of the people. Chinese at every social level accepted them and generally tried to live in accordance with them. Thus Confucianism cultivated a profound social integration expressed by similar patterns of life in all parts of the country, and by values and a world view shared by peasants as well as the elite.

Confucianist integration was flawed, however, by conflicting class interests. Members of the gentry, as landowners, exploited the peasantry economically, and as allies of the bureaucracy they exercised political power, as in the collection and remission of taxes, at the expense of the peasantry. There were, of course, many other groups in Chinese society whose interests connected with, but were not exactly the same as, those of either the peasantry or the elite. Porters, pedlars, vagabonds, secret societies, and bandit groups were all important strands in the complex fabric of Chinese society. But even these diverse elements fell naturally into local groups, and by and large they accepted the fundamentals of the Confucian value system in which they all lived and functioned. Perhaps the simplest illustration of that fact is that most peasant revolts were local in nature and aimed to change the personnel who manipulated the Confucian order—officials and the emperor himself—but not the order itself.

Confucianism advanced territorial integration by promoting the idea of a broad political community of all men under Heaven, and it specifically legitimized the rule of the emperor and his officials over all parts of the country. But other aspects of Confucianism had an opposite influence. Confucian emphasis on the primacy of family relations inhibited the development of truly national loyalties. And Confucian economic ideas were at least partly responsible for China's very weak economic integration. The chief integrative force of Confucianism was social, and over the centuries it produced an extraordinarily high degree of social integration. Premodern China often disintegrated territorially, but because of Confucianism the social cohesion of the Chinese people was never significantly damaged.

Only in the twentieth century did China disintegrate both socially and territorially.

Disintegration

In the late nineteenth and early twentieth centuries, the traditional bonds of national integration in China began to fray, to weaken in effectiveness. Ultimately, they broke almost completely. Through the second half of the nineteenth century, the monarchy's power to exact obedience steadily diminished. After the English defeated China in the Opium War (1839–1842), China suffered a successive series of defeats by foreigners through the remainder of the nineteenth century, and each defeat reduced the moral and physical resources of the monarchy. In the wake of a great agrarian-millenarian revolution in the middle of the century, regional armies under provincial officials emerged as the predominant military power in the country. The expansion of provincial power, growing domestic distress, the court's failure to deal effectively with foreign missionary, commercial, and military incursions, and a growing movement for constitutional government, combined to undermine the legitimacy of the monarchy. The Chinese attributed their troubles to the alien origins of the ruling Ch'ing Dynasty, which also undercut the dynasty's authority. By 1911, the Manchu Court was so devoid of power and legitimacy that revolutionaries overthrew it with ease, thus severing completely that traditionally integrative bond.

The cohesive influence of the traditional bureaucracy also declined during this period. The waning of monarchical power from the middle of the nineteenth century meant a reduction in the effective authority of court officials. In 1905 the court abolished the civil-service-examination system as a means of selecting officials; thus the Confucian intellectual and institutional aspects of the civil-service system, which had been such important sources of national cohesion, disappeared. The whole future of the bureaucracy became problematical, and Chinese education no longer hewed strictly to Confucian orthodoxy. The status of the bureaucracy was further undermined when, as the first phase of a series of constitutional reforms, the court in 1908 created elected provincial assemblies. These assemblies promptly became centers of provincial power that, in effect, challenged the remnants of central authority.

In this context, local gentry looked less and less to the national government as the source of wealth and honor, and increasingly occupied itself with local and provincial matters. In the last years of the Ch'ing Dynasty, many members of the gentry were active in the provincial assemblies, where they vigorously asserted local and provincial interests. The local elite also began to acquire a smattering of Western education and began to venture into new kinds of business activities and to express new political ideas. Some advocated vigorous anti-imperialist policies, others economic modernization, in most instances with a strong local or provincial orientation.

In this fashion, the major elements of territorial integration virtually disappeared. Confucianism, the major bastion of social integration, was also under attack. Confucian philosophy was incompatible with Western industrial civilization, but under the pressure of militarily superior imperialist powers, Chinese literati in the mid-nineteenth century were forced to borrow a few elements of Western weaponry and technology in an attempt to give China the strength to resist further Western encroachments. When that proved inadequate, Confucian reformers declared that more thorough Westernization was acceptable as long as it was for expedient utilitarian purposes only; they maintained, however, that Confucianism should continue to be the source of China's basic values. When this adaptation of Confucianism also proved too limiting, some reformers were driven to claim that Confucianism, if properly understood, approved of modernizing innovation, an argument tantamount to admitting that Westernization was inevitable, as indeed it appeared to be by the end of the nineteenth century. The termination of the civil-service system and its rewards at the beginning of the twentieth century confirmed that impression, and demonstrated that Confucian political philosophy and moral values were no longer the direct path to political power; this change in policy also diminished the appeal and relevance of Confucianism. By the early 1900s, a few intellectuals had gone so far as to repudiate Confucianism, though they represented only a minute portion of the Chinese elite. A larger number was reconciled to accepting some Western ways, but hoped to preserve the Confucian core of Chinese civilization. Even before this time, Chinese businessmen had adopted Western modes of business, especially in the treaty ports, and after the turn of the century there began to emerge a small group of professionals trained along Western lines. Despite these portentous changes, however, the basic moral and social values of Chinese life were still essentially Confucian, and the bulk of the elite as well as the mass of the peasantry were still committed to them. Thus, while territorial disintegration was far advanced, social disintegration had only begun.

The Revolution of 1911 greatly accelerated territorial disintegration. With the elimination of the monarchy, the last major check on provincial autonomy disappeared, and warlordism emerged. Between 1916 and 1928, the struggle among independent militarists—warlords—tore China into fragments, and the formal political machinery of the republic that had succeeded the monarchy—the parliament, ministries, and so forth—became largely irrelevant to the realities of Chinese political life. At the head of their personal armies, the warlords dominated districts, provinces, and regions, and warred with neighboring generals for additional territory and revenues. The Chinese people, particularly the peasants, paid for warlord anarchy with blood, possessions, and hope.

The establishment in 1912 of a Western-style republic, however, opened the floodgates to new and larger waves of Western influence, which further subverted traditional social integration. During the early years of the republic, an increasing number of intellectuals concluded that selective Westernization could never meet China's needs, and that the entire Confucian tradition would have to be repudiated as irrelevant to the modern world. This view was especially convincing to ardently anti-imperialistic young Chinese who had been educated in some measure along Western lines. In the years after 1915 to the early 1920s—in what was called the May Fourth Movement—these youngsters led a great national drive to repudiate Confucianism, and they immersed themselves in an orgy of Westernization. Yet the May Fourth Movement was above all an intellectual one, centered in the cities and in the universities and spread by periodicals and books. The intellectuals seized upon many aspects of Western thought, some of which, however, were incompatible with others. Out of this movement came converts to Marxism, to anarchism, liberalism, and a host of other isms. The May Fourth Movement signaled the coming of age of a new, Westernized intellectual elite, with deep internal divisions. The new elite was not a functioning part of existing institutions, and it was largely cut off from the peasant masses of China. Indeed, rural China—the China of the peasants—was hardly touched by it, and continued to live by its Confucian values and traditional institutions. This dichotomy between the elite and the masses resulted in acute social disintegration.

By the early 1920s, with central government a shambles, with provincial and local independence backed by a welter of warlord armies large and small, with the nation's ethical and philosophical guidelines in disarray and disrepute, and the intellectual elite internally divided and alienated from the Chinese peasantry, national disintegration could hardly have been more extreme.

Reintegration

In the midst of this disunity and turmoil, one thing was clear: the reintegration of China required the destruction of warlord power. But beyond that there was much disagreement; leading politicians and intellectuals held conflicting views about such basic issues as the form of the next government, the role of the masses in the nation's political life, the goals of government policies, and the rate and kind of Westernization needed.

In the early 1920s, two political parties arose to seek national unity, and the power to realize their own respective visions of the nation's future. One was the Kuomintang, which traced its history to the revolutionaries who fought to overthrow the Manchu Dynasty.* It had declined in vigor since those days, but in 1924 it was

---

* Kuomintang is variously translated as the National Party, the National People's Party, and in other ways, but most commonly the Nationalist Party. However, it is often not translated at all; the transliterated Chinese name has acquired widespread currency throughout the world, and will be used here. One great advantage of this practice is that it avoids the possibility of confusing "nationalist" as a noun or adjective with the name of the party. The transliter-

restructured as a disciplined, vibrant revolutionary organization. The other was the Communist Party, established in 1921 by intellectuals who had been moved by the Russian Revolution and the persuasiveness of Marxism-Leninism. The two parties at first joined forces to destroy warlordism and to establish a strong national government that could resist imperialism and improve the lives of China's millions. The coalition also conducted a military campaign that successfully gained control of most of China south of the Yangtze River. At that point, however, internal contradictions split it asunder. Cooperation turned into hostility, and the two parties began the civil war that would continue sporadically until 1949. Nonetheless, Kuomintang General Chiang Kai-shek continued the military expedition to achieve national unification. In 1928 the armies he led defeated the remaining northern warlords. The Kuomintang declared the nation unified, and organized what was proclaimed to be a new national government for all of China.

Chiang Kai-shek acknowledged that China badly needed an "integrating force," and he thought the Kuomintang represented that force. In that he was wrong. The Kuomintang failed in its unifying efforts, and it was left to the Communists to bring the nation together again.

Chiang made some progress in integrating China territorially. Although the provinces nominally accepted the establishment of the new central government, the warlords after 1928 continued to rule most of the provinces with high-handed independence. Nonetheless, through military and political actions, Chiang did gradually reduce their autonomy, so that by 1936 the national government's writ had at least limited effectiveness in most provinces. By that time, too, Chiang had successfully forced the Communists out of regions in central China, where for several years they had resisted government campaigns against them, and driven them into the barren reaches of the northwest. Chiang's accomplishments in territorial integra-

---

ated name of the Communist Party, Kungch'antang, is rarely used, though during the Second World War the Communists briefly followed a policy of using only the transliteration in English language news releases to put themselves in the same category as the Kuomintang—thereby avoiding some of the unfavorable connotations that the English name had to American readers.

tion were largely achieved by exacting political obedience through military and political pressure, but he also undertook a number of economic reforms. His government built some roads, unified the national currency, improved banking facilities, and initiated other measures of economic modernization. Presumably, the effects of Chiang's programs, and similar projects that would have come later, would have ultimately filtered through the country, creating territorial integration by means of greater communication and economic cohesion and producing within the Chinese community changes that would have finally facilitated social integration. But that required time, and time was short in China. In 1937 Japan invaded the country, occupied northern China, the Yangtze Valley, and the whole coastal region, and the Kuomintang's modernization programs were disrupted and eventually brought to an end.

Under Chiang's government, there were two Chinas: one was the modern, semi-Westernized cities of the eastern coastal provinces, inhabited by an urban elite of Westernized intellectuals, businessmen, merchants, professionals, and officials who had little contact with life in the countryside; the other was rural China, unchanged in its poverty, ignorance, and hardship, the helpless prey of local officials, warlords, and the conservative local gentry. The national elite was itself divided, and even that portion that accepted Kuomintang leadership was not unified. It included old and new militarists who were satisfied to rule by the gun; it included traditionalists who dreamed of restoring the past; and it included Westernized Chinese who lived and thought almost exclusively in the Western fashion, somewhat like aliens in their own land. But it included too few Chinese who had the capacity to apply modern concepts and skills in a pragmatic fashion to solve Chinese problems in a Chinese context. This elite was therefore completely unprepared to meet the needs of China's millions, to spur and inspire the peasants to break with the old ways, institutions, and thoughts and to work to create a new and modern nation.

Chiang not only failed to promote social integration, but his own party and government were shot through with factionalism, corruption, and inefficiency. They ignored in practice the most progressive aspects of the ideology they preached. Party and government personnel so abused their authority that their actions gave the lie to

Kuomintang ideology, which thus lost any power to persuade or inspire China's vast population.

Those who supported the Kuomintang inside and outside of China often maintained that the efforts of Chiang and his party during the prewar decade, 1927–1937, represented reasonable and practicable moves in the direction of political and economic modernization, and would have produced national reintegration. That may, indeed, be true. This book will not argue that the Communists offered the only possible route—the "inevitable" route—to modernization and national integration. But whatever unifying potential was inherent in the Kuomintang's programs ended abruptly when Japan invaded China in earnest in 1937. As we have noted, the "threshold of integration" is difficult to define with precision, but in any case the Kuomintang did not reach it. The Communists, on the other hand, did. And here, too, the Japanese invasion was critical, for it provided the opportunity—indeed, the necessity—for new integrative alternatives to emerge.

During the anti-Japanese war, the Communists came to control large territories behind Japanese lines in northern China. There they mobilized the peasants along nationalist lines by effectively fulfilling their urgent local needs. The Communists thereby gained the confidence and support of the peasantry whose energies they then channeled toward achieving nationalist and modernizing goals —and victory over the Kuomintang.

One compelling need of the peasantry was defense. When the Japanese invaded north China, central government troops and officials retreated, leaving the peasants defenseless. The Japanese occupied only the cities and lines of communication, not the countryside. However, they repeatedly raided the rural areas and treated the peasants with great cruelty. In response, the Communists organized local defense efforts and, indeed, complete local and regional governments behind Japanese lines. These military and political organizations fostered nationalistic and patriotic feelings of pride. Under Communist guidance the peasant quickly came to understand that the defense of his life, his family, and his village was part of a larger defense of the Chinese people and nation as a whole. In that fashion, vast numbers of peasants, by seeking to protect themselves and their villages, were swept into a larger national movement of resistance. At the same time, the Communists initiated political and economic reforms that destroyed the traditional economic and political power structures in the rural communities, and, in effect, began the modernization of the peasantry. They gave the peasant honest government and reduced extortionate rent, taxes, and interest payments. Ultimately, they redistributed the land and properties of landlords and organizations. New political institutions were created that tied the peasants more closely to central governmental authority and gave them a participatory role they never had before. There was a surprisingly successful attempt to reduce or eliminate the most oppressive aspects of the traditional rural social order, perhaps best symbolized by the emancipation of women from their age-old subservience. Communist education and propaganda stressed the need for a new social order for the new Chinese nation.

In this way, the Communists organized a de facto state within a de jure state they did not yet control; theirs was a cohesive, dynamic, modernizing enclave state in the midst of disintegrated, demoralized China. By the end of the war against Japan, the Communists governed almost 100 million people, perhaps a fifth of the total population of China. Through Communist education and propaganda, and especially through their own participation in a national endeavor, these millions acquired a new national spirit; mass nationalism—modern nationalism—was born in China. Somewhat paradoxically, it was on the solid basis of this mass nationalism that the Communists swept to victory over the "Nationalist" leader, Chiang Kai-shek.

Whereas Chiang had expected economic modernization to produce territorial and, ultimately, social integration, the Communists achieved a high level of social integration through social mobilization and reform before they had much of an opportunity to undertake economic modernization. That opportunity finally came when the civil war ended in 1949 and the People's Republic of China was founded. The Communist government swiftly launched a comprehensive program of economic and technological development. At the same time, educational and propaganda facilities were used intensively to cultivate in the Chinese people throughout the country a firm commitment to national development and power as conceived by the Communist government. Many new organizations came into being, organizations for youth, labor, women, peasants, students. Old associational ties and behavioral patterns were destroyed and new bonds of national scope were strengthened. Frequent "rectification campaigns" have served, among other things, to reduce the gap between the elite and the masses which intense technological modernization works to broaden. In these and other ways, China has moved toward stronger and stronger territorial and social integration. The process has not been smooth and unilinear, but unquestionably China since 1949 has achieved an extent of national integration it has never known before.

This chapter has offered the most cursory sketch of China's disintegration and reintegration. Now it is time to examine in more detail one part of that process, the four decades of disintegration that began with the birth of the republic from the 1911 Revolution.

II

The Birth of the Republic

IN THE AUTUMN of 1911, a few soldiers in central China launched a desperate revolt against the monarchy. Small in scope and lacking effective leadership, their uprising appeared doomed. It was but a puff when measured against the vast upheavals that had punctuated China's long history. Yet within a few short months the age-old Chinese monarchy had disappeared, and a Chinese republic had come into being. What lay behind these dramatic changes? What did they augur for China?

Revolutionary hagiography and myth have long obscured the Revolution of 1911. The Kuomintang has cultivated the notion that the revolution was largely the work of Sun Yat-sen and his revolutionary party, the precursor of the Kuomintang, fighting selflessly for nationalism and democracy. This version of the revolt is an incomplete and highly idealized view of history. The Revolution of 1911 was produced by the convergence of several historical currents that flowed out of the nineteenth century. It is an oversimplification, but basically true, to say that the erosion of Manchu legitimacy fatally weakened the monarchy, so that only a mild push was necessary to topple it; that the revolutionary movement provided the push, and also the goal of a republican form of government; and that autonomous provinces and independent armed forces determined the course of the revolution and the distribution of real power after the dust had settled.

The Revolutionary Movement

After three years of sporadic violence, the British in 1842 defeated China in the Opium War and exacted certain commercial concessions in the treaty that followed. That defeat was the first in a long series suffered by China at the hands of imperialist powers during the nineteenth and twentieth centuries, and the first in a network of one-sided agreements that the Chinese call the "unequal treaties." Each defeat persuaded more Chinese that governmental reform was necessary. Immediately after the Opium War, in which China was unable to defend itself against modern weapons, a handful of officials declared that China should build Western-style guns and ships—but they were isolated voices. By the 1860s, a number of leading officials had accepted the idea that China would have to strengthen itself through limited borrowing from the West, particularly for weapons but also for industry, communications, and organization. By the end of the century reformers were prepared to go much further and adopt even Western political concepts, such as parliamentary government. The Manchu Court countenanced some modernization, particularly in the military field, but lagged far behind what the most radical reformers advocated. A few Chinese finally concluded that reform under the emperor was impossible, or would come so slowly as to be too late. They decided that China could save itself only by removing the Manchu rulers, and that meant revolution.

Until 1900 the revolutionary movement was tiny and feeble. In the years that immediately followed, however, it expanded with rapidity as Chinese impotence in foreign affairs made drastic remedies seem necessary. Ironically, it was the implementation by the court of educational reforms in the early years of the twentieth century that abetted this expansion. The reforms included the creation of Western-type schools in China and the dispatch of Chinese abroad to study. The students who went to Europe, America, and Japan learned how backward China was in some realms compared with industrial nations. This honed their desire to change that state of affairs quickly, and led them increasingly to condemn the Manchus for China's retarded development.

By 1905 several small revolutionary organizations had come into existence, and in that year most of them were brought together into a single revolutionary organization led by Sun Yat-sen, the T'ung-meng-hui. The name is variously translated, most often as Revolutionary Alliance, Chinese League, or United League. Sun Yat-sen did not share the gentry-intellectual background that was more or less typical of the young intellectuals who made up the bulk of the membership of the new organization. Born in a peasant family in Kwangtung, Sun left home as a boy to live with a brother in Hawaii, where he was educated in Christian schools along Western lines. He later studied medicine in a British school in Hong Kong. For several years, Sun divided his interest between medicine and political reform, but finally rejected both for revolution. As his biographer says, Sun became the country's first professional revolutionary. He founded his first revolutionary organization in 1895 and, with secret society allies, launched an attack on Canton. It was a fiasco, but it marked the beginning of Sun's reputation as a revolutionary. Subsequent revolutionary activity—and the frantic Manchu reaction to Sun—enhanced his reputation and largely accounted for the welcome accorded him when he arrived in Tokyo in 1905, where young Chinese intellectuals had despaired of the nation's salvation as long as the Manchus ruled in Peking. It was in this context that the United League was organized in Tokyo, and though it embraced an enormous diversity of views, ranging from anarchism to Buddhism, it represented the mainstream of the revolutionary movement from then until 1911.

The overriding goal of the league was to end Manchu rule in China; all other declared political and social ends were completely secondary. The revolutionaries claimed that the Manchu conquest of China some three centuries earlier had been barbarous in its cruelty, that the Manchus had discriminated against Chinese ever since, and that racial inferiority rendered the Manchus incompetent to deal with imperialist aggressions against China. By emphasizing alleged racial differences between Manchus and Chinese, the revolutionaries tried to marshal the full force of Chinese ethnocentrism against them. Moreover, the issue of race was one on which all the revolutionaries could agree. The revolutionary camp was divided by personalities, factions, regional differences, divergent political views, and other factors, but everyone in it sought to overturn the Manchu Dynasty. Unfortunately, by blaming the Manchus for all of China's troubles, the radicals avoided the hard necessity of examining Chinese social and political history to find the sources of China's weakness during the nineteenth and twentieth centuries.

The revolutionaries also criticized the Manchus for unwillingness to modernize. That criticism became less persuasive after the turn of the century, however, when the court instituted a series of reform measures designed to achieve precisely the kind of changes the radicals had been demanding for years. The revolutionary camp declared that the Manchu reforms were nothing but a smokescreen, a cruel hoax on those Chinese who were foolish enough to believe in them, and it demanded additional changes that the Manchus simply could not accept. The United League sought a cluster of interconnected goals, including the formation of a republic, national unity and military strength, and the establishment of equality and freedom. The republic was the key. The revolutionaries held that a republic was the most advanced form of government, and that China should leap into the vanguard of history by adopting it. To do otherwise, Sun Yat-sen often argued, would be the same as building a railroad and using the earliest, most primitive type of locomotive instead of the most modern engine. Moreover, a republic would best assure democracy and freedom in China. Sun claimed that elements of republican government had existed in the Chinese past, and that some even persisted in aspects of local institutions. It was only Manchu rule that had suppressed them and restricted their growth; once the Manchus were driven out, China would provide congenial soil for a republic. Furthermore, the creation of a republic would assure China a vigorous, dynamic government that could protect it in international affairs. The revolutionaries seldom tried to show in specific detail how a republican government could withstand foreign incursions; it was an assumed consequence. The League was not sharply antiforeign: its spokesman emphasized that China would continue to observe its treaties with foreign powers after the revolution.

The United League formulated another goal, social revolution, but it was an objective so ill-defined and ambiguous that it was clearly not a central aim. League writers espoused socialism as a means of securing economic and social justice, but they did not spell out what socialism meant or attempt to relate it to Chinese conditions. The revolutionaries did not try to organize the peasant masses or to orient their movement to the peasants' needs. The official manifesto of the league called for the equalization of land ownership, which was significant as one of the earliest attempts to relate the revolutionary movement to the peasant question. Yet nothing was done to analyze that relationship in any systematic fashion or to implement the equal-ownership principle. In fact, when the league was reorganized after the revolution as the Kuomintang, the equal-ownership principle was removed from the party's platform.

A strong current of romanticism ran through the entire revolutionary movement. Many of the young intellectuals were more preoccupied with the glamor and drama and heroism of a revolutionary assault on the bastions of Manchu reaction than they were with the study and planning required to define the problems, clarify revolutionary goals, and ascertain effective methods to achieve them. Even the top leaders of the league attempted little in the way of specific plans for the republic they hoped to establish, or the transition to it.

In the long run, the weaknesses of the revolutionary movement were more significant than its strengths. The founding of the United League created a facade of unity, but in actuality the movement was riven by factionalism, regionalism, and personal and ideological disagreement. Personal conflict was intense and marked by gross insults. Rampant provincialism further impaired the effectiveness of the league; it was more like a loose union of provincial organizations than a unified group of individuals, and party members generally gave their first loyalty to provincial leaders, not to the central party authorities. The provincial leaders often devised their own plans for provincial activities, and implemented them without concern for the league leadership. Central headquarters had little staff, money, or authority. The revolutionaries sought to augment their strength through alliances with secret societies, but these had their own goals and methods and the alliances were rarely satisfactory. Narrow anti-Manchuism provided the glue that held the revolutionaries together, and there was nothing in the organization or spirit of the movement that promised cohesion once the Manchus had been driven from the scene. The number of committed revolutionaries was not large. Although the records that could reveal the total membership of the league have been lost, reconstruction from partial statistics indicates that the organization may have had a membership of only about 10,000 by the time of the 1911 Revolution.[1] A large percentage of its members, however, consisted of overseas Chinese who provided moral and financial support from the safety of other countries. Some 1,400 to 1,500 were in the United States alone: others lived in various cities in Japan and Southeast Asia. Moreover, by 1911 a substantial portion of the membership consisted of soldiers and other uneducated people who looked to the intellectuals for leadership. Probably no more than 3,000 were intellectuals, and no more than a few hundred of these constituted a nucleus of activists who kept the organization together and planned and implemented its operations. Of course, the power and influence of a group, particularly a revolutionary group, is not necessarily directly proportional to its numbers. But numbers are nevertheless important. Certainly they were in China, where the revolution, once it started, would assume such a diffuse character. Given its size and its weaknesses, the revolutionary movement would probably have been far less influential than it was had it not operated in the context of diminishing Manchu authority.

The Erosion of Manchu Legitimacy

In the closing decades of the nineteenth century and the first decade of the twentieth, a host of factors brought Manchu legitimacy into question. The alien origins of the Manchus now came back to haunt them. The Manchus had come to China in the seventeenth century as barbarian invaders from the region now called Manchuria. Partly sinified even then, after the conquest they adopted Chinese culture in full, and ruled in the Chinese way. Indeed, they became staunch defenders of the Confucian order, and Chinese hostility toward them was muted as long as that order was sacrosanct. By the late nineteenth century, as Confucian political ideas came increasingly under attack, the rationalization for the Manchu position in China was inevitably undermined. After the turn of the century, revolutionary propaganda encouraged Chinese to think of the Manchus as an inferior race that conquered China by cruel force, as merciless rapists of their country, and as their tyrannical oppressors for nearly three centuries.

The Manchus also had to bear the chief responsibility for China's impotence vis-à-vis foreign imperialism. Their defenders might argue that because the Manchus ruled in accordance with Chinese values and through Chinese political institutions, China's weaknesses were inherent in the Chinese system and were not created by Manchu rule. But blame is a corollary of power, and as long as the Manchus sat on the throne in Peking they were blamed for China's defeats. If they could not defend the country against foreign attack or encroachments, they had failed in their most fundamental duty as rulers, and no longer deserved to rule. The Japanese victory over China only made the antagonism toward the Manchus more acute. The Chinese had, of course, resented Western exploitation from the outset, but the strangeness of it, the exotic quality of Western technological and organizational superiority, made the relative impotence of the Chinese somehow understandable and acceptable. But when China in 1895 and Russia in 1905 were humbled by an Asian neighbor who had adopted Chinese arts, writing, and philosophy, and whom the Chinese had always viewed with patronizing superiority, the Manchu failure seemed more abysmal in contrast with the Japanese achievement.

The right to rule was also slipping from Manchu hands in a traditional sense. In the Confucian scheme of things, the monarch's authority was justified by the happiness and prosperity of the people. In the late nineteenth and early twentieth centuries, however, economic distress was endemic and social violence was on the rise. In the three years preceding the 1911 Revolution, high taxes, food shortages, and misgovernment sparked hundreds of violent outbreaks, particularly in the Yangtze Valley. In the spring of 1910 large-scale battles took place between clans in Kwangtung; looting, kidnapping, and robbery were widespread in the provinces; and a Canton newspaper reported that murder was "almost a pastime." In the summer of the same year, the rapacity of officials in Shantung engendered a revolt in which the magistrate was killed and roughly 100,000 people fought with government troops. Such outbreaks threatened the monarchy directly; they also strengthened the notion that the Manchu government had simply lost the capacity to deal with the problems of China.

The shortcomings of Manchu leadership became even more conspicuous after the deaths of the Empress Dowager and the Emperor in 1908. A child was left on the throne, under a regent who was generally considered to be a mediocrity—perhaps an unduly harsh judgment. Given the domestic and international pressures within which the government had to operate, the wonder is that the Ch'ing Court achieved as much as it did in asserting Chinese sovereignty against foreign powers and in promoting reform. But the Manchus could not win; every measure taken to improve the nation's position seemed also to undercut their power. The Manchus sent students abroad to study, but the students promptly became radicalized. The government promoted military modernization, but that only created stronger provincial military establishments to challenge the central government. The court stimulated the growth of Chinese nationalism by wielding the concept of national sovereignty in diplomatic struggles, but nationalistic intellectuals were increasingly effective in stamping the Manchus as being outside the national pale.

Of all the policies that boomeranged against the Manchus, the most important were the constitutional reforms. Shortly after the turn of the century, a demand arose that the court institute a constitutional system of government with representative organs. The Manchus acquiesced, guided by their own inadequacies and by the apparent success of the Japanese monarchy in fostering a constitution that allowed for representation while protecting its own prerogatives. In 1907 the court announced that constitutional government would be gradually introduced during the following nine years. The first stage occurred in 1908 when it authorized elected provincial assemblies through which the advice of the local gentry could be made available to the government.

The gentry assemblymen quickly showed themselves to be surprisingly effective parliamentarians, and the assemblies became potent centers of provincial strength. Although their powers were to be advisory only, they immediately began to assume legislative functions. Under threat of mass resignation, the gentry insisted that provincial governors accept assembly recommendations and act upon them. The popular sovereignty inherent in the elected character of the assemblies tended to usurp the legitimacy of the monarch as expressed in the concept of the Mandate of Heaven. The Mandate of Heaven was supposed to be revealed through the welfare of the people. But the people presumably now spoke through elections, which constituted a more direct, specific, and formal mandate than that claimed by the court. The provincial assemblies thus undermined Manchu legitimacy and at the same time became centers of gentry power.

Growth of Provincial Autonomy

The growth of provincial autonomy was less important as a proximate cause of the 1911 Revolution than it was in determining the course and consequences of the revolt once it began. It was rooted in popular feeling, in geography and economics, and in the structure of Ch'ing government.

Strong local, provincial, and regional feelings have flourished throughout Chinese history. They might be conceived as three concentric circles, with localism in the center, and with loyalties and attachments diminishing in intensity from the center to the periphery. As we have already noted, a cluster of villages formed the basic unit of rural life, and each person had a particular feeling for his native village and surrounding locality.

People were also strongly aware of their provincial identity. The Chinese traditionally accepted a whole lexicon of alleged provincial characteristics: the Hunanese were fiery, and superb warriors; the resident of Kwangtung was quick and crafty; the Chihli (Hopei) peasant was frank, stolid, and cheerful. These stereotypes reflected provincial differences in customs, diet, history, institutions, and attitudes. Linguistic differences also separated provinces from one another. Many provincial boundaries were determined by topographical features that embraced natural regions, thus emphasizing their separate identities.

Local and provincial identities fell within a larger and looser circle of regionalism. People thought of themselves as southerners or northerners or southeasterners as distinct from southwesterners, and so on. The chief regional distinction was between southerners and northerners, and it was associated with alleged social, political, intellectual, and behavioral differences.

Regionalism also had an economic dimension, particularly in connection with military power. In premodern China, regional resources—the resources of a large and wealthy province, or of two or three provinces—might well compare with those that the central government could effectively tap. The size of the country was too vast, geographic obstacles too formidable, transportation too expensive, and provincial elites too jealous of their own power and possessions to permit the central government to obtain more than a limited portion of provincial revenues. One economist has recently argued persuasively that premodern economic forces in China favored regionalism rather than centralized power, "and that only conditions outside economics prevented a breakup of China."[2]

In the Ch'ing bureaucracy, the authority of the viceroys faintly reflected this regionalism in the sense that a viceroy normally headed two provinces. (Occasionally, he represented one particularly important province, rarely three.) The viceroy stood at the head of two provincial political structures, however, not one regional organization. In the late Ch'ing period the viceroy tended to act primarily as governor of the province in which his headquarters were located—a province, not a region, being the key political unit. Tension of one sort or another always existed between the provinces and the central government; a strong ruler tried to tie the provinces more closely to the court, and the provinces assumed more independence when the ruler was weak. Even under a powerful monarch, though, the traditional organization of the state recognized the unique sociological, geographical, and economic identity of the provinces by according them substantial autonomy.

Under a series of weak monarchs, the accretion of provincial power over a long time could reach a point where regional clusters of provinces might coalesce to challenge the dynasty itself. But that was normally a late development in the life of a dynasty. In its early stages, provincialism did not signify a conspiracy to overthrow the monarchy as much as a strong tendency for independent action in provincial affairs, and a reluctance to brook interference from the court. Just such trends appeared in the late Ch'ing period.

In the 1850s the great Taiping Rebellion exploded across central China. The Manchu military establishment had long before shown its incompetence to deal with even small-scale rebellion, and was utterly useless in the face of this huge movement. As a consequence, leading provincial officials assumed the task of defending the dynasty—and the traditional Confucian social order—against the heterodox Taipings. Tseng Kuo-fan, Li Hung-chang, and other provincial leaders created new and relatively efficient armies that ultimately quelled the Taiping Rebellion and the disorders that arose in its wake. These armies were recruited regionally and financed with regional sources of revenue. They were organized to be loyal to their commanders, who also created personal political organizations to protect and assert their newfound power.

The regional army leaders used their armies on behalf of the monarchy. More than that, they were personally subject to the authority of the monarchy. (The political-military machines they created did not flourish into the twentieth century and then overthrow the monarchy, as is sometimes suggested.) Nonetheless, they accumulated enormous practical independence. The normal balance between provinces and center was tipped in favor of the provinces, and the central government was never able to restore it. This slippage of central authority was particularly noteworthy in the key areas of finance and military.

In the best of times, the fiscal structure of the empire was extremely decentralized, with collection and control of revenue largely in provincial hands, although subject to central authority. But when the court was weakened or on the defensive, provinces could easily thwart central financial control. During his campaigns against the Taiping rebels in the 1850s and 1860s, Tseng Kuo-fan created his own, virtually independent, financial organization. It was at that time that *likin*, a tax on goods in transit, came into existence. From then until well into the twentieth century, it would provide the provinces additional financial muscle. By the end of the nineteenth century, a leading reformer could lament that "the power of financial control is now vested not with the central government but with the provincial authorities. . . . The Board of Revenue exerts no direct [financial] control over the nation."[3]

Similarly, the nation's military strength remained largely under the control of provincial officials, which was one source of China's weakness in the Sino-Japanese War. An American scholar, John Rawlinson, reports that the captain of a Chinese ship captured by the enemy asked the Japanese commander to allow him to keep his ship on the ground that it belonged to the Kwangtung provincial squadron, which had taken no part in the war. Japan's victory in the war prompted the Chinese Court to initiate a program of military modernization. A high-ranking officer, Yuan Shih-k'ai, was ordered to organize an army along Western lines, and arm it and train it in the Western fashion. Yuan immediately undertook the task, and swiftly created the most modern military establishment in China. Known as the Peiyang Army, it expanded during the last years of the nineteenth century and the first years of the twentieth to become the most powerful single force in the country. However, this added power for the central government was offset by the fact that the provinces were simultaneously increasing their military might.

As part of its program of military modernization, the court ordered all provinces to establish military academies and to train their officers and troops according to foreign methods. The monarchy tried to control these innovations through central government representatives in the provinces, but they were never more than visitors, and could not gain substantive control over provincial military affairs. Thus, the monarchy achieved little in the way of reducing provincial political and military powers. The importance of provincial military expansion lay not only in its effect on relations between the provinces and the court, but also in its impact inside the provinces: provincial military organizations acquired increasing clout in provincial politics.

We referred briefly in the first chapter to the dominant role of the gentry in local and provincial politics. Though widely used, the term "gentry" is somewhat confusing and inappropriate for China; there is some dispute about what it precisely denotes when applied to traditional China, although there is general agreement that a Confucian education, as marked by examination success, was a central qualification. But whatever the former situation, by the early 1900s the impact of modernizing trends was broadening the nature of the gentry. Not only Confucian learning but Western learning as well qualified one for elite status, particularly after the abolition of the examination system in 1905. Further, the establishment of Western-style economic enterprises—mines and industries, railroads, banks, modern shipping firms, and similar commercial ventures—produced the nucleus of a new bourgeoisie that took its place in the provincial elite. Provincial military leaders also played a part. Thus, by the last decade of the Ch'ing period, local gentry had come to include those who controlled wealth, troops, new learning, businesses and business organizations such as chambers of commerce, and professional men; the weight of traditional scholarship and examination status had declined, although it was by no means insignificant by 1911.

As noted earlier, the gentry had functioned in a dual capacity, as a spokesman for local interests and as an unofficial agency of the bureaucracy. By the early twentieth century, as Manchu legitimacy and power waned, members of the new gentry became less amenable to official control and asserted themselves more vigorously as local and provincial leaders, explicitly or implicitly in opposition to the central government. It was their thrust for independence that made a constitutional system of government attractive to many of the gentry in the early twentieth century, for it seemed to offer a means of legitimizing provincial autonomy. Consequently, they welcomed the Manchu constitutional reforms launched in 1907, and they promptly transformed the new provincial advisory assemblies into centers of provincial authority, which became the chief agencies of provincial interests in conflict with the central government. Many a conflict there proved to be, and none more acrimonious than the railroad issue.

The question of railroad construction exacerbated the tensions between provincial and central interests in the early twentieth century. Regional officials had originally taken the lead in building railroads, and early in the century the gentry in several provinces organized railway societies to undertake the construction of provincial lines. The central government understandably sought a centralized railway system. It therefore planned to obtain money through a foreign loan in order to create a national network of railroads and buy up the provincial rail investments. The provinces involved became agitated over the court's plan because they saw it as a threat to provincial interests and their own investments, and because they felt the court's dependence on a foreign loan would open the door further to foreign encroachments on China's sovereignty. Nowhere was opposition more vigorous than in the province of Szechwan, where the problem was compounded by the fact that a portion of the money raised for railroad construction had been lost through corrupt and incompetent management. In the spring of 1911, when the Manchu Court announced the nationalization of the railways, widespread disturbances erupted in Szechwan. Finally, in the late summer, the court sent troops into the province. In a sense, this confrontation was the beginning of the 1911 Revolution.

In sum, by the eve of the 1911 Revolution, the provinces had drained substantial military, political, and financial power from the central government, had asserted themselves politically against the court through the provincial assemblies, and in the process had emphasized the legitimacy of provincial power. The monarchy was not entirely without authority or influence. It was more than a facade concealing the reality of provincial independence. But perhaps not a great deal more.

The Wuhan Revolution, 1911*

On October 9, 1911, several revolutionaries were preparing explosives in a basement hideaway located in the Russian section of Wuchang. They accidentally exploded a bomb, and a police officer rushed to investigate. Among other things, the officer found a list of members of the Wuchang revolutionary organization. The following day, authorities began to arrest revolutionaries and those suspected of revolutionary inclinations. The rebels therefore decided it would be better to revolt immediately than to await certain arrest, and they launched an uprising that evening by seizing control of an army camp in Wuchang. The Manchu governor and army commander of Hupei Province both fled, leaving the antirevolutionary forces without leadership. As a result, Wuchang was in the hands of

* Wuhan is the collective name for the cluster of three cities: Wuchang, Hanyang, and Hankow. The 1911 Revolution is often called the Wuhan Revolution.

the revolutionaries by the following morning. The Revolution of 1911 had begun.

It was not an auspicious beginning. Despite the flight of the two government leaders, most of the armed forces in Wuchang remained loyal, at least for the moment. The core of the rebel group consisted of little-known soldiers, most of low rank and reluctant to lead the revolution. They had only the most tenuous ties with Sun Yat-sen's United League, and, in any event, none of the league leaders was on the scene. The revolutionaries decided to force Li Yuan-hung, a well-known colonel in the imperial army, to serve as their leader. Li had absolutely no inclination to revolt, but accepted the leadership as an alternative to being shot, and it was over his name that the first proclamations of the revolution went out to the rest of the country on October 12.

The revolutionary call elicited no response for little more than a week, while the country waited to see what would happen. Then, in rapid succession, the provinces responded sympathetically. The revolution took place in the form of provincial declarations of independence from Peking. In essence, one province after another seceded from the central government. Hupei started the ball rolling by its proclamation on October 12; and the provinces carried it in the following order: Shensi and Hunan, October 22; Kiangsi, October 24; Shansi, October 29; Yunnan, October 30; Kweichow, Chekiang, and Kiangsu, November 4; Kwangsi, November 7; Anhwei, November 8; Fukien and Kwangtung, November 9; Shantung, November 13; and Szechwan, November 22. Except for outlying territories not centrally involved in Chinese political struggles (Tibet, Mongolia, Manchuria) and two distant border provinces (Sinkiang, Kansu) only two of China's central provinces remained in the imperial camp: the metropolitan province of Chihli, and its neighbor Honan.

Immediately after the outbreak of the revolt in early October, the court summoned Yuan Shih-k'ai to lead the Peiyang Army against the rebellion. Yuan delayed, and set conditions for his return to office, until in desperation the Manchu Court gave him virtually full powers to handle the situation as he saw fit. And as Yuan saw it, it was time to negotiate with the revolutionaries. They willingly offered him the presidency of the new republic if he would abandon the Manchu cause. Their offer foreshadowed the arrangement that was finally made. On February 12, 1912, a Manchu decree of abdication was published, and a month later Yuan Shih-k'ai was inaugurated as President of the Chinese Republic.

It is natural that Chinese and foreigners alike think of these events as the fruit of the propaganda and conspiracy of the United League. The league was the best known of the revolutionary organizations at that time, and historians associated with the Kuomintang—the successor of the United League—have long looked upon the 1911 Revolution as "their" revolution; for example, they revised the Chinese calendar to date from 1912. Yet in fact the league was only one of a broad range of groups and individuals who were involved in bringing the Manchu Dynasty to an end, and in some ways not the most important. Many people besides revolutionaries were involved in effecting the change of government, and their actions generally served three goals: (1) to end the rule of the Manchus; (2) to retain a large measure of provincial autonomy; and (3) to assure that no radical changes occurred in property rights, class relations, or in local and provincial power structures.

The driving force behind the spread of revolution throughout China in the autumn of 1911 was not a desire for a republic, and certainly not a desire for social revolution. It was simple opposition to continued rule by the Manchus on racial, nationalistic, and practical grounds. Some radical intellectuals had more far-reaching and multiple goals, of course, but the radicals did not provide the chief force of the revolution. The Manchus were overthrown because their legitimacy had been so eroded that many people who were *not* members of the United League or of any other revolutionary organization thought that the monarchy had run its course. Moreover, many of those who were revolutionaries also thought almost exclusively in terms of ousting the Manchus, giving only token attention to what would follow. This lone objective was certainly the motivation of those who originally launched the revolution at Wuchang, and it explains partly their forcing Li Yuan-hung to become a revolutionary leader, the last thing he wanted to do. Li was selected for two reasons. First, he was of high rank and fairly well known, and the revolutionaries thought the public would respond more sympathetically to the revolution if such a person were at its head. Second, Li was Chinese, a member of the Han race, an important qualification for any revolutionary leader precisely because the revolt so specifically focused on the alien origins of the Manchus. If the aims of the revolutionaries had been more sweeping, Li would not have been considered suitable.

The anti-Manchu emphasis of the revolution was widely recognized at the time. American diplomats in China reported that hostility to the dynasty was almost universal among the Chinese, and that even many Chinese officials sympathized with the revolutionary movement. They sympathized with it because they saw it as designed to achieve little more than the overthrow of the Manchus, a point on which many individuals and groups with diverse interests and views were able to come together. An American financier in China at that time aptly summarized the causes of the revolution by saying that "the hatred of the Manchus is the common denominator of many different numerators."[4] Indeed, even after the revolution had been going on for two months, the revolutionary headquarters at Wuhan acknowledged that anti-Manchuism took priority over republicanism by offering to accept a constitutional monarchy as long as the ruler was Chinese.

However, though opposition to the Manchus was primary, it had an inherent republican logic that emerged very clearly once the revolution had begun. A republic was the only practicable alternative to Manchu rule. What other options existed? Theoretically, a new dynasty might be set up, but who would rule and under what circumstances? There was no acceptable candidate to found a new dynasty, with the possible exception of Yuan Shih-k'ai, and he was in no position to do so. In the absence of any contender for the monarchy, the only available alternative was that which had been defined by years of revolutionary propaganda and agitation, a republic. Yuan Shih-k'ai's assumption of the presidency seemed to guarantee that it would not be socially radical. Moreover, even conservative Chinese had come to accept the need for Westernization in China, and a Western form of government was not inappropriate, particularly a form identified with highly admired Western nations. More important, everyone feared foreign intervention if disorder was prolonged, so many constitutionalists and others who had not advocated a republic were pressured to accept it, if only to settle matters swiftly.*

There was still a more vital reason to turn to a republic as an alternative to the Manchus. A republic, as understood—or misunderstood—by the Chinese, offered a high degree of provincial autonomy, a crucial point to those who enjoyed and profited from the semi-independence that the provinces had acquired over the preceding four or five decades. The prevailing view in Shansi in December, 1911, when the form of national government was still under debate, illustrates the position of the provinces. Shansi was prepared to accept any reasonable solution, including constitutional monarchy, but: "The essential point is that local autonomy, to the extent recognized in modern constitutional government, shall be guaranteed . . . members of the [provincial] government are quite indifferent as to who occupies the Throne . . . as this will have little connection, under the new proposed form of government, with their local affairs."[6] This view was held even more firmly at the other end of the empire, in Kwangtung, where the "general idea among the thinking Chinese" was "to inaugurate a government on the system of the American republic and that the provinces . . . shall be, within certain limits, independent of the control of the Central Government. Others hope, on the contrary, that each province will be given a republic absolutely independent of the others."[7] The revolution is sometimes said to have started several months earlier than the Wuhan revolt, when the Szechwanese rose up in violent protest

---

* The intense fear of foreign intervention hung over all the activities of the Revolution of 1911. It was not an idle fear. Not only did the Chinese have the entire background of imperialism in China to prompt their concern, but foreign powers did, in fact, intervene on a number of occasions. In November and December of 1911, the American minister to China sent repeated messages to the Secretary of State emphasizing Yuan Shih-k'ai's need for money and the desirability of the department's supporting a loan to Yuan. In December, 1911, representatives of the United States, France, Germany, Great Britain, Japan, and Russia presented identical notes to the commissioners at Shanghai which said, in essence, that the powers considered the Chinese struggle to affect seriously the material interests and security of foreigners, and thus, though they wanted to maintain an attitude of neutrality, they wished to stress the need to arrive at a settlement as quickly as possible. In mid-January, 1912, the French minister to China visited Prince Ch'ing to urge Manchu abdication. At the same time, Russia pressured China to acknowledge the independence of Mongolia, and England denied the Chinese the right to intervene in the internal administration of Tibet.[5]

against Ch'ing government's plans to nationalize the Szechwan-Hankow Railroad, a line the Szechwanese were financing and intended to control. But here again is an illustration that provincial interests were a prime factor in the revolution and its outcome; control of the railroad was a provincial interest the Szechwanese were willing to fight for. They were not prepared to accept a form of government that would limit their interests.

The powerful concern for provincial autonomy was, at the same time, a concern to maintain the provincial status quo in economic and political relations. In fact, most provincial declarations of independence had two aspects, one revolutionary and one conservative. As a blow against the dynasty, they were revolutionary. But they were also a way of keeping fiery revolutionaries out of the provinces, thus protecting them against radical social ideas and the spread of agrarian revolt. Nobody was more sensitive to revolutionary movements than foreigners in China, whose opportunities and profits depended upon maintenance of the status quo, so it is of more than passing interest that foreign observers were elated with the conservative character of the revolution as they watched it unfold. An American naval officer reported that the Chinese at Amoy, having joined the revolution, were electing a new council, and it was taken for granted that it would be a "representative body of reliable and conservative revolutionary Chinese."[8] The American consul general in Hong Kong reported to the Secretary of State at the beginning of 1912 that the revolutionary movement "represents the business and property holding classes of Chinese. The remarkably small disturbance to the finances and general business conditions of the Far East caused by this immense revolutionary movement is in itself demonstration of the conservative nature of the movement and of the ability of the conservative classes to ultimately control the situation."[9] The same kind of reports came from north China. One diplomat reported that the merchants in Tientsin agreed "that the old regime had outlived its usefulness and they would welcome the abdication of the Manchus and the organization of a new form of government, if the change can be effected without great disorder."[10] His report fairly well described the view of the majority of anti-Manchu revolutionaries in 1911. They wanted to get rid of the Manchus; they would accept the republic, but it should all be done with speed and order to preclude the spread of a peasant revolution, and with care not to jeopardize profits or disrupt either socioeconomic relations or real political power.

Chuzo Ichiko has traced the sequence of events by which each province joined the revolutionary movement, and his data reveal the jealously provincial character of the revolution as well as its conservative social quality.[11] In nine of the fifteen provinces that declared independence before the end of 1911, the gentry and rich merchants, led by members of the provincial assemblies, took the initiative in making the declarations, and thus kept provincial power in nonrevolutionary hands. Kwangtung is a good example; the provincial assembly, the guilds, charitable associations, and the General Commercial Association joined to petition the Ch'ing viceroy to declare the province independent.[12] The viceroy acquiesced.

Ichiko shows that in nine provinces high-ranking Ch'ing officials were selected as governors after declaring provincial independence; four declined, but five took office. In only six provinces were professional revolutionaries in the leading positions; in three of these, the administration was heavily weighted by the presence of gentry and provincial assemblymen, and in two others the radicals held power only temporarily.

If dissatisfaction with the Manchus was so widespread that officials and gentry were willing to join in overthrowing them, why had previous attempts at revolt failed to elicit support? Why did so many provinces respond to just this revolt? There were two major reasons. One was simply luck, the fact that the viceroy and the commander of the army in Hupei both fled as soon as the revolt began. Sun Yat-sen himself acknowledged that this accidental circumstance was crucial to the success of the 1911 Revolution. Because their flight left a vacuum in antirevolutionary leadership, and delayed any vigorous attempt to put down the revolt, the revolutionaries had the priceless gift of time. Time, in the eyes of those watching from other provinces, was the equivalent of success. With the Wuchang revolutionists still in control after nearly two weeks, and nothing being done to quash them, two other provinces took the cue and declared independence. After that the bandwagon effect was increasingly operative. But there was another and more important reason for the widespread response to the Wuchang revolt. The first declaration of revolution that went out from Wuchang on

October 12 was over the names of Li Yuan-hung and T'ang Hua-lung. T'ang was the president of the Hupei Provincial Assembly, and, like Li, no revolutionary. To the other provinces the revolt was obviously being led by "solid citizens," and other solid citizens suddenly became more inclined to take the crucial step toward independence than they had been when revolts had been started by provincial revolutionaries or secret societies.

We have already observed that from the late nineteenth century provincial power structures had come under strong military influence or military domination. It is therefore not surprising that in ten provinces military men became governors immediately after the revolution, or within the following two or three months. Moreover, the troops in the various provinces, both new and old, were largely recruited from within the provinces in which they served; their loyalties were strongly provincial and personal, so that provincial military leaders had, in effect, personal armies at their disposal—a measure of just how "national" the new Army was. The "nationalism" of the provinces was aimed at the expulsion of the Manchus; it envisioned an end to imperialist exploitation of China, but it did not countenance the subordination of provincial aspirations that genuine national unity would require.

It was the high degree of provincial autonomy, under gentry-merchant-military control, that explains why the Revolution of 1911 took place as a series of provincial declarations of independence. It was a form of revolt that was anti-Manchu and that limited the threat of agrarian revolt, the scope of substantial social change, and the modification of local power structures. It was also one that promised continued provincial autonomy. In some instances, the declaration of provincial independence may also have been a pre-emptive tactic to avoid conflict with revolutionaries until the dust settled and the results of the conflict became clearer.

Presidency of Yuan Shih-k'ai

Ernest Young's study of Yuan Shih-k'ai has persuasively shown the fallacy of the thesis that Yuan's rise to the presidency of the republic was a result of his talent for intrigue, deception, and

Machiavellian politics. Revolutionaries and monarchists alike thought Yuan was the indispensable man, the one person who might be able to maintain a semblance of national order and unity, and preclude foreign intervention. Yuan was willing to accept leadership of the republic not only to satisfy his own ambitions, but because he had little choice: his military position vis-à-vis the revolutionaries was precarious, and he had good reason to believe that he could receive foreign support only if he supported a republic. Thus, because everybody wanted him, and because all other options looked more dangerous and less promising, Yuan Shih-k'ai became President of the republic.

Yuan's contemporaries agreed that he was a very able man, but beyond that there was a wide range of opinion about his values, character, and actions. Most historical writing about him has been critical, even denunciatory. The celebrated reformer Liang Ch'i-ch'ao expressed a generally accepted view that "Yuan thought that it was human nature to tremble before a flashing knife and to go wild for yellow gold, both of which weapons he used to rule the empire." True, he used force and bribery to gain his ends, and these activities influenced the political atmosphere of the early republic. Yet it is possible to view Yuan as a man who was not as bad as his detractors claim.

Yuan was President of China for almost four and a half years, from March, 1912, to his death in June, 1916. During that time, two related phenomena occurred that were of significance for the future of China. One was the failure to create an orderly and effective system of parliamentary government; the other was the further development of provincial militarism—warlordism.

The failure to develop a functioning parliamentary system was perhaps due less to the negative aspects of Yuan's presidency than to the absence of any powerful force or effort on behalf of the republic. A small number of intellectuals sincerely hoped for a republic, and Western-style businessmen had similar aspirations. But for many, a republic was simply not a primary goal. Advocates of constitutional monarchy, and others who had been in the non-revolutionary camp before the Wuhan Revolt, now bent every effort to thwart the revolutionaries who sought to consolidate republican institutions; they preferred domination by Yuan Shih-k'ai, at the expense of the republic, to the rise of their traditional rivals. The gentry and the military who controlled provincial power structures were far more concerned with preserving their provincial power than with working to create an efficient parliamentary government in Peking. Furthermore, the customary Chinese ways of doing political business were simply not appropriate for a republic. The mass of the population was virtually uninvolved in the issue. If their attitudes had been known, they would probably have turned out to be more concerned with being well governed than with operating strange republican institutions. The political parties that came into existence in 1912 and 1913 were monopolized by intellectuals; they did not represent the mass of the population, and they were torn by jealousies, factionalism, and prejudices. Republican politicians frequently absented themselves from sessions of Parliament, and in debate often showed themselves to be more preoccupied with discomfiting their parliamentary enemies—and the President—than with the needs of the masses or with honest efforts to make the parliamentary system work. Even members of the Kuomintang, between denunciations of Yuan Shih-k'ai, accepted bribes from him. In this absence of positive pressure and effort to create a viable republic, anti-republican forces in Yuan's presidency were doubly effective.

One such force was Yuan himself, who used violence and threats to attain domestic political ends. It was widely believed that Yuan was responsible for several political assassinations, including that of Sung Chiao-jen, the Kuomintang leader who hoped to lead a responsible cabinet under Yuan's presidency. Moreover, Yuan did compel the Parliament to remain in its meeting hall until it elected him President. He also used the thinly veiled threat of telegraphed requests and demands from his own generals to justify actions that he himself wished to take. He flouted the law on several occasions; for example, he executed two officers without a trial, transferred the properly elected governor of Chihli (Hopei) without the countersignature of his Premier, and concluded a huge foreign loan without the participation or approval of Parliament. Finally, he ordered the largest party, the Kuomintang, dissolved, and two months later suspended Parliament and ruled, in effect, as military dictator. In the spring of 1914, he promulgated the Constitutional Compact, which essentially formalized his autocratic power, but he still ruled through his army, not civil political agencies. These actions badly undercut the authority of the newly formed republican institutions, constituted new precedents for the use of force in domestic political struggles, and confirmed to many that Yuan was not interested in maintaining a republican system of government. The inability of the republicans to respond seemed to prove the widespread claim that a republic was inappropriate for China.

Yuan has been denounced for many of his actions, but the most furious condemnation has been leveled at his attempt to restore the monarchy. One of the arguments used by Yuan's supporters to justify this action was the memorandum prepared by Yuan's American adviser, Dr. Frank J. Goodnow, which argued that a monarchy might be more appropriate to China's conditions than the republican form of government. Goodnow's views have often been dismissed with a sarcastic phrase, or interpreted as a manufactured rationalization for Yuan Shih-k'ai to do what he had always intended to do. Yet the fact is that Goodnow's arguments were reasonable, and indeed were partially confirmed by the subsequent history of China. Goodnow contended that China had for centuries been accustomed to autocratic rule, that recent attempts to introduce constitutional government had occurred in most unfavorable circumstances, and that all the current turmoil augured great difficulty when it came time for Yuan to pass on his office to his successor. Such difficulties would endanger the independence of the country. The creation of a monarchy, on the contrary, would resolve the succession problem, and thus help insure the peace of the nation and obviate foreign intervention. Goodnow cautioned, however, that the change from a republic to a monarchy would only be successful if three conditions existed: (1) the change not be strongly opposed by the Chinese people or by the foreign powers; (2) the law of succession be fixed so as to leave no doubt about the legal successor; and (3) provision be made for the development of some form of constitutional government under the restored monarchy.

At the time of the Revolution of 1911, Yuan had advocated constitutional monarchy. The circumstances of the revolution forced him to give up that goal as impracticable in 1911 and 1912, but there is no reason to believe that he was persuaded of the superiority of the republican form of government for China when he did so. Indeed, his experiences during the first few years of the republic may well have convinced him of the correctness of his original views, views that were further confirmed by the analysis of Goodnow, a respected foreign scholar and adviser. By the beginning of 1915, Yuan already had as much power as an emperor, and therefore his monarchical attempt can hardly be interpreted as the first sign of overweening vanity and ambition. Because his motives must inevitably be obscure, it is also reasonable to think that Yuan was concerned with the fate of the country when the expected disorders attendant upon the swearing in of his successor occurred. The Twenty-one Demands presented by Japan to China in January, 1915 —which would have transformed China into a Japanese protectorate —could only have heightened Yuan's sense of danger to China; if Japan could present such far-reaching demands when China was not torn by civil strife, what would happen if factions were struggling over the presidency?

Whatever Yuan's motives, his attempt to restore the monarchy promptly engendered military opposition that spread throughout the country. In March, 1916, Yuan canceled the monarchy and tried to continue as president. But it was too late. Hostility toward Yuan the Emperor continued toward Yuan the President until his death in 1916 brought the crisis to an end.

The complete inadequacy of the efforts to create a viable republic under Yuan reflected the weakness of the republican element in the movement that overthrew the Manchus. Provincial militarism, on the other hand, was a powerful element in that movement, and it continued to flourish under Yuan's presidency. It is customary, and reasonable, to date the beginning of the warlord period from 1916, when Yuan died. But the warlords already existed under Yuan's presidency, and already enjoyed some of the freedom that would make them notorious in the decade after his death. No less an authority than Li Yuan-hung himself described the situation in the middle of 1912 in words that might apply as well to any moment during the later warlord period:

> A province is the territory of the man who rules it, the army is the possession of its general. This disposition finds imitation far

and wide, as a sound is repeated by its echo. At the beginning it was a small matter, but in the end it has become like a spreading conflagration. For the measuring out and the partition of the country they care nothing.[13]

Throughout the years of Yuan's presidency, the generals worked steadily to strengthen their armies. Amid frequent reports of troop disbandment, there were also those on the steady recruitment of new men. It is difficult to say whether the recruits outnumbered the disbanded troops, but because the latter certainly consisted of the least competent and the least fit, the result was unquestionably to strengthen the units involved. Without much doubt, the number of men under arms in the provinces expanded significantly. Yuan's own force, the Peiyang Army, also expanded; he recruited three new brigades and two reserve battalions, and enlarged two brigades into divisions and four battalions into mixed brigades.

Provincial officials on occasion simply bypassed the central government and dealt directly with foreign financiers regarding the development of provincial resources or the arrangements for a foreign loan. Honan, Chekiang, Kwangsi, Kwangtung, and Fengtien all engaged in such direct negotiations. The United States consul at Foochow tried to interest American capitalists in negotiating with Fukien, but without success; perhaps the Americans were dissuaded by the fact that the province was already more than $6 million in debt. With the exception of revenues from the maritime customs, which were collected under foreign supervision, almost all important sources of revenue were appropriated by local authorities. Moreover, even before the end of 1912, some provinces were printing paper money with no backing. Consequently, Yuan's administration hovered on the brink of bankruptcy from the outset. In the spring of 1914, the American minister to China reported that, except for the revenues under foreign control, Yuan's government was receiving no more than 5 percent of the tax revenue due from the provinces, and that the central government was living "from hand to mouth."[14]

The term "provincial autonomy," or, more accurately, the "semi-autonomy of the provinces," refers, of course, to a wide range of situations. Some provincial governors gave more attention to national unity than did others; some supported Yuan, others distrusted him; some felt more vulnerable to Yuan's power than others because of geographical, military, or other reasons; and some governors were more willing to assert their military strength openly and arbitrarily, others were more inclined to follow the dictates of the central government or the provincial civilian leaders in most routine matters. The essential points are that the provinces had the capacity to act more or less independently if the issue required, and that at all times provincial authorities retained basic control of provincial troops and revenues. Obviously, no provincial governor could control the central government, but the semi-independence of the entire group of provinces was a profound limitation on the power of Peking. Even so, the provinces did acknowledge its authority, and often followed its orders, especially when the alternative was to stand alone in open defiance of the President.

In the early summer of 1913, Yuan Shih-k'ai dismissed the governors of Kiangsi, Kwangtung, and Anhwei, all members of the Kuomintang. The governors decided to resist, and launched the so-called Second Revolution, in 1913. Although seven provinces joined in the opposition to the government, Yuan quickly put down the rebellion with little fighting. He then appointed other generals to be governors of six of the defeated provinces, and in that fashion extended his control more tightly over most of the nation. Only Yunnan and Szechwan could be considered independent of Yuan, though Kwangsi and Kweichow were more loosely tied to him than the remaining provinces. In the long run, the uprising of 1913 was another setback for the republic, and another step in the development of warlordism. In one sense it produced a somewhat more effective national unity than had existed since the Revolution of 1911 because more governors were willing to obey Yuan in more matters. In another, however, it worked against national unity; the ousted military governors were members of the Kuomintang, men presumably more committed to the republic and to ultimate civilian rule than the officers who replaced them. Whatever the effect on national unity, the quelling of the revolt did not fundamentally alter the bases of provincial independence.

In the final analysis, whatever unity existed in China by 1916 was a unity imposed by the military dictatorship of Yuan Shih-k'ai, a dictatorship made possible by the loyalty of leading generals in the Peiyang Army. Behind that dictatorship, the reality of provincial militarism existed; Chinese warlordism was about to be born. Not only was real power in the hands of the generals, but the extensive disorder and lawlessness that would characterize the warlord period already appeared during Yuan's presidency. Reports of brigandage, looting, kidnappings, murders, came from many parts of the country in 1912—and every year thereafter. In some instances, purposeful and systematic violence was perpetrated by the military, as when General Chang Hsün allowed his army three days to loot Nanking during the Second Revolution. But more commonplace was the rise of local brigands who struck out on their own in the villages and rural areas away from provincial capitals. Instead of returning to peaceful occupations after their separation from the army, many disbanded soldiers formed bandit gangs to live off the country. From this time on, the demand for firearms in China was insatiable; pistols and rifles, even of ancient vintage, commanded extraordinary prices as long as they functioned and were sold with a few hundred cartridges. At the beginning of the republic, an American consul in Szechwan telegraphed a description of the situation in that province as follows: "Superfluous troops, shortage money, unsettled authority indefinite menace."[15] Those eight words could just as well have applied to any other part of China throughout the period of Yuan's presidency.

Yuan Shih-k'ai's control of the powerful Peiyang Army remained sufficient to allow him to keep most of the provinces obedient to the central government, except in matters that would basically undermine provincial power. Thus the semblance of national unity persisted through his presidency, despite the fundamental disintegration and disorder that was setting in. But when Yuan Shih-k'ai died in 1916, the removal of the one accepted national symbol and the keystone of the Peiyang hierarchy also dispelled the illusion of national unity. The reality of provincial militarism that had been growing behind the facade of unity for several decades now emerged unobscured.

In sum, the revolutionaries defined the political goal of the Revolution of 1911, the republic, but the socially conservative, anti-Manchu movement determined the content of the republic. The institutions of the new republic were utterly at odds with the thinking and values of the overwhelming majority of Chinese, including the Chinese elite who held the reins of political and social power at the national and provincial levels. At the beginning of the People's Republic of China in 1949, it was still common for Chinese to see political action in highly personalized terms, believing that social order should be based on the guidance of talented and cultivated men; certainly, this feeling was even more widespread 40 years earlier. Moreover, the republican institutions were not only at odds with the thinking and values of the Chinese people, they were at variance with the distribution of power in the country. This disparity was the fundamental weakness of the republic. In a basic sense, the republic was irrelevant to the Chinese facts of life.

The Revolution of 1911 was nationalistic, but only in a limited sense. It was in opposition to alien rule, Manchu rule. Furthermore, it was indirectly motivated by anti-imperialism, though in fact the revolution itself was marked by virtually no anti-Westernism or antiforeignism. Nevertheless, there was little sense of a national community, little cooperative effort toward a national end. The orientation was anti-Manchu, anti-imperialist, and strongly provincialistic. There was no national hero or leader who could become the symbol of national aspirations, and thereby stimulate nationalist feelings. Sun Yat-sen did not have the capacity for that role, and in any event Sun was not a central figure in 1911, except to his own United League, which, after all, was not the major force behind the revolution. Yuan Shih-k'ai, accepted as the indispensable man, was still not a great leader, indeed, not even an effective leader in the circumstances. He did not have the charisma or the vision or the capacity to become a center for nationalist emotions; in a sense, Yuan was indispensable by default. But the most important limitation on Chinese nationalism was the limited involvement of the mass of the Chinese people. Peasants joined the revolt, of course, but their participation was localized in character and restrictive in goals. For most, the revolution ended with provincial secession. That is why, despite the bloodshed that did occur, the revolution seems curiously bland. In 1911, Chinese nationalism was only skin deep.

The revolution nevertheless signified profound changes in China. It brought to an end the monarchical system of government that had

existed in China for well over two thousand years. Nothing could
have shown more clearly that Confucian society could not be put
back together again. The creation of the Western-style republic, in
spite of its deficiencies, served to license the extension and acceleration of Westernization in all areas of Chinese urban life. Finally,
it destroyed the strongest remaining political link between the
provinces and localities on the one hand and the central government
on the other. As a consequence, it opened the way to extreme territorial disintegration.

The Warlords

THE PEIYANG ARMY, as long as it was unified, imposed a certain unity on China. What held the army together was loyalty and obedience to Yuan Shih-k'ai; when he died it began to break into smaller constituencies under Yuan's chief commanders. These army fragments then fought for regional and national power by every means available, including war. The collapse of Peiyang unity allowed non-Peiyang units—other central government armies as well as provincial troops—to assert themselves and seek their own goals to an extent that had not been possible earlier. Yuan's death opened an era in which military leaders in every province acted without restraint to seek provincial or personal goals, and tortured the country with incessant warfare, rapacious exploitation, and banditry. It was the period of the warlord.

The Warlord Period

Scholars seem rarely to agree about definitions, and they have offered several to describe the characteristics of a warlord. Defined in the simplest and most practical terms, a warlord was a commander of a personal army, ruling or seeking to rule territory, and acting more or less independently. His independence might be qualified by alliances with other warlords, or by political or military exigencies, and he might even at times assume a position subordinate to another leader. Basically, however, a warlord decided his own policies in the light of his own interests and goals.*

Warlords dominated Chinese political life from 1916 to 1928, the "warlord period," a full one-third of the republican era. For those twelve years, China was politically fragmented, divided among a host of warlords, large and small. Some controlled a district or two, some ruled a province; the most powerful exercised authority over two or three provinces. A national government continued to exist in Peking; that is, the Peking government was formally recognized by foreign states as the government of China, and Chinese politicians spoke of it as such. For most purposes, however, the national government's writ extended no farther than the guns of the Peking warlord. For the Peking government was also a warlord government; it was the creature of whatever warlord or warlord clique ruled the capital and its environs.

The warlords fought literally dozens and dozens of wars against one another. Most were short-lived and small, but some were on a vast scale. Together, they brought terrible suffering to the Chinese people. The military power relations among the warlords changed constantly, and those changes were reflected in a shuffling of government offices as victors took the posts of political honor and losers resigned or fled. The most conspicuous feature of warlord politics was the extraordinary rapidity and frequency with which national and provincial posts changed hands. In those dozen years of the warlord period, China had more than seven heads of state (one person served on two occasions), not counting one imperial restoration and several brief periods of regency or caretaker governments. Twenty-five cabinets tumbled one after another, each marked by dissension, with an average life-span of four months.

It would be tedious and not particularly instructive to trace

---

* The word "warlord" as I use it with regard to twentieth-century China is less value laden than its Chinese equivalent, *chün-fa.* I apply the word to all the men who exemplified a specific sociomilitary phenomenon, whether their political policies were reactionary or enlightened. To the Chinese, *chün-fa* is a term of opprobrium; enemies were chün-fa, never friends. This view has carried over to influence modern scholarship, so that some writers consider it inappropriate to apply the term "warlord" to a military leader, regardless of his independence and personal army, if he sponsored constructive government policies. *Tuchün* was the title of provincial military governors. They were the protagonists of the warlord period, and *tuchün* is therefore sometimes used as a loose equivalent of warlord.

these convoluted political changes and the wars that produced them. The warlord period exemplified the extremity of China's territorial disintegration. But more than that, it formed the context within which some of the most significant trends and events in modern Chinese history took place. It was during those years that young China repudiated Confucianism, that Chinese anti-imperialism entered a more intense phase, that the Literary Revolution occurred, that Marxism was introduced to China on a significant scale, that the Communist Party was established and the Kuomintang reorganized, and that Chinese social disintegration accelerated. Moreover, warlords continued to influence national politics right up to 1949. The types of warlords, and the essential characteristics of warlord organizations and warlord politics therefore demand our attention.

The Warlords

The warlords numbered in the hundreds. Noone has yet worked out a complete typology of warlords, and it will not be attempted here. But it will be useful to discuss a few of them, because their careers provide an outline political history of the warlord years. Moreover, they show the extraordinarily diverse backgrounds and characteristics of the warlords. Some came from impoverished families at the very bottom of society; others boasted of aristocratic lineage and family wealth. A few were Confucian scholars who had won degrees in the civil-service system. Others were illiterate, and still others were fairly well versed in modern Western knowledge. Their political views and military abilities were similarly varied. The following brief sketches of outstanding warlords illustrate most of these traits.

PEIYANG ARMY LEADERS: FENG KUO-CHANG AND TUAN CH'I-JUI

Feng Kuo-chang and Tuan Ch'i-jui were the two outstanding warlords to emerge in the first years following the death of Yuan Shih-k'ai. Both began their military careers in the Tientsin Military

Academy, a school that Li Hung-chang established in 1885 to train modern army officers. For Tuan, it was a natural step; his grandfather and father had served in Li's army, and Tuan apparently had no doubts about seeking a career in the military. Feng, on the contrary, came from a family of landowners that had fallen on hard times, and financial straits led him to a military career only after his failure to obtain the second civil-service degree dashed his hopes for a post in the civilian bureaucracy.

Feng and Tuan acquired good records as officers who understood modern military principles. Yuan Shih-k'ai invited them to join him in creating the Peiyang Army after the Sino-Japanese War, and they soon rose to join the inner circle of Yuan's chief subordinates. Though Yuan was forced into retirement in 1908, Tuan and Feng maintained close contact with him, and when he was called back to deal with the Revolution of 1911 they served him faithfully. They showed publicly that they would lead their troops against the monarchy or against the revolutionaries as Yuan commanded.

During the years of Yuan's presidency, both Tuan and Feng remained his leading subordinates, and both enjoyed high office in the central government as well as stints as provincial governor. The two, however, disapproved of Yuan's attempt to become emperor, perhaps partly because they realized that the hereditary basis of imperial succession would leave them subordinates of Yuan's son. Although they did not engage in active, vigorous opposition, their obvious disapproval of Yuan's plans encouraged other warlords to withhold approval and to come out openly against Yuan's monarchy.

When Yuan died, Vice President Li Yuan-hung took over the presidency, but Li had no military power of his own and little influence among the Peiyang generals. As a result, the real power flowed to the two senior Peiyang leaders—Feng and Tuan—who became the outstanding figures in the first generation of warlords. Each tried to install his supporters in provincial governorships and in other high positions. Feng's followers came to be called the Chihli Clique, and Tuan's group of warlords as the Anhwei Clique. The maneuvers, intrigues, and battles between these two groups dominated the early warlord years. In the course of their rivalry, Feng attained the presidency of the republic and Tuan was at one time Prime Minister. The government of neither man, however, was

genuinely effective over more than a portion of the country—
essentially the provinces ruled by their respective subordinates and
allies. Feng died in 1919 but his Chihli Clique, under the leadership
of Ts'ao K'un and Wu P'ei-fu, defeated Tuan and his followers in
the Anhwei-Chihli War of 1920. After that, Tuan remained on the
periphery of Chinese political life until 1924, when the dominant
northern warlords installed him briefly as head of a compromise
government in Peking. In 1926 he fled into retirement, and never
again played a significant role in Chinese politics.

CONSERVATIVE WARLORDS: WU P'EI-FU
AND CHANG TSO-LIN

Wu P'ei-fu and Chang Tso-lin were among the best known of the
northern warlords during the 1920s, and each controlled the Peking
government for several years.

Like Feng Kuo-chang, Wu was a Confucian scholar turned
soldier.[1] He was born in a poor family in 1874, received a traditional
education, and passed the first civil-service examinations in 1897.
But Wu evidently recognized that times were changing, and that
the military modernization program offered unprecedented career
opportunities for ambitious young men. Moreover, Japan's victory
over China in 1895 had persuaded Wu that China had to create a
powerful national army, and he wanted to take part in it. He therefore enrolled in one of the new military academies, and in 1903
graduated as second lieutenant in the Peiyang Army.

About two years later, Wu was assigned to the Peiyang Army's
Third Division, then commanded by Ts'ao K'un. That began a relationship that lasted for almost two decades: Wu enjoyed Ts'ao's
patronage, and Ts'ao relied upon Wu's military talents. Ts'ao became leader of the Chihli Clique after the death of Feng Kuo-
chang, but his preoccupation with political affairs, and Wu's superiority as a military leader, made Wu the effective head of the Chihli
warlords.

With the defeat of Tuan Ch'i-jui and his followers in the Anwhei-
Chihli War of 1920, the Chihli warlords, headed by Wu, dominated
the national government in Peking. Wu used this position to launch

a policy of national unification by military force, a policy of simply beating the other warlords into submission in order to end national disunity. But Wu suffered the fate of most ambitious warlords: his expanding power was finally undercut by defections of key subordinates. In 1924, while Wu was locked in a struggle with the Manchurian warlord, Chang Tso-lin, one of his commanders turned against him and brought about the collapse of Wu's armies. Although Wu later recovered enough of a following to take part in the warlord resistance to the National Revolutionary Army in 1926–1928, he never again dominated affairs as he had earlier in the decade. After 1928, he retired to Szechwan, and in 1931 moved to Peking, where he spent his time studying Buddhist and Confucian classics, practicing calligraphy, writing poetry, and engaging in serious drinking. When the Japanese conquered north China in 1937–1938, they urged Wu to become head of a puppet government, but Wu steadfastly refused except under conditions that would have rendered his regime independent of Japanese control.

To the end, Wu was an avowed and articulate Confucianist. As he ruminated about his career late in life, he concluded that his misfortunes and those of the nation all derived from the breakdown of the traditional order. Social harmony required filial piety, loyalty, sincerity, selflessness, and modesty, he argued, but loyalty above all. Loyalty to one's superior and loyalty to one's country were two facets of the same thing, and both he and the country had suffered from the breakdown of that kind of loyalty. Wu cited Kuan Yu and Yo Fei as the outstanding examples of loyalty and filial piety, and exhorted his countrymen to emulate those great military heroes of antiquity.

Wu's own unshakable loyalty to his superior illustrated one of the shortcomings of the Confucian system. He refused to denounce Ts'ao K'un, or interfere with his political ambitions, even when Ts'ao turned to wholesale bribery in order to be elected President. This refusal did not reduce Wu's personal stature in the eyes of the Chinese, but it did undermine confidence in his ability to clean up the country, whatever his personal virtues. Moreover, Wu's administration of his own provinces illustrated that Confucian loyalty was no substitute for vigorous administrative action. His provinces were infested with bandits, water control and education were badly neglected, and many other social problems were unresolved while Wu pursued the elusive goal of unification by force.

Wu's sometime enemy, Chang Tso-lin, did not look the part of a warlord; certainly his appearance belied his nickname, "The Tiger of Manchuria." He was slender, almost frail, and seemed overwhelmed by the bemedaled and braided uniform that he occasionally wore. His face was thin and rather sad, and he had a droopy mustache and a soft voice. But despite his appearance, he was a shrewd man, and held greater power over a longer time than any other warlord in China.

Chang was born in a peasant family, and started his career as an enlisted soldier in the Sino-Japanese War. After the war, he returned to his home in Fengtien, one of the three provinces that then constituted Manchuria. There he organized a small militia force to defend the locality, and this became the nucleus of a personal army. Scholars disagree over whether or not Chang was ever a bandit; some claim that he led a bandit gang, others assert that he was accused of banditry only because the local defense unit he commanded was not part of the regular military establishment. Chang used his followers to harass the Russians during the Russo-Japanese War, and after the war he arranged with the military governor of Fengtien to have his troops become a regiment in the regular army. Through the next decade, Chang gradually went up in rank, and expanded the number of his troops.

When Yuan Shih-k'ai maneuvered to become emperor, Chang traded his support for appointment as military governor of Fengtien. By 1919 he had succeeded in having his nominees assume the post of governor in the other two Manchurian provinces, Kirin and Heilungkiang, while he took the position of inspector general of the Three Eastern Provinces (Manchuria). Although Chang conferred with the other two *tuchüns* on important matters, and they were largely independent as far as affairs in their own provinces were concerned, they never challenged Chang's superiority. Not only was he responsible for their appointments, but he was supported by the Japanese, who could be expected to intervene in any internal conflict in Manchuria. Thus Chang's power over the entire region was complete, and until his death in 1928 he ruled it as a sovereign state, even concluding treaties with foreign governments.

Having consolidated his position in Manchuria, Chang attempted to expand his influence into north China, and this brought him into conflict with other warlords. Wu P'ei-fu defeated Chang in 1922 but could not invade Chang's Manchurian base. Therefore Chang was able to rebuild his army and try again in 1924. In that war, Wu was betrayed by one of his officers, Feng Yü-hsiang, and Feng and Chang shared the fruits of victory. But they did not share them long; in 1925–1926 they fought a bitter war, and Chang and his allies finally defeated Feng and conquered much of north China. Chang took over the Peking government and declared himself Grand Marshal of China. In the meantime, however, a revived revolutionary movement in the south launched the so-called Northern Expedition, a military campaign to unify the country. The revolutionary army moved steadily northward and drove Chang from Peking in June, 1928. On his way back to Manchuria, Japanese soldiers bombed his train, and Chang was killed.

The Japanese were as intimately involved with Chang's life as they were with his death. Japan's ambitions on the mainland were focused on Manchuria, and throughout Chang's career he had to accept some measure of Japanese involvement in Manchurian politics and economy. He was never a Japanese puppet, and, in fact, tried to limit Japanese influence as much as he dared. But he could not reject it completely, and therefore yielded what he had to, taking in exchange Japanese aid in the form of advice and material. This aid was partly responsible for the high quality of Chang's army. Chang served Japanese ends by allowing Japanese influence in Manchuria and China generally. The Japanese who assassinated him hoped to create an opportunity for Japan to seize Manchuria. Although that did not take place in 1928, it did in 1931–1932, when Chang Hsüeh-liang, Chang Tso-lin's son, headed Manchuria.

Chang seems to have been one of the most thoroughly pragmatic and least ideological of the major warlords. Wu P'ei-fu's conservatism stemmed from his Confucianism, but Chang gave little indication that he was concerned with Confucianism or any other ideology. He wanted to maintain his military dictatorship, and he supported what would contribute to that end and opposed whatever would interfere with it. Anything that smacked of revolution was therefore anathema to him. For example, he responded harshly in

1919 to student demonstrations in Peking protesting the Versailles decision to turn over German concessions in China to Japan. Chang ordered that all student mail be censored, that students be forbidden to read newspapers from Tientsin or Shanghai, and that they not be permitted to hold meetings of any kind. Doubtless, this extreme conservatism partly accounted for Chang's hostility to the Russians, although his fear of Russian intentions in Manchuria, and the anti-Russian bias of his Japanese sponsors, also fostered that attitude. It also accounts for the character of his administration in Manchuria and, during the last two years of his life, in north China. The military dominated all levels of government, and virtually nothing was done in the way of social reform.

REACTIONARY WARLORDS: CHANG HSÜN,
CHANG TSUNG-CH'ANG

Chang Hsün and Chang Tsung-ch'ang were probably the most notorious of the warlords. Both were ruthless men, but Chang Hsün's most conspicuous trait was his commitment to past customs and loyalties. He was the complete anachronism, a twentieth-century general with an eighteenth-century mind. Chang Tsung-ch'ang, on the other hand, was as contemporary as cruelty; he demonstrated unequivocally how much damage an insensitive and brutal man can do when he has an army at his disposal.

Except for the facts that his family was very poor and that he was orphaned by the age of ten, little is known of Chang Hsün's origins. He joined the army during the Sino-French War of 1884–1885, and after the war continued to serve in south China. However, he got into trouble with his superior, allegedly because he was assigned to buy weapons in Shanghai but squandered the money on women and wine. He then went north about 1895, and shortly afterward became one of Yuan Shih-k'ai's officers. He served Yuan in several capacities until the Revolution of 1911.

After the revolution, Chang Hsün emerged as the most conspicuous and forceful defender of prerevolutionary institutions. He remained fiercely loyal to the Manchu imperial house, and symbolized his fealty by retaining his queue and ordering his troops to retain theirs. For this reason, he was called the "Pig-Tailed General." He supported continuation of the cult of Confucius, and was hostile to most manifestations of new thought in China. Since he was loyal to the Manchu Emperor, Chang opposed Yuan Shih-k'ai's attempt to become Emperor, but he did not join the military struggle against Yuan, whom he regarded as his patron.

After Yuan's death had resolved Chang's conflict of loyalties, he began to plot the restoration of the Manchu emperor. His opportunity came in the spring of 1917 when President Li Yuan-hung called Chang to go to Peking to help resolve a political crisis in the relations between himself and the National Assembly. Chang went to the capital, and promptly announced the restoration of the Manchu Dynasty and the imperial administrative system. Chang had earlier discussed his plans with leading Peiyang warlords, who had led him to believe they would support his restoration plans. The Peiyang leaders, however, were using Chang in their own complicated plots; as soon as Chang declared the restoration, they announced their devotion to the republic, and sent their armies against the pig-tailed troops in Peking. The restoration was thus brought to an end two weeks after it started, and Chang Hsün was forced into hiding. He was pardoned a year later, but he did not resume his active career; he lived quietly in north China until his death in 1923.

Chang was utterly arrogant and independent. Except for his loyalty to the Manchu Court and to Yuan Shih-k'ai, he seemed to acknowledge no authority and brook no restraints. During the Second Revolution of 1913, Chang allowed his troops to loot and rape the great city of Nanking with appalling ferocity. His was not the only army involved, but he is generally considered responsible for the terror. Wherever his pig-tailed army went, people were a little nervous. A popular ditty of the warlord period hinted at the difficulty of living in a time of change when enemies of change such as Chang Hsün were around:

> One cannot mix with people if he does not cut his queue.
> But if he cuts it he must fear what old Chang Hsün will do.[2]

Chang Tsung-ch'ang, the Dog Meat General, is perhaps the best exemplification of the brutality and exploitation of which warlords were capable. He was born in 1881 in an impoverished and marginal family; his father was a trumpeter and head shaver, and his mother exorcised evil spirits. The family moved to Manchuria when Chang was in his teens, and there he worked his way up from petty crime in Harbin to banditry in the countryside. During the Russo-Japanese War of 1904–1905, Chang fought on the side of the Russians, after which he again took up life as a bandit. Chang's activities during the confusion of the 1911 Revolution are not completely clear, but when the dust settled he emerged with regular military status; by 1913 he was commander of a division. In subsequent years he had various commands, and in 1922 he went to Manchuria to serve under Chang Tso-lin. He fought well for Chang, and in 1925 he became military governor of Shantung, under the auspices of the Manchurian warlord. He held the position until he was chased out of the province by the Nationalist armies in 1928, which, for practical purposes, ended his career.

Chang was once described as a dinosaur, a figure of great physical power moving across the landscape in a mindlessly brutal way. He had the physique to go with the simile; he was a huge, powerful man, about six and a half feet tall. He squeezed out the wealth of Shantung without mercy, and left it in poverty and disorder. When a newspaper criticized him, he promptly had the editor shot, a solution that typified Chang's approach to problems of noncooperation or opposition. His troops were well known for their facility in "opening melons," splitting skulls, and hanging strings of severed heads from telegraph poles as warnings to those who would question Chang's authority. When he fled in 1928, between a third and a half of the province was in virtual anarchy, the impoverished prey of roaming bandit gangs.

Like Chang Hsün's conservatism, Chang Tsung-ch'ang's propensity for destruction found reflection in a ditty that children used to sing in Peking. A translation does not convey the rhythm that gave it part of its childish appeal, but it does indicate the kind of impression Chang Tsung-ch'ang made on the population:

> Chang Tsung-ch'ang, wicked and wasteful;
> Wrecks shoes, wrecks stockings, wrecks army equipment.[3]

Besides his rapacity and brutality, Chang was known for his concubines and his colorful personal habits. The number of his concubines has been variously reported between 30 and 50, although it is perhaps presumptuous for historians to try to fix the number when Chang himself allegedly did not know. Popular gossip had it that Chang had "three don't-knows": he did not know how many women, how many troops, or how much money he had. John Gunther demonstrated his enviably thorough research techniques by reporting that Chang had concubines of 26 different nationalities, each with her own washbowl marked with the flag of her nation. Occasionally, Chang took a large number of his concubines to restaurants or public functions, and they served as hostesses for his sometimes lavish parties, where huge quantities of Western liquor and giant cigars were consumed.

With Japanese support behind the scenes, Chang went back to Shantung early in 1929, hastily organized a motley army, and tried to reestablish himself as a power in the province. He was quickly defeated, and again fled. A few years later, while on a railroad station platform, he was assassinated by the adopted son of a man Chang had murdered a few years earlier.

REFORMIST WARLORDS: CH'EN CHIUNG-MING, LI TSUNG-JEN, FENG YÜ-HSIANG, YEN HSI-SHAN

The wonder is not that there were conservative or reactionary warlords, but that there were so many who accepted or advocated some measure of iconoclasm and social reform. Ch'en Chiung-ming and Li Tsung-jen were both southerners. Ch'en exemplified the warlord who began as revolutionary. Li moved in the other direction; he started his career as a young officer in the warlord wars of Kwangsi and later emerged as a national leader. Reformist warlords also appeared in the north, Feng Yü-hsiang and Yen Hsi-shan being the best known and the most influential. Yen maintained the most stable warlord administration in north China, ruling Shansi virtually unopposed for two decades. Feng, on the other hand, was one of several warlords who could never get a firm grip on substantial territory and shifted from one region to another. Both men guarded their independence against revolutionary movements as long as possible. However, during the Northern Expedition, Yen and Feng joined the Kuomintang and continued to fight for their independence from inside the party.

Ch'en Chiung-ming was born in 1878 in a gentry family in Kwangtung. He received a traditional Confucian education, and won the first degree in 1898. Even before that time, however, Ch'en had been attracted by the new ideas entering China from the West, and early in the twentieth century he enrolled in a school where Western learning was taught. He graduated in 1907, and shortly afterward became editor of a reformist newspaper. When the Manchus created provincial assemblies in 1909, Ch'en was elected to the Kwangtung Assembly. A few months later he joined the United League, Sun Yat-sen's revolutionary party.

It was the 1911 Revolution that brought Ch'en into military affairs. When the revolt broke out, Ch'en promptly raised a military force that played a critical role in swinging Kwangtung into the revolutionary camp, and he was rewarded by being named vice-governor of the province. He successively held several other positions of influence in the province, but he joined the rebellion against Yuan Shih-k'ai in 1913, and had to flee when the revolt was put down. Ch'en returned to China in 1916 to fight Yuan's monarchical movement, and in 1917–1918 he succeeded in carving out a military base in eastern Kwangtung and southern Fukien provinces.

By 1920, while Ch'en was still organizing his regional administration in south China, Sun Yat-sen concluded that the best hope for his revolutionary movement lay in creating a military base in Kwangtung from which to launch military campaigns to unite the country. But Kwangtung was at that time in the hands of Kwangsi warlords, so Sun urged Ch'en Chiung-ming to oust the Kwangsi armies. Ch'en succeeded in doing that in 1920, and in the following year, again at Sun's urging, Ch'en invaded Kwangsi and conquered that province.

Sun Yat-sen was naturally pleased with Ch'en's success, and felt that the provinces of Kwangsi and Kwangtung would serve as an adequate base for the revolution. Sun now began to plan a northern expedition to eliminate the warlords, and he counted upon Ch'en to lead it. But Ch'en was not really interested. Though he had joined Sun's revolutionary party in 1910, he had had little connection with Sun or his movement since 1913. In fact, he disapproved of some of

Sun's policies, particularly the plan to use Kwangtung as a base from which to conquer the rest of the country. Such a plan promised to tax Kwangtung's human and economic resources, yet offered little prospect of success. Ch'en's personal ambition and intellectual conviction alike argued against such a policy. He was also jealous of his position in Kwangtung, and wanted to diminish Sun's influence rather than enhance it. Moreover, Ch'en, like other southern warlords, was persuaded that China's best hope lay not in unification by force, but in a federation of autonomous provinces. As a consequence, friction between Sun and Ch'en mounted until, in the summer of 1922, Ch'en's troops attacked Sun's headquarters, and the revolutionary leader barely escaped with his life. Shortly afterward, however, warlord allies of Sun from Yunnan and Kwangsi drove Ch'en from Canton. He maintained fragments of military power until 1925 when they were completely destroyed, thus ending his career as a warlord. Ch'en remained on the periphery of Chinese politics for the next eight years, but his influence was negligible once his army was gone. He died in 1933.

Ch'en's regional administration from 1918 to 1922 reflected some of his earlier progressive ideas, though he was not in power long enough to effect permanent reforms. He was particularly interested in improving education. He established dozens of new primary schools, and set up a provincial educational committee of outstanding educators. To preside over it, he invited Ch'en Tu-hsiu, who, as publisher and editor of the radical journal *New Youth*, was the leading Westernizing intellectual of the time. Ch'en Chiung-ming also talked of provincial self-government, but that seems to have meant a rejection of Peking's control more than a democratic government within the province. Although at one time Ch'en encouraged labor unions and peasant unions, his policies became increasingly conservative as these unions became more radical. His conservatism seems to have derived partly from his sympathy with the gentry class, the class of his origins, and, more substantially, from a core of Confucian belief that Ch'en never quite got rid of. Like other reforming warlords, Ch'en was at heart a benevolent despot.

Like Ch'en, Li Tsung-jen had an education that combined the old and the new. Li was born in 1891 in a family that had once been wealthy, but at that time owned only a small farm.[4] His father was an unsuccessful scholar who tutored in the Chinese classics when he was not working the land. He gave his son an elementary education along traditional lines, and, surprisingly for a Confucian scholar, also sent him to a modern elementary school that had been established near the family's home early in the twentieth century. But Li did not show much aptitude for academic studies, and he was accordingly sent to the Cotton Weaving Institute for practical training. He graduated but could find no work, and shortly afterward enrolled in another practical institution, the Kwangsi Military Elementary School. It was here that he started his life's career, and also where he met the men who were later to become, with Li, the leaders of the Kwangsi Clique.

After several years in military school, and a brief stint as a physical education teacher, Li joined a unit of the Kwangsi Army in 1916, where he gained steady promotion during the following five years. But that army was shattered and dispersed by Ch'en Chiung-ming's invasion of Kwangsi in 1921. Li led his men into the mountains to escape the invader, a move that marked the beginning of his creation of an independent, personal army. When Ch'en withdrew from Kwangsi in 1922, no single group was capable of taking over provincial authority. The province was in complete turmoil, divided among many small bands and tiny armies. There were at least fifteen separate armies in the province, each numbering several thousand troops, to say nothing of bandit gangs and even smaller armed groups. Li's army numbered about 2,000 men and dominated five rural districts. From this base, he and his allies used a combination of force and guile to eliminate their rivals, until by late 1925 they controlled the entire province of Kwangsi.

In the years Li and his partners were unifying Kwangsi, the Kuomintang was establishing its supremacy in the neighboring province of Kwangtung. Economic and geographic factors have always made Kwangtung the natural ally of Kwangsi, because if Kwangsi were to be cut off from Kwangtung, it would become only a poor and isolated hinterland. This circumstance, as much as ideological affinity, prompted Li and his associates to join the Kuomintang early in 1926. For practical purposes, the Kwangsi Clique continued to manage internal provincial matters pretty much as they wished, though they generally accepted Kuomintang authority in matters of national scope. The most pressing national task at that time was a military expedition to the north to capture the national capital and unify the country under a Kuomintang government. Units participating in the expedition were organized as the National Revolutionary Army. The Kwangsi Army was named the Seventh Army of the National Revolutionary Army, and Li Tsung-jen was its commander.

Li played an active and a crucial role during the Northern Expedition. His troops fought effectively in several important campaigns, and he supported Chiang Kai-shek's anti-Communist policy. When the expedition reached the Yangtze, Chiang suddenly split with the Communists and the Kuomintang Left, rupturing the revolutionary movement and laying the seeds for the long internecine civil war. Through participation in the revolutionary expedition, the Kwangsi army penetrated Hupei and Hunan, thus bringing Kwangsi power into the Yangtze Valley. However, control of these Yangtze provinces became an issue of conflict between Li and Chiang Kai-shek in 1929, and the Kwangsi leaders were finally forced out of central China and back to their home province.

Through the first half of the 1930s, Kwangsi remained essentially independent. Li and other Kwangsi leaders were remarkably successful in the administration and development of their province. Crime was virtually eliminated, official corruption was almost nonexistent, and conspicuous progress was made in developing industry, in public construction, and in expending educational programs. A remarkable militia system was developed that created an armed populace and that was linked with other socially constructive activities. Li and his associates became famous as superb administrators and organizers devoting their talents to the public good.

Li was brought actively back into national affairs with the outbreak of the Sino-Japanese War in 1937. He held high military posts throughout the war, and in 1948 was elected Vice President of China. When Communist victories in the civil war finally compelled Chiang Kai-shek to resign as President in January, 1949, Li became Acting President. It was too late for Li to alter the situation, however, particularly because Chiang continued to exercise control informally through personal influence and through his position as leader of the party. In 1949, when the Communist victory was already certain, Li went to the United States for treatment of a stomach disorder. He lived in America until 1965, when he suddenly went to the People's Republic of China and was received as a returning hero. He died there in 1969.

In north China, Yen Hsi-shan and Feng Yü-hsiang were the most powerful and most colorful of the reformist warlords. The two were strikingly different in personality and appearance. Feng was a huge man, a compelling speaker with a flair for the dramatic gesture. Yen, a man of medium build, maintained a solemn reserve; he rarely laughed, and seldom revealed his inner feelings. Feng, on the contrary, was extremely emotional and not infrequently wept publicly. He also affected great simplicity in life and dress; his garb was of the plainest, and he often traveled in a freight car or truck; he denied accumulating money for personal ends, and no evidence exists that he did so. Yen, however, amassed a fortune and lived in conspicuous luxury.

Feng was the son of a low-ranking army officer, and he spent his childhood in and around army camps. When he was only 16, he joined Li Hung-chang's army, and in 1902 he transferred to Yuan Shih-k'ai's command. Feng advanced steadily in rank, primarily because of his own ability and his extraordinary energy and diligence. With virtually no formal education, he struggled hard to educate himself. He aspired to be first in examinations and competitions, and very often gained that distinction. His career was also helped by the fact that he married the niece of one of Yuan Shih-k'ai's trusted subordinates.

Until about 1911 Feng held traditionalistic and conservative views—not unexpected in an ignorant peasant youth. The death of the Manchu Emperor in 1907 reduced Feng to tears. On the eve of the revolution, however, he came under the influence of some radical officers who persuaded him to help overthrow the monarchy. His superiors put him under arrest, and he was only saved from execution by the influence of his father-in-law, who also managed to get Feng back into Yuan's army shortly after the establishment of the republic.

By the early twentieth century, Westerners had extensive political and economic power over China. At a time of domestic crisis, therefore, the support of Westerners could be helpful. Partly with that in mind, Feng formally adopted the Christian religion in 1914; he had strong puritanical tendencies, and he was impressed by the personal behavior of Christians he observed in China. They did not smoke opium, or drink, or gamble; they educated their children and worked hard, traits Feng admired. He tried to convert his troops to Christianity because he felt they would be more loyal and better disciplined soldiers if they followed Christian moral injunctions. Years later, when Feng was nationally and internationally known, he was called the "Christian General," and many stories circulated about his unique mixture of Christian moralism and Chinese militarism.

It was not only its Christian coloration that made Feng's army unique in China. Feng demanded extraordinary physical fitness, and subjected his officers and men to constant and rigorous training to achieve it. At a time when soldiers were generally expected to be disorderly and officers were assumed to be venal, Feng enforced the most rigid discipline and punished the slightest hint of corruption. He prohibited drinking, gambling, visiting prostitutes, even swearing. Officers were selected on the basis of merit, and were expected to be able to do anything they ordered their men to do. Feng indoctrinated his troops in Christian and Confucian values, stressing both the importance of moral life and the existence of the army as the servant of the people.

Like a number of warlords, Feng controlled many different regions during his career, from a few districts to a province to several provinces. His civil administration demonstrated the same kind of moralistic concerns that his military-training programs did. He vigorously suppressed banditry and disorder, and prohibited vices such as prostitution, gambling, and opium smoking. Feng established several kinds of social-welfare institutions, including rehabilitation centers for beggars, sanatoriums for narcotics addicts, and orphanages. In peacetime, he put his men to work on public projects such as road building, tree planting, and flood control.

Unfortunately, few of Feng's reforms were permanent. The vicissitudes of warlord politics seldom allowed him to remain in one province long enough to carry the programs through, and his successors never concerned themselves with continuing his innovations. Also, Feng seldom had enough money to support his reform proposals adequately; from the outset some were more in the nature of paper changes than substantial realistic innovations. Perhaps the chief weakness of Feng's reform program was his failure to marshal the support and participation of the people he presumably served. Despite the aura of Westernization and innovation given by Feng's Christianity and by the promulgation of reform directives in the context of warlordism, Feng was basically traditional in his thinking. He thought in authoritarian and moralistic terms, not in terms of organizational or institutional change.

Feng participated in many of the warlord wars, and seems to have hoped at one time that he would be able to unify China by force. However, this did not happen, and in 1926 he and his army joined the Kuomintang's Northern Expedition, partly because Feng sympathized with Kuomintang objectives, partly because the prospects of the Northern Expedition looked good, but mainly because the revolutionary army opposed his enemies, Chang Tso-lin and Wu P'ei-fu. When the country was ostensibly united in 1928, Feng was in a powerful position, with high office in the national government and several provinces under his control. Like other warlords, however, he would not accept the leadership of Chiang Kai-shek, and in 1929–30 he joined with Yen Hsi-shan in a bitter, bloody war against Chiang. Chiang won the war and deprived Feng of troop command. His defeat brought his career as a warlord to a close, though he held various sinecures in the national government until his death in 1948.

Yen Hsi-shan had a much more stable career than Feng. Yen was born in Shansi where his family had for generations been minor bankers and merchants. After a brief period studying the classics in a traditional Chinese school, Yen was enrolled in one of the new military academies established as part of the Manchu program of military modernization. In 1904 he went to Japan to continue his military education, and was graduated from the Imperial Military Academy in 1909.

At that time, Japan was a center of activity for Chinese radicals, and, like so many Chinese youngsters sent to study abroad, Yen learned as much from revolutionaries as from his military teachers. He joined Sun Yat-sen's revolutionary group, the United League. He returned to China in 1908 to become brigade commander in the

New Shansi Army and found that many of the officers and men of this unit were also members of Sun's party. When the Wuhan revolt started in 1911, Yen and his fellow revolutionaries responded by attacking the Manchu garrison in Shansi, and the Shansi provincial assembly declared the province independent. Because Yen combined military authority with revolutionary legitimacy, he was made military governor of the province, a position he was to hold virtually without interruption for the next two decades.

In most of China warlords rose and fell with bewildering speed, but Yen was able to rule Shansi undisturbed, largely because of the province's geographical isolation. Steep mountains enclose it on three sides, and the Yellow River on the fourth is not navigable. Through most of the warlord period, Yen Hsi-shan was able to stay out of the civil wars that tortured the country and made tenure of office so uncertain. He devoted his energies to the administration of his own province, and created such a reputation for peace and prosperity that he was known as the "Model Governor." His reputation, in fact, exceeded the reality, but he nevertheless promoted a variety of reforms.

Like Feng Yü-hsiang, Yen attempted to eliminate a number of traditional practices. He ordered that queues no longer be worn, and authorized his police to cut them off whenever they spotted them. Yen set up a Society for the Liberation of Feet, and urged students to wear badges announcing that they would refuse to marry girls with bound feet. He deplored the traditional idea that women needed no education; they should have some learning, he said, although very little.

Like most of China's people, only an infinitesimal portion of the Shansi population could read or write. In 1918 Yen launched a campaign to reduce illiteracy by giving at least four years of education to the maximum possible number of children. By 1923 his program had resulted in about 800,000 children in his province receiving some kind of elementary education; in that year, education was the largest single item in the Shansi provincial budget. The school curriculum showed the influence of John Dewey, who gave several lectures in Shansi in 1919, and whose pragmatism found a strong response in Yen's own concern for practicability. Schoolwork was geared as closely as possible to the daily life and needs of the people.

Yen also viewed his schools as major agencies of political indoctrination, as instruments for the creation of a pattern of proper behavior and political obedience. Like Feng Yü-hsiang, Yen was very much concerned with public morality and behavior. He set up an Early Rising Society to see that people did not dawdle in bed after six in the morning. He outlawed idleness, gambling, brawling, and excessive partying. Yen attacked prostitution in an original way by convening a conference to determine methods of "ensuring constancy and regularity of sexual intercourse between husbands and wives."[5]

Yen was ideologically eclectic, borrowing ideas from a range of theories and ideologies in both East and West. Yet the core of his ideology was the Confucian belief that political problems were essentially moral, and that political authority was the prerogative of moral men who would wield it in a benevolent but nonetheless authoritarian fashion.

Yen, like Feng Yü-hsiang, often spoke in nationalistic terms, particularly in denouncing imperialism in China. Yet he resisted the spread of Sun Yat-sen's political ideas in Shansi, despite his own early membership in Sun's party. Moreover, he condemned the 1919 student demonstrations against Japanese imperialism as disorderly. It was only when the Northern Expedition appeared to be irresistible, and Yen was forced to take sides before he was engulfed, that he joined the National Revolutionary Army and ordered the people of Shansi to embrace Kuomintang nationalism.

After the nominal unification of the country in 1928, Yen opposed the extension into Shansi of effective control by the central government, and in 1929–1930 joined with Feng Yü-hsiang in the decisive war against Chiang Kai-shek. After Feng and Yen lost the war, Yen announced his retirement from public life, but two years later he returned to power in Shansi with the acquiescence of the central government. He then launched a widespread program of provincial development. He also attempted to resist the spread of communism in his province by military opposition to Communist forces and by developing social and economic reforms that would steal the thunder of the Communists. Like the rest of the Kuomintang, though, Yen was forced off the mainland in 1949. He went to Taiwan, where he lived until his death in May, 1960.

Warlord Armies

The indispensable qualification for a warlord was command of a personal army, an army that obeyed only him. The most important warlord units were nominal parts of the national army, and therefore presumably subject to the orders of the government in Peking. Their inclusion in the national army, however, was merely a formal matter with little relation to reality. As one warlord recalled, "Military men were told to obey, but that did not mean obedience to civil authorities. . . . A battalion or regimental commander nearly always obeyed his divisional commander's orders to fight or refrain from fighting. He himself never analyzed the question, nor did he consider whether he was fighting for the country, the people, or for his divisional commander."[6]

Warlords cultivated and maintained the obedience of their armies through military discipline, personal loyalty and obligations, regional feeling, patriotism, and identification of officers' personal advantage with the warlord's. Military discipline and the military ethos of obedience varied from one warlord army to another, but together they must be considered a powerful cohesive force. Many officers were professional military men, the products of Western-style military academies. They were well grounded in the military virtue of obedience, and a few armies conducted continuous training and indoctrination programs to maintain a high level of discipline among officers and men.

The force of such training was supplemented by bonds of personal loyalty and obligation between the warlord and his officers. Personal ties had always been primary in China, and they assumed an even more critical role in the early twentieth century as the monarchy declined in importance as a focus of allegiance. Tseng Kuo-fan and Li Hung-chang, who organized the armies that suppressed the Taiping Rebellion in the nineteenth century, selected officers who would be personally loyal to them, and these officers used similar criteria in selecting their own subordinates. In that fashion they forged a chain of loyalties stretching from the lowest officer to the general. In later armies, notably that of Yuan Shih-k'ai, the same practices were followed. Virtually every military officer was bound to some of his superiors and subordinates by obligations in addition to those of military rank and office. These included ties of family and marriage, teacher-student and patron-protégé relations, and friendship.

Provincial patriotism was also a cohesive force. Traditionally strong provincial feelings were intensified by the provincial character of the Revolution of 1911 and the weak republican government. It was often expressed in the warlord era by the use of slogans demanding that provinces be governed by natives: "Hunan for the Hunanese," "Szechwan for the Szechwanese," and so forth. The composition of most warlord armies showed strong regional characteristics, particularly in the officer corps. An officer would hesitate to leave an army composed of men whose language and values were familiar, especially if the alternative was an army with different regional traits. Thus, regional feeling tended to inhibit defections, and to that extent helped maintain army unity. At the same time, regionalism was one obstacle to the creation of a larger unity. Regional patriotism, in other words, obstructed efforts to merge armies into new, larger organizations that transcended the province.

Another important cohesive factor in warlord armies was the expectation of officers that they would rise in proportion to their army's success. When a warlord gained in power, his subordinates expected advancement in rank, promotion in office, or at the very least expanded opportunities to gain wealth.

The defection of officers, who would take their entire units with them, was the chief threat to the unity and strength of warlord armies. Defection of complete units was facilitated by the fact that officers were bound in a chain of loyalties, the primary link being between an officer and his immediate superior; only through his superior was an officer loyal and obedient to the commanding general. If an officer defected, the link of loyalty was broken at that point; the chain on both sides, however, remained intact, with all the men and officers under the defector's command normally following him. The chief reason for defection was disappointment over rewards. When an officer did not receive the promotion or advancement he expected, he became more susceptible to an invitation to change sides, particularly when the blandishments were sweetened with offers of money, rank, or office, as they usually were; in some cases, huge sums were offered to entice high officers to change their loyalties. A warlord's involvement in what seemed clearly a losing cause also encouraged defection among his subordinates.

Not only did inadequate rewards nourish defection, but, somewhat ironically, the granting of rewards could also engender disunity in warlord organizations. Leading subordinates had to be rewarded in the only coin that had meaning in warlord China: enlarged command and territorial authority. Yet military and territorial authority were the sinews of independence; the more soldiers and territory a warlord's subordinates had at their disposal, the more they tended to become allies instead of subalterns. The warlord naturally called upon his chief lieutenants to administer his expanded domains, but he found it increasingly difficult to exact obedience from them; he had to consult with them, but he was well aware that his subordinates might go off on their own or ally themselves with others if they found it in their own best interests to do so. The growth of warlord organization, therefore, had its own built-in limits.

When an officer defected not to another army, but to become an independent agent, he became a warlord. In the same way, when a warlord's subordinate acquired so much military and territorial power that he became an ally of his former superior, he became a warlord. In short, every military unit from a company to an entire army was potentially a warlord unit, and every officer a potential warlord. He actually became a warlord at the moment he assumed an independent stance, when he no longer acknowledged the orders of a superior.

The many ties between officers and their commander are often summed up—somewhat imprecisely—as loyalty. For the rank-and-file troops, however, loyalty was less important than obedience. Obedience of soldiers to their officers was inherent in the discipline and authoritarian nature of military organization. The soldier obeyed his immediate superior; he did not judge the legitimacy or illegitimacy of his commander's actions. That obedience to their superior and not loyalty to the warlord was what held the troops in line was evidenced by the facility with which defeated soldiers were absorbed into victorious armies where they served new commanders with no apparent difficulty.

Warlord armies mushroomed in size after the death of Yuan Shih-k'ai. Despite the dangers and discomforts of army life, and the low social status of the common soldier, armies seldom lacked recruits. Perhaps a few were attracted by a romantic image of army life, and an occasional recruit may have joined from nationalistic or patriotic motives. But unquestionably the pressure of rural poverty was the most effective recruiting agent. Most recruits were impoverished peasants who joined the army for subsistence and fellowship that did not seem to be available elsewhere. This fact explains the apparent paradox that soldiers often objected to attempts to disband them and return them to civilian life but they often deserted when battle seemed imminent or their treatment particularly brutal.[7] They joined the army to make a living, not to die. The most ambitious among them felt that in the army, more than any other sector of Chinese society at that time, they could expect their ability to be rewarded without regard to family background, social status, or formal education. If a poor man rose to officer rank, he found a modicum of prestige and wealth that was otherwise not available to him. One Chinese anthropologist, Fei Hsiao-tung, reported that in the community he was studying,

> A family which we knew to have been in debt for several hundred dollars cleared up all its obligations and acquired more than 10 kung of land in one year after the son had entered the army. The richest family in the village has a son who is the commander of a regiment.[8]

One young officer, whose salary was $128 a month, discovered that he could receive $3,000 a month if he could wangle the post as garrison head in a town where salt was stored and sold.[9] High-ranking officers amassed enormous sums, and acquired vast land holdings. Such seductive prospects doubtless attracted many able young men from the poor peasantry. Indeed, Fei noted that during the two years he studied the village, 27 out of the 100 males in the 16 to 30 age group left home to seek opportunity and 18 of them went into the army.

According to national army regulations, recruits were to be between 19 and 26 years of age, but most warlords were not that particular. Chang Fa-k'uei, whose "Ironsides" troops were a crack fighting unit, recalls that "in practice we took anybody we could get. We accepted young boys and men older than [26]. We took men with one eye, anyone as long as he could walk. They could serve as cooks."[10] Chang, like several other warlords, often sent his officers to their home districts to recruit their friends, neighbors, and contemporaries. In this way, the ties of localism, friendship, and regional feeling lent cohesion and stability to the units recruited.

Enlistment was for an indefinite period, and many men served 10 or 20 years or more in the army. If a soldier wanted to leave the army, he requested a long leave, often for the ostensible purpose of visiting a sick parent or relative. Chang Fa-k'uei reports that many of his soldiers asked for such leaves at about the age of 40, when their physical strength began to decline. Commanders normally did not try to retain these men. If war was not imminent, insistent leave requests of younger soldiers might also be approved, for they were considered potential deserters. The treatment of captured deserters varied from army to army, but the death penalty was likely only when the deserter took his rifle with him, deserted on the eve of battle, or when the commander wished to make a conspicuous show of rigorous discipline. In Chang Fa-k'uei's army, recruits were told that if they deserted after a request for leave had been denied they would not be executed, but that the death penalty would be applied to anyone who deserted without first having asked for leave.[11]

Conditions of life for the common soldiers varied enormously from one warlord army to another. In some armies, men underwent regular training, systematic discipline was enforced, and life went on in an organized military pattern. Feng Yü-hsiang trained his troops rigorously, with emphasis on physical labor and strict obedience to puritanical regulations. Chang Fa-k'uei had one of his men shot for stealing a few bananas to stress to his troops that he would not tolerate a breach of discipline. A number of other warlords, though less conspicuously strict, nevertheless maintained vigorous and obedient armies. In other units, discipline was lax, training was careless or nonexistent, and life was irregular and disorderly. Some troops were notorious for waging drunken brawls, smoking opium freely, and spending more time gambling than on the drill field.

The Control of Territory

Each warlord has to find sources of support for his army. Only taxation provided adequate and reliable revenue and therefore a warlord needed control of territory to tax. Consequently, command of territory is sometimes considered one defining characteristic of a warlord. Li Tsung-jen learned the importance of territorial control at the very beginning of the warlord period. As he later recalled, 1916 was the most troublesome time of his career:

> Our difficulty resulted from the fact that we were the only army under the direct command of General Headquarters without a "territory." When the Anti-Yuan Movement started early that year, local militias were organized everywhere. Once a local militia was organized, its commander would petition General Headquarters for recognition and for an official title. As soon as they were formally recognized, they would draw rations from the local government, so all these local armies had their respective "territories"!
>
> Our Sixth Army, however, was under the direct command of General Headquarters. We did not have a local "territory" from which we could tax the people. We depended entirely upon Headquarters for our daily maintenance. When General Headquarters was disbanded after the war, we were transferred to the command of the Military Governor of Kwangtung. In those days, however, the Provincial Government of Kwangtung could hardly support itself. As a result of this financial hardship, not only was our pay deferred from month to month, but even our daily maintenance could not be met.[12]

Li's statement incidentally reveals the way small warlord units could come into existence. The local militias he described, with their local commanders dominating particular areas, however small, were essentially warlord units, and their commanders were petty warlords. Unquestionably, innumerable petty warlords were scattered over the length and breadth of China behind the facade of national and provincial authority claimed by the more powerful warlords.

Not every warlord had control of territory at all times, and a typology of warlords might reasonably distinguish between those who had an area and those who were looking for one. But every warlord needed territory as a source of support; without it, he could not exist for long. Without territory, a warlord was also at a military disadvantage: he could not make long-range defensive plans, the supply lines for arms and material were inevitably precarious, and his very presence in another warlord's bailiwick usually meant that he had to fight frequently. Such a warlord inevitably had to obtain support through alliances or accept subordination to another militarist—relations that were usually unstable and temporary. The independence that was the essence of the warlord required regional authority. The size of the regions varied enormously, but there was a rough correlation between territory and the strength of the warlord's army. The commander of a powerful force might control one or more provinces; smaller units might dominate only a few districts.

Regardless of the size of a warlord's territory, he craved the legitimacy of official position in the republic's political-military structure whenever that was possible. This was easy to obtain when allied with the warlord holding Peking, the source of office and titles. When a warlord's enemy held Peking, he might simply deny the validity of the national government and give himself a flowery title in opposition to the Peking regime. Even in such cases, however, warlords went to surprising lengths to try to acquire some semblance of legitimacy. "Elections" were a favorite method. For example, when Chang Tso-lin was driven from north China in 1922 and stripped of his titles by the Peking government, he ruled Manchuria independently; he simply cut it off from the rest of the country. However, he was careful to arrange a joint conference of delegates of both the three provincial assemblies in Manchuria and the various other Manchurian organizations alleged to be representative of the people. This conference approved Manchuria's independence and conferred upon the Manchurian warlord the title "Protector of Peace of Manchuria."

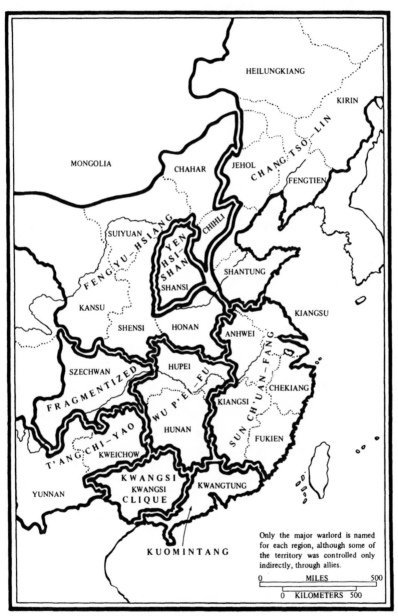

HEILUNGKIANG

KIRIN

MONGOLIA

CHANG-TSO-LIN

CHAHAR

JEHOL

FENGTIEN

SUIYUAN

CHIHLI

F E N G - Y U - H S I A N G

YEN
HSI-
SHAN

SHANSI

SHANTUNG

KANSU

SHENSI

HONAN

ANHWEI

KIANGSU

SZECHWAN

HUPEI

S U N - C H ' U A N - F A N G

F R A G M E N T I Z E D

W U - P ' E - F U

KIANGSI

CHEKIANG

HUNAN

FUKIEN

T ' A N G - C H I - Y A O

KWEICHOW

YUNNAN

KWANGSI
KWANGSI
CLIQUE

KWANGTUNG

KUOMINTANG

Only the major warlord is named
for each region, although some of
the territory was controlled only
indirectly, through allies.

0   MILES   500

0   KILOMETERS   500

Warlord Division of China, c. January 1, 1926

Warlords were responsible for civil and military administration in their domains. Normally, each province had a civil governor; provincial assemblies continued to function in some, but in almost every instance they were completely subordinate to the military governor, the *tuchün*. In some measure, petty militarists limited the *tuchün*'s effective authority by controlling districts or regions in parts of his province. Usually, though, provincial warlords tried to get their own appointees into important positions all the way down to the district level, and probably succeeded except in those instances where districts were completely in the hands of petty warlords whom the provincial warlord for some reason or other did not wish to challenge. About a year after Ch'en Shu-fan became *tuchün* of Shensi in 1916, for example, all the district magistrates in that province, with only two or three exceptions, held their appointments from Ch'en.* In many instances, magistrates would be permitted to continue in office under a new *tuchün* if he made a satisfactory donation to the new ruler's treasury. In 1921, when Wu P'ei-fu took over Hupei, he considered $50,000 a satisfactory donation.

Warlords differed in their approach to the responsibility of governing. In some areas, warlord government was simply a euphemism for rapacious exploitation and brutality. In others, warlords worked closely with the local and provincial gentry to maintain law and order, to develop educational institutions, and to formulate reasonable programs to deal with local and provincial needs. No matter how responsible and able an individual warlord might be, however, the people inevitably suffered from the warlord system, if only because of its insatiable demand for money.

Warlords exploited every source of revenue that experience or imagination suggested. They increased the land tax in many areas, collected for years in advance in some regions, and occasionally collected the same year's taxes more than once. Commodities were also taxed. Salt was so heavily taxed that it produced huge revenues. Opium was also a major source of money, and warlords encouraged

---

* Strictly speaking, they were acting appointments. District magistrates were supposed to be appointed by the central government from among men who had either passed examinations for such a position or who had qualified by serving in that capacity for a certain number of years under the former dynasty. However, the provincial government had the right to appoint acting magistrates, and Ch'en's appointees were therefore all "acting magistrates."

its cultivation; some levied a "laziness tax" on those who did not plant it. They exacted protection money from opium and gambling houses. Large sums were drained from railroad incomes, with virtually nothing returned in the form of maintenance. Every region was dotted with illegal tax stations to tax goods in transit. Chambers of commerce were forced to contribute "donations" under threat of looting the city. When regular and supplementary taxes did not produce all the revenue a warlord wanted, he levied special taxes ostensibly for specific purposes, such as taxes for "university expenses" or "self-government expenses." In Shantung, when the harvest was good, there was a "rich harvest tax." When all else failed, warlords did not hesitate to turn to the printing press to make money; one produced it on a manually operated duplicating machine.

Wars

Wars, understandably enough—real, bloody, and devastating—typified the warlord years. Some warlords sought constantly to expand their territories; others, landless, sought to acquire their own regions. Either reason meant that it was necessary to encroach upon another militarist's domain—and that meant war. Some warlords were moved to expand through simple ambition or greed; others thought in terms of unifying the country under their command, and saw each victory as a step toward national unification. Somewhat paradoxically, "self-defense" was also a reason for attacking one's neighbor. Because each warlord expected the worst from other warlords, he not only had his own defenses in perpetual readiness, but would on occasion seize an opportunity to strike first when he considered the chances of success particularly good.

Most warlords were bound to others in cliques, and the major wars during the period were those between the important warlord cliques.[13] The first notable cliques to emerge were those that developed around Yuan Shih-k'ai's lieutenants, Feng Kuo-chang and Tuan Ch'i-jui. As described earlier, Feng's followers were called the Chihli Clique, and Tuan led the Anhwei, or Anfu, Clique; these two groups fought in 1920, and the Chihli Clique won. Two years later the three provinces of Manchuria, formed as the Fengtien Clique, or Manchurian Clique, and led by Chang Tso-lin, fought inconclusively against the Chihli militarists; in 1924, however, they were victorious after the defection of Feng Yu-hsiang brought the Chihli group down. Feng then formed his own group of warlords, known as the Kuominchün, or National People's Army, which was defeated by Chang Tso-lin after a long struggle in 1926–1927. The Kwangsi Clique became the best-known clique in the south. Led by Li Tsung-jen and his associates, the clique for short periods extended its control to other provinces, though it remained in Kwangsi most of the time.

The same bonds that cemented warlord armies played a role in maintaining cliques: regional and provincial bonds, family relationships, marriage connections, superior-subordinate military relationships, teacher-student obligations, and friendship. As the warlord period wore on, however, these bonds diminished in importance and bald power considerations increasingly came to the fore—and wars increased in scope and became bloodier.

Historians agree that war was endemic during the warlord period, but do not concur on how many wars were fought. One scholar asserts there were more than 140 wars between 1916 and 1928; another writer has counted more than 400 large and small civil wars after 1911 in the province of Szechwan alone. Some students of the period have also deprecated the dimension of this warfare by picturing it as a kind of comic opera in which each side put up a fierce show but nobody really got hurt. They reason that it made no sense for men to kill one another for a cause no more serious than the personal aggrandizement of their commander. This view, however, is completely erroneous. By and large, warlord wars were real, and spilled real blood.

It is true that on occasion an element of make-believe surfaced in warlord wars. Sometimes opposing commanders would arrange to have their men fire into the air to avoid bloodshed when negotiation or obvious power disparity guaranteed the result. Also defeated warlords were often permitted to retire with their lives and their wealth. But these were minor incidents in a larger and bloodier process. The factor that decided how hard troops fought was not the personal gain of the commander but the degree of their training and discipline. Undisciplined and untrained troops tended to avoid serious battle whenever possible, though even they fought fiercely when regional prejudices were awakened. But disciplined armies, like those of Feng Yü-hsiang and Chang Fa-k'uei fought with skill and stubborn courage on most occasions, and the casualty figures proved it. The major warlord wars were fought by men of ambition, contending for high stakes, and casualties were heavy. In the war of 1929–1930 in which Yen Hsi-shan and Feng Yü-hsiang battled Chiang Kai-shek, casualties on both sides exceeded 300,000 and damage to property was incalculable. When regional prejudices were involved, civilian casualties could also be extremely high. After one brief conflict between Yunnanese and Szechwanese troops in Chengtu in 1917, an estimated 3,000 civilians lost their lives from rifle and shell fire and more than 600 houses were burned, though casualties among the troops did not exceed 50 on either side.[14]

Poor or nonexistent army medical care was partly responsible for high fatality figures. In the absence of competent treatment, even relatively light wounds could prove fatal or crippling. After a battle, the victorious side normally incorporated able-bodied soldiers from the defeated army, but nobody took responsibility for the defeated wounded. As one warlord recalls:

> In cases where we were defeated, our wounded were pathetic.
> The enemy would not take care of them but they would not kill
> them either. If at all possible, the wounded retreated with us.
> They just hobbled along. . . . When we were victorious, . . . we
> did not take care of their wounded either. We could hardly take
> care of our own casualties. The enemy wounded could return to
> their units if they wanted to. They could do whatever they liked.
> We were usually too busy pursuing the enemy. We buried our
> own dead but left the enemy dead on the battlefield. We took
> only able-bodied men as prisoners of war.[15]

Because personal loyalties played such a major role in warlord armies and organizations, the elimination of a single individual could have important results. As a consequence, assassination was a significant mode of warlord conflict. All warlords feared assassination, and some took elaborate precautions to prevent it. Chang Tso-lin tried never to give advance notice of his movements, and often had a subordinate ride in his car while he traveled in another vehicle. That these were not unreasonable precautions may be indicated by a Chinese newspaper report that of 30 prominent Chinese who died in 1925, 12 were assassinated. A common method of murder was to invite the victim to a feast where he was seized and killed.

Occasionally, hostages were also a factor in warlord conflicts, though obviously only under a special combination of circumstances. In 1916 during the war over Yuan Shih-k'ai's monarchical movement, for example, one of Feng Yü-hsiang's officers was captured by Szechwanese troops under Chou Chun. Feng promptly wired Chou that if his subordinate were not released immediately, he would kill Chou's father, who happened to live in the area controlled by Feng. Chou promptly freed Feng's lieutenant.

The Abuse of Civilians

For the mass of the population, the terror, oppression, tax demands, bloodshed, intrigue, and pillaging of the warlord era made those dozen years a nightmare. It was a nightmare the masses did not forget, for warlord misgovernment and rapacity constituted the backdrop against which the Kuomintang and Communists would later compete.

The warlords squeezed the peasants pitilessly by raising normal taxes and instituting dozens of supplementary taxes. In Kwangtung, there were at least 30 different supplementary taxes, and by 1924 in Szechwan 26 supplementary taxes were imposed on salt alone. Not only their possessions, but the peasants' labor was forced from them. An English diplomat reported in 1924:

> A feature of life in Szechuan for many years has been the commandeering of labour by the troops engaged in preparations for or the prosecution of civil war; almost every day, even in the Treaty Port of Chungking, gangs of men may be seen roped together with cords round their wrists being carried off by soldiers

to act as transport coolies and no soldier in Szechuan ever carries his own baggage on the march and sometimes not even his rifle. These commandeered baggage coolies receive no pay but sometimes are given a kind of certificate for labour done which entitles them to preferential treatment when the next commandeering takes place, and often they are snatched away in the streets and forced to accompany the troops to distant places at a moment's notice from which journeys they may not return for weeks, if at all.[16]

The incessant wars wrought unbelievable hardships on villagers and town dwellers alike. Troops looted and lived off the countryside, pillaging large and small towns with ruthless thoroughness. Chang Fa-k'uei, after a defeat in 1922, led his men into the mountains where they stayed for more than half a year. He later recalled:

> Whenever we ran out of food, we would raid a little village to get a few chickens, etc. A village was inhabited by ten families or less. My men would surround a village before dawn and fire several shots to intimidate the people. We told them to come out and give up. This was the classic method of raiding a village. Sometimes we killed and carried away little pigs weighing around thirty catties. We took corn, rice, potatoes, taro. Did we take money? No. There was no money to be had anyway.
>
> We had moral principles. We were a different kind of bandit. We never indulged in fornication or rape. We only robbed because we had nothing to eat. I maintained military discipline and organization among my men.[17]

In 1920 the troops of Chang Ching-yao, a particularly unsavory warlord, looted the town of Yochow in Hunan. A British official described it as follows:

> The arrival of Chang himself on June 13th was the signal for a general looting of the city. I have never seen more thorough work. Every shop, every house in this beautiful and prosperous city has been literally stripped. There is not a vestige of any usable commodity from one end of the city to the other, including the great old yamen used by Chang himself. The place is furnished only by troops, who lie disconsolate, dirty, hungry and demoralized on the floors and the counters of the shops and on

every flat surface that is shaded from the sun. Most of the population has fled, but some 10,000 remain all crowded into the American Mission Hospital.[18]

There is a Chinese saying that "bandits and soldiers are breath from the same nostrils," and it is certainly true that they are frequently indistinguishable. In fact, many warlords started their careers as bandits. From banditry they moved into the army, and ultimately declared their independence and the quest for territory that qualified them as warlords. Because the object of regional administration was so often little more than organized exploitation, it might be argued that the size of a man's appetite largely determined whether he was considered a bandit or a warlord. The bandit had no official position; he killed and stole and fled. The warlord had military rank; he killed and stole and stayed. In his case, the kernel of truth in the exaggeration that greed and murder on a large enough scale pass for ambition, or even statesmanship, was applicable.

Warlords and Foreign Powers

The widespread disorder and violence of the warlord period disrupted foreign trade and endangered foreigners. At the same time, of course, the impotence of the Chinese central government during the warlord years served as an open invitation to foreigners to fish in China's troubled waters. Foreign interference occurred in several ways and at several levels, but the two most important involved further control over China's economic resources and supplying aid to selected warlords.

The foreign grip on China began to tighten during the 1911 Revolution, when the diplomatic corps took over complete control of China's maritime customs. Since the nineteenth century, the maritime Customs Administration had been administered by a largely foreign staff under a foreign director, though foreigners had never handled the actual cash; Chinese authorities had banked and disposed of the money. During the Revolution of 1911, however, foreign commissioners of customs took over the collecting, banking, and remitting of customs revenues, and not long afterward an agreement was signed at Peking whereby the foreign diplomatic corps became trustees of the revenue, with the duty of seeing that the money was used to discharge the obligations secured upon the customs—foreign-loan payments—and that only the surplus was to be released to the Peking government. Later, when revolutionaries set up a rival government in Canton, they protested furiously against the surplus of Canton's customs being paid to their enemies in Peking, but there was nothing that they could do about it.

The Japanese had long had their eyes on the industrial complex at Wuhan, and made it one of the targets of their Twenty-one Demands to the Chinese Government in 1915. As a result, the Chinese agreed not to confiscate the Hanyehping Iron and Coal Company in Wuhan, to convert it into a state enterprise without Japanese consent, or to allow it to borrow or use foreign capital other than Japanese. Japanese capitalists were thereby able to acquire a controlling interest in the major enterprises of the iron-steel-coal complex at Wuhan. In the warlord period, the Japanese further tightened their control over these properties.

When the immediate furor over the Twenty-one Demands had subsided, the Japanese embarked on a policy of loaning such vast sums to the warlord government in Peking that they amounted to massive bribes. In return for these Nishihara loans, which totaled well over 100 million yen during 1917 and 1918, Japan gained additional economic privileges. Japanese merchants and investors, backed by their government, were active throughout China, though they considered some regions—Fukien, and especially Manchuria—to be their particular domains.

Manchuria was so completely under the economic domination of Japan that an anti-Japanese boycott, which started in 1919 in most of China, was completely ineffectual there. A British consul in Mukden reported that there had been no boycott of Japanese goods in Manchuria not only because of Chang Tso-lin's harsh rule, but because the Japanese so completely monopolized the import of foreign goods that no other goods could be found to take the place of boycotted Japanese supplies. At another Manchurian port, Newchwang, the British consul reported the extent to which the Japanese controlled the economy and life of that port by 1919:

Already preponderating Japanese influence is encountered in every department of life in Newchwang. Much of the currency consists of Japanese Gold and Silver Yen notes, and the principal bank is the Yokohama Specie Bank. Not only is the South Manchurian Railway Japanese, but a zone on each side of it is under Japanese jurisdiction, and is policed by Japanese gendarmerie. The Newchwang Electric Light and Waterworks are Japanese. So is the only fully staffed and equipped modern hospital. Most of the shipping and wharf accommodation is Japanese, and so are the chief buildings in the non-Japanese quarter even. . . . Most of the goods on sale in the shops are Japanese, the boycott having had little effect. All the soft coal is supplied by the Japanese, who even control to a great extent the Chinese supply. Aerated waters are Japanese and most of the beer. Whiskey, on sale everywhere under various Scotch labels, is really Japanese, as are the Worcester Sauce, and many other apparently British goods. Even the straw hats worn by the Chinese are of Japanese make.[19]

Japan was by far the worst offender in using warlord disunity to force new economic concessions from China. The other powers, generally, were satisfied to wring the maximum profit from the privileges already permitted under treaties dating from the Ch'ing era. Nonetheless, for them the warlord period was a mixed blessing. The impotence of the national government meant that the Chinese could muster little effective opposition to imperialist interpretations of the treaties, and their implementation. Yet the treaty agreements signed by the central government were not consistently honored by provincial warlords, and the disorder and danger in warlord China threatened and inconvenienced foreigners as well as Chinese. Foreign investment in China was overwhelmingly direct—in railroads, mines, and various businesses, enterprises that required orderly conditions for efficient functioning. Without doubt the imperialist nations, with the possible exception of Japan, would have much preferred a stable Chinese Government to the anarchy of warlordism, and they kept a wary eye open for the warlord strong enough to bring a steady hand to Peking.

In the meantime the foreign powers had to deal with existing circumstances, which often meant dealing directly with warlords. Only in that way could they assure their treaty rights, and possibly stretch them. According to one American diplomat, for example, it was "reliably stated" that the English paid substantial sums annually to the *tuchün* of Honan and his commissioner for foreign affairs for their extending protection to a British concern operating contrary to its charter and in violation of the treaties.

Many of the weapons with which warlord armies fought one another and abused the Chinese people were sold to them by foreigners. In 1919 the American minister to China suggested that it would be difficult for the Chinese to fight if the supply of weapons were cut off, and thus recommended an international agreement prohibiting the sale of arms and munitions in China. The result was the Arms Embargo Agreement of 1919, but it was so widely and flagrantly violated that it was formally canceled ten years later. Throughout the warlord period, foreigners sold weapons by the gun and by the shipload to eager warlords.

Two foreign powers—Japan and Russia—provided overt support for their favorite warlords. Japan, most energetic along these lines, extended huge loans to the Anhwei Clique in 1917–1918, was apparently involved in the plotting that led to Feng Yü-hsiang's overthrow of Wu P'ei-fu in 1924, and gave continued financial and material assistance to Chang Tso-lin in Manchuria. The Russians provided Feng with aid in the form of military instructors and political advisers, arms and material, and money. It was rumored that Wu P'ei-fu was supported by Great Britain; fairly thorough research has shown, however, that although Wu's relations with the British were generally friendly—and included a few loans from British merchants—Britain never supplied him with significant material aid.[20]

Some writers have also said that foreign powers moved into the tumult of warlordism to manipulate warlords like puppets, in the hope of profiting enormously if "their" warlord triumphed over the others and united the country under himself. There is a grain of truth in this view, but no more than a grain. The warlords proved to be very good manipulators themselves. The Russians, for instance, gave military aid to Feng Yü-hsiang in return for his agreement to permit political activity by Kuomintang instructors in his army, and to cooperate generally with the Kuomintang and the National Revolutionary Army, then being guided by Russian advisers. The

Russians kept their part of the bargain, but Feng tightly restricted the role of Russians among his troops. He did not permit them to act as political instructors, and in those instances where Russian activities threatened to have radical consequences in his army—which occurred when some of his cadets put out a political newspaper—Feng instantly and unequivocally squelched them. As for Chang Tso-lin in Manchuria, he had a much more difficult situation to deal with. The Japanese were extremely sensitive to conditions in Manchuria, and they were willing to act much more boldly and arbitrarily than were the Russians wherever they considered their interests in China to be threatened. Nevertheless, Chang was far from a Japanese puppet, and seems to have maneuvered as effectively as possible to retain some degree of independence.

The Federalist Movement

The chief prize for the leading northern warlords was the control of Peking and the machinery of the national government. With that in hand, they received certain national tax revenues, the most important being the surplus of the maritime customs and the salt revenues, the collection of which was handled by foreigners. Moreover, they could claim to speak for the nation in foreign and domestic matters, and they had the authority to negotiate foreign loans in the name of the national government. As a consequence, the northern warlords usually insisted upon the need for centralized government and national unity; the chief advocates of unification by force were invariably found in the north. Southern warlords, who had no hope of gaining control of the national capital, spoke strongly for a federal system of government in which the provinces would retain very substantial powers.

Federalism along these lines had been discussed by Chinese intellectuals at least as early as 1898, and had never lacked advocates. Some intellectuals argued that the provinces were the largest effective political units in the country, and thus formed the natural building blocks of the nation; they also believed that realism demanded a high degree of provincial autonomy until national territorial integration was further developed. It will be recalled that some provincial leaders hoped to create a federal system of government at the time of the 1911 Revolution. Federalist ideas became particularly popular at the beginning of the 1920s. Warlords used them to defend their own independence of the Peking government. Provincial gentry and bourgeoisie thought the federal idea justified their staying out of—and not helping to pay for—national civil wars. Intellectuals, disappointed with the immediate political results of the May Fourth Movement, hoped that federalism would prove a means of eliminating warlordism and encouraging the development of democracy.

Despite these varied sources of support, the federalist movement made little genuine progress. At least five provinces drafted provincial constitutions as a first step towards realization of a federal system. But there were almost no practical efforts to coordinate the activities of the various provinces, so that provincial constitutions were merely a device to assert the autonomy of the specific provinces in which they were drafted. Only one province—Hunan—actually claimed to function in accord with its constitution. The Hunan document, proclaimed in January 1922, described a highly advanced, democratic system of provincial government, but it did not alter the reality of warlord control. In other provinces, federalism was even more of an empty cliché, a facade to cover the self-serving policies of provincial gentry and provincial military leaders. With the advent of a new revolutionary movement after 1923 led by a coalition of the Kuomintang and the Chinese Communist Party, the popularity of the federalist movement declined. It remained a subject of intellectual debate, but never emerged as a realistic political alternative in China.

Warlords and the Confucian Tradition

It has been argued that warlords were Confucianists, and that a regional militarist should only be called a warlord if he held to Confucian ideology. That view is misleading on at least two counts. First, it implies that warlords held a much more coherent and systematic ideology than they actually did; in general, the warlords were weak ideologically. They did not use ideology to determine or define their political goals, though they often rationalized their political actions in ideological terms. Generally, the warlord was inclined to be pragmatic; he left the theorizing to his secretary. Second, the warlords represented a rather wide range of ideologies, from federalism to Kuomintang nationalism, from Christianity to anarchism. It is true that most of these foreign-derived ideologies were superficially understood and were welded onto an ideological base that derived from Chinese tradition. Yet even that ideological base was not purely Confucian as the term is normally understood. It had a substantial element of orthodox Confucianism, to be sure, but it was also comprised of Chinese popular beliefs and China's popular military tradition.

One of the most widely accepted clichés about premodern Chinese society is that the military was despised. To illustrate how disliked the military was, writers have time and again cited the Confucian maxim that "Good iron is not used to make nails; good men are not used to make soldiers." If society were ruled by Confucian virtue, as orthodoxy dictated, force would not be necessary. In a society where status and wealth were associated with civil office, talented and ambitious men simply did not seek military careers. In short, good men were not needed as soldiers and would not want to become soldiers.

Yet the ideals of Confucian orthodoxy were often modified in Chinese life. The law was extensively used despite Confucian injunctions about its inadequacies. As for the military, the facts of life were at odds with Confucian theory. Every dynasty in Chinese history was founded by military action, and every dynasty came to an end through force. Moreover, there was in traditional China a powerful current of military heroism that is often ignored in evaluations of Chinese civilization. It was nourished by the exaltation or apotheosis of Chinese military heroes and by popular literature.

The greatest military hero and most revered warrior in Chinese history is Kuan Yü. Kuan Yü (*died* 219) lived in the closing decades of the Han Dynasty, and was deeply involved in the struggles that led to the creation of the so-called Three Kingdoms that emerged from the collapse of the Han. Kuan Yü received little official attention in the centuries immediately following his death, but during the Sung Dynasty temples began to be erected to him and his cult spread from that time on. Every dynasty piled honors upon his name and ultimately Kuan Yü, the man, became Kuan Ti, a god. Although called the God of War, Kuan Ti's supernatural functions multiplied and came to involve all sorts of nonmilitary activities, such as supervising the weather and curing various diseases. Most important, Kuan Ti became an enormously popular figure. His temples were everywhere, in myriad tiny villages. His reputation among the masses and literati alike was enhanced by the novel *The Romance of the Three Kingdoms*, which relates his adventures with two other celebrated warriors of the time; largely through this novel, Kuan Yü became a symbol of loyalty. In short, for the past thousand years or so one of the most popular gods and most widely admired romantic figures of Chinese history was a warrior.

Yo Fei was another warrior who became a symbol for integrity and self-sacrifice. Yo lived from 1103 to 1141, a time when several groups of nomadic warriors were pressing in upon northern China, which they finally conquered. General Yo led a vigorous struggle to recapture the lost territory, but he was eventually imprisoned as a result of court intrigues and later executed. A few years after his death the state restored his titles and honors and built a temple to him. Even though later alien dynasties, the Yuan and the Ch'ing, did not give Yo Fei much official notice, his reputation for selfless devotion to the country gradually grew, and by the nineteenth century he had come to represent national opposition to foreign aggression.

Many warlords were very conscious of these heroic warriors of history. Yuan Shih-k'ai, for example, expanded the formal cult of military heroes by decreeing that the Military Temple, which had been devoted to Kuan Ti alone, should thereafter include Yo Fei and 24 other celebrated military leaders. Yen Hsi-shan, the warlord of Shansi, also built shrines to Kuan Ti and Yo Fei, and the remarks and writings of other warlords show that these two heroes especially were often in their minds and provided them with a vague model of what a military man should be.

The use of history in this way—great commanders inspiring later generations—is familiar to people of all countries. Nonetheless, it is perhaps difficult for foreigners to understand the extent to which Chinese literature supplied examples of attitudes and behavior to emulate. Many warlords had little, if any, formal education, and their learning derived largely from the tales and novels that were known among the people. Tales of military heroism were more popular than ever in the late nineteenth century, when most of the warlords were growing up. One modern scholar suggests that this popularity reflected the wishful thinking of a weak nation confronted by foreign powers with superior military strength. Whatever the reason, ideals of military heroism spread.

Two great novels were particularly influential in shaping attitudes. One, as noted above, was *The Romance of the Three Kingdoms,* a novel of war, intrigue, and personal heroism rooted in the history of the third and fourth centuries. The other was *The Water Margin,* a novel about men forced into banditry by official corruption. Both are attributed to Lo Kuan-chung, a writer of the fourteenth century, although both were current in the realm of public story-tellers long before that time. A high Chinese official in the twentieth century went so far as to attribute many of the conspicuous features of the warlord period to the influence of these two works. Doubtless, he overstates the case, but the two novels and heroic tales did indeed affect general views and specific behavior. The Taiping rebels of the nineteenth century are said to have taken some of their military tactics and strategy from these novels. More important, they absorbed a feeling of legitimacy and righteousness by identifying their own movement with the struggle against corruption and evil described in these novels. These two books, more than any other literary works, spread the concept of the righteous warrior fighting corruption and greed, which was usually personified by a bad official. Military characters also have a central and popular place in the Chinese theater. And there are Chinese tales of chivalry that though less formally military, are peopled with heroic swordsmen who have the power to fly, to kill monsters, and to command supernatural powers.

Chinese history and popular literature, therefore, contributed to a mood and an orientation far closer to the military than to the ideals of Confucian civil society. They combined to create a generalized concept of heroism that had a strong military element. The

scholar might hold the preeminent place in Chinese society and tradition, but scholarly ability alone was not enough to make a Chinese
hero; the true hero was an amalgam of both literary and martial
virtues, and even the scholar knew it. This concept of the true hero
is perfectly expressed in a short poem by a Ming poet:

> He who is a fine scholar but lacks courage has no dignity;
> He who is a good soldier but no scholar is not a complete hero.
> Who is to be compared with Kuan Ti, who combined military
> genius with literary capacity, and would study at night without
> taking off his armor?[21]

Kao Ch'i, a poet of the fourteenth century, wrote of his youth:
"Astride my horse I betook myself off to distant places, hoping to
achieve glory by deeds of daring. But in the end my plans accomplished nothing, and I returned home, to take up the scholar's mode
of life anew."[22] Elsewhere Kao denies that he was always a "useless
scholar," and describes his earlier ambitions to be like the heroes of
history who commanded troops, led campaigns, and arranged alliances. Kao Ch'i, the very exemplification of the classical scholar-
poet, clearly felt that military activity was not to be despised, but
that it was one of the chief elements of which heroes—even Confucian heroes—are made.

Few warlords have yet been studied in detail, but there are indications that many of them found inspiration and justification in
this heroic tradition. It not only provided them with some of their
ideological assumptions, it shaped the image they held of themselves. And they saw themselves as romantic heroes unfettered by
the rules that apply to ordinary men. Biographies and autobiographies of warlords are modeled directly on the pattern of heroic
romances. Virtues are always vast and never sullied by qualities
merely human, and sometimes the hero consciously copies the behavior of a literary figure. For example, two of the leading warlords,
Feng Yü-hsiang and Li Tsung-jen wrote lengthy autobiographies,
and each work is clearly designed to show its author as a hero in
the great classical tradition of romantic heroes. Both men present
themselves as above caring for mere social amenities, for honors,
awards, profit, rank; they are candid, straight-talking revolutionaries
who often elicit the hostility of lesser men because, in their honest

revolutionary frankness and simplicity, they ignore social forms, which somehow inevitably smack of hypocrisy and insincerity. In each work, the following sequence frequently appears: the hero decides on a course of action; widespread disapproval, criticism, and denunciation are encountered, but the hero, with determination and uncompromising integrity, persists in what he believes to be right; the results invariably prove the hero correct and dismay and abash all opposition. This succession of events is precisely the dramatic sequence by which the romantic literary heroes show themselves to be heroes.

Feng and Li were not the only warlords who displayed some of the characteristics of literary heroes. Good or bad, they all seemed larger than life. Many were incredibly greedy, and retired with huge fortunes. Some were capriciously cruel, and chopped off heads with little provocation. Even those who were not unnecessarily cruel were ruthless when it was necessary to protect their power. They were feudal lords with a twentieth-century vocabulary, and this curious combination gripped the imagination of the common people. Countless stories circulated about the warlord's cruelty, his extraordinary prowess in battle and bed, even his supernatural origins. The warlords were colorful and dramatic, and many acquired something of the status of folk heroes despite the hardships they brought upon the Chinese people.

The Effects of Warlordism

The twelve years of the warlord period affected China in many ways. Unquestionably, warlordism had a damaging and inhibiting effect on the Chinese economy. Chronic warfare and the disorderly conditions associated with warlordism devastated crops and farming facilities. Orderly and productive agriculture was constantly disrupted by the threat of hostilities, the conscription of peasants as soldiers or carriers, the seizure of farm vehicles and animals, the omnipresent danger of bandit raids, and the ruthless exploitation of the peasantry. The production of opium had almost been eliminated before 1916, but under the warlords large areas of land were given over to raising the profitable poppies. The amount of cultivated land used for opium jumped from 3 percent in 1914–1919 to 20 percent in 1929–1933.[23] One dramatic index of the state of Chinese agriculture under the warlords is the fact that by 1929 famine conditions existed in at least nine provinces in north and central China, and in every case warlordism was a major contributing factor.

Trade was also restricted during the warlord era by multifarious and arbitrary taxes. In 1921, for example, there were 735 customs barriers in China to tax goods in transit; many of them had substations so that the total number of tax points was in the thousands.[24] The seizure of goods by troops or bandits, the frequent warlord manipulation of currency, the military control of transport systems, all damaged trade. Long-range economic projects were not feasible where the future was so uncertain. Moreover, wardlordism produced an economic data gap; after 1916 one province after another stopped submitting statistical reports to Peking about many economic matters.

In the long run, perhaps the most significant economic consequence of warlordism was that it retarded the kind of progress that China needed so badly for its international standing and domestic well being. China needed a modern, efficient agriculture and a flourishing, growing industry; warlordism obstructed the former and precluded systematic and comprehensive progress toward the latter.

Was democracy discredited in China because the oppression and disorder of warlordism existed within the formal political framework of a parliamentary democracy? Chinese sufficiently sophisticated to think in terms of democracy and its political alternatives were perfectly capable of recognizing that the republic which existed in name never really existed in fact; democracy had never been achieved after the fall of the Manchus, so the warlords could not discredit it. The persistence of warlordism after 1912, however, did indicate that a parliamentary republic might not be the most suitable road to democracy. The Chinese were, therefore, willing to consider alternative routes, but they had to be realistic alternatives. The warlord republic was well equipped with glittering generalities about concern for the common people, justice, and anti-imperialism, but the reality was far different and it was the reality that counted. The warlord republic may well have cultivated a skeptical realism that encouraged intellectuals to evaluate the later contenders in the Kuomintang-Communist civil war in terms of results rather than rhetoric.

The warlords certainly contributed to the militarization of Chinese politics that had been going on since the late nineteenth century. The Japanese invasion of China and the Communist-Kuomintang civil war strengthened the trend. As a consequence, the leaders of both the Communist Party and the Kuomintang were military men or men with extensive military experience.

Most important, and most relevant here, is that warlordism expressed and intensified the continuing territorial disintegration of China that had begun with the waning of central control in the mid-nineteenth century. The national government became completely impotent during the warlord years—lacking money, prestige, and power. The national bureaucracy, shaken but not destroyed by the late Ch'ing reforms and the Revolution of 1911, disappeared as provinces became openly autonomous and officials were either forced out of office or absorbed by warlord organizations.

The warlords also stimulated social disintegration. The ubiquitous threat of violence accelerated the process, already begun in the nineteenth century, by which control over the use of force became more and more a central feature of local power. Moreover, the old notions of the local elite's obligation to the peasants, and the fulfillment of various political and social functions on behalf of the peasantry, gave way to more naked exploitation. These social changes, along with a rise in banditry associated with warlordism, produced a desperate need among peasants for protection, which they sought largely through so-called secret societies. During the 1920s, that need was also a major factor in producing a massive enrollment in peasant unions. But whatever the organizational form this need took, the need itself demonstrated a deepening chasm between the peasantry and the local gentry.

Warlordism also undermined the traditional rural order by fostering social and geographic mobility. For example, the Chinese military elite was broadened and democratized during the warlord period; because of the single ladder of promotion in Chinese armies

—no distinction was made between "commissioned" and "non-commissioned" officers—peasants were able to aspire to the highest positions, and many actually rose to middle and high rank. Jerome Ch'en has analyzed the careers of 1,300 officers during the warlord era and found that 70 percent were illiterate or semiliterate, an extraordinary indication of the extent of social mobility that warlordism fostered. A large number of the best-known warlords typified this rise from backward poverty.

The military upheavals of the warlord era tossed individuals and armies here and there across the face of China, introducing numberless Chinese to compatriots in different regions, to cities, and to some elements of modern technology. In this way, of course, their intellectual horizons were extended a bit beyond the scope of village and field. The significance of this phenomenon must not be overemphasized; soldiers in a campaigning army are inevitably insulated from the people among whom they travel. Nevertheless, many Chinese first acquired some idea of the human and geographic dimensions of their country, and of the world outside the village, during marches with warlord armies. If nothing else, these military treks may have prepared the way for an understanding of nationalistic propaganda by many Chinese during the 1930s and 1940s.

Warlordism fostered nationalism in other ways as well. Some warlords systematically disseminated nationalistic and patriotic ideas, because they believed in them and as a means of legitimizing their actions. Troops were never called upon to fight for their commander's personal aggrandizement, but to "destroy imperialism," "to save China," or "for the welfare of the masses." Warlords cloaked many selfish policies in such verbiage, but in the process they introduced nationalistic and broad social concepts to their troops, and, to a much lesser extent, to the populations under their influence. A young man who joined Feng Yü-hsiang's army simply to find a profession later recalled how moved he was to hear Feng lecture to his troops on patriotic themes, how he then began to understand the meaning of becoming a soldier and the national function of the army. Whatever the real motives of such ostensibly nationalistic warlords, they subtly and indirectly advanced the idea that the only goals the Chinese *should be* fighting for were national and social.

Warlordism also encouraged the growth of nationalism indirectly—as a reaction to its own misgovernment. Warlordism promoted disunity, squandered the nation's physical and human resources, prompted interference in Chinese affairs by imperialist powers, and inhibited the development of modernizing trends. All these factors intensified the frustration of politically thoughtful Chinese and spurred them to intense study and speculation about the sources of national power and how to develop them. The warlord milieu was surprisingly favorable for such activity, because there was no single national power, espousing one authoritative ideology, to limit intellectual experimentation. Warlords generally did not like radical intellectual currents, but they were in no position to stop them effectively or to offer feasible intellectual alternatives. Neither before nor after the warlord era was there such exciting and significant intellectual activity as that which emerged with force and dynamism during the warlord years. It is often called the Intellectual Revolution, but, more precisely, it marked a major phase in China's social disintegration and the beginnings of a new integration.

Urban Intellectual Revolution

THROUGH THE CENTURIES, the dynasties of China had collapsed in a welter of war and revolution, but before the 1900s social integration had remained strong. The Confucian elite had continued largely intact; its economic, intellectual, cultural, and social values had gone essentially unchallenged, and it had maintained close cultural and functional ties with the mass of the population, the peasantry. The result was that wars and revolutions notwithstanding, the country ultimately reintegrated along Confucian lines. In the twentieth century that did not happen. China not only disintegrated territorially—a disintegration exemplified by the warlords—but it fell apart socially as well. Confucian orthodoxy crumbled under the pressure of Westernizing trends. Intellectuals became increasingly iconoclastic, despite divisions among themselves over fundamental social, political, and philosophical issues. This trend was apparent from the late nineteenth century, but not until the May Fourth Era, from about 1915 to the early 1920s, did the transformation of values among Chinese intellectuals accelerate so suddenly and dramatically that it came to be called the Intellectual Revolution.

Confucianism, Nationalism, Westernization

Many writers have emphasized the intensification of Chinese nationalism in the years around 1919. But scholars have stressed the "rise of nationalism" at every stage of Chinese history since the late nineteenth century. During the Sino-French War in 1884, Chinese were provoked to a remarkable "display of mass nationalism." Japanese demands in China in 1915 produced a "rising tide of nationalism." Four years later China was still marked "by the steadily rising tide of Chinese nationalism," and in the early 1920s there was an "increasingly fervent nationalism." In the mid-twenties the "spirit of nationalism grew and intensified to a point unattained before." And in the decade after 1927, "China's national consciousness advanced by leaps and bounds."[1] To the very end of the republican period, in every phase, the "rise in nationalism" has been cited.

For the same years similar statements have been made about two phenomena intimately related to the rise of nationalism: the "increase of Westernization" and the "decline of Confucianism." As nationalism "rose," Westernization "increased" and Confucianism "declined."

Each of these statements is correct in its context, but their cumulative effect is confusing. With all the rises, increases, and declines over such a long period of time, it is difficult to know what the balance was at any given moment. Writers discussing the last decades of the Ch'ing emphasize the rapidity of change, and the reader wonders what was left for the Intellectual Revolution to revolt against. Other writers stress the comprehensive iconoclasm of the Intellectual Revolution, and thus seem to imply that changes preceding it were minimal. We simply have no clear base line from which to measure specific surges of Chinese nationalism and Westernization, or to judge the nature of the Chinese intellectual elite at a specific time. Before discussing the intensification of nationalist fervor and antitraditionalism that characterized the May Fourth Era, therefore, we shall look at the state of nationalism, Confucianism, and Westernization on the eve of that great change.

The Opium War was the first dramatic revelation of China's weakness vis-à-vis the West. After its disastrous conclusion in 1842, a slowly growing number of Chinese became interested in Western learning and institutions as a source of strength. Until the end of the nineteenth century, this trend lay, by and large, within the bounds of traditional political conceptions. Confucian statesmanship recognized the need for defense, and the self-strengtheners of the mid-nineteenth century moved toward meeting that need when they borrowed elements of military technology from the West. The purpose of the borrowing was to gain sufficient strength to resist further foreign influences, and keep unaltered the core of traditional institutions and values. By the middle of the 1890s leading reformers had concluded that more far-reaching changes were necessary, and they reinterpreted the Confucian classics to justify innovation. That very process, however, signified continued acceptance of the authority of the classics. Moreover, the reformers sought to preserve the monarchy and critical elements of the Chinese tradition.

The explosion of events at the turn of the century—China's defeat by Japan in the war of 1894–1895, the scramble of imperialist 'powers for economic and territorial concessions in China in 1897–1898, the humiliating defeat of China by the powers during the Boxer Rebellion of 1900, Japan's stunning victory over Russia in a war fought on Chinese territory in 1904–1905—demonstrated the inadequacy of China's self-strengthening endeavors and the real possibility that foreign nations might simply carve up China and bring its independent existence to an end. Even Chinese conservatives finally recognized the danger. As a result, China turned from the search for means to protect the traditional way of life to a quest for national power even at the expense of tradition. Survival of the nation became the primary goal, and with that switch Chinese nationalism was born.

Chinese nationalism at that stage had a powerful anti-imperialist orientation; indeed, for the most part the nationalism of that era can be defined as concern for the existence of China as a political unit in the face of foreign penetration, depredations, and threats. As a conscious sentiment, nationalism was largely the province of a portion of the politically aware elite: officials, some merchants and professionals, and intellectuals. In China, a country of illiterate peasant masses, "intellectuals" comprised virtually all who were educated, although by the early twentieth century the lines were sometimes blurred; an educated merchant, for example, might or might not be considered an intellectual, depending upon his interests and activities and the inclinations of the person doing the classifying. The most active and significant core of intellectuals, however, consisted quite clearly of students, teachers, and writers, and their con-

ception of Chinese nationalism became steadily more sophisticated
in the second decade of the twentieth century. A nationalist, it
should be noted, was not necessarily a revolutionary; indeed, many
of the anti-imperialist nationalists did not support revolution.

In the last decade of the Ch'ing Dynasty, the Chinese expressed
their indignation and opposition to foreign encroachments and insults in various ways. The government implemented a vigorous forward policy on its borders in an attempt to preclude England in
the south and Russia in the north from taking over regions traditionally under Chinese suzerainty. Public demonstrations protested incidents that illustrated the extent of foreign power on Chinese soil.
When the United States passed the Exclusion Act of 1905 to limit
Asian immigration, Chinese student nationalists launched an anti-
American boycott, the first political boycott in Chinese history.
The Chinese Government, the provincial gentry, and merchants per-
sistently sought to recover mining concessions and railway rights
that had been relinquished to foreigners.

The birth of nationalism in China greatly stimulated Westernization, because it was the Western nations who knew the "secrets" of
wealth and power—as they had proved time and again to China's
dismay. The Chinese accelerated their attempts to acquire Western
machines, to expand Chinese industry, to study Western science and
emulate Western economic practices. It was the old self-strengthening policy, but no longer limited by the need to remain within the
bounds of Confucian political and economic conceptions. The dissolution of those earlier restrictions now cleared the way for conflict among Westernizers about the scope and approach to Westernization most appropriate for China.

At the turn of the century a small number of Chinese intellectuals concluded that Western secrets of wealth and power consisted
not alone of technological knowledge but included political theories
and sociopolitical institutions that China would also have to emulate. Westernization thus conceived implied the purposeful displace-
ment of Confucian political institutions and social values in order
to serve the transcendent need of building national power. But this
conception engendered serious disagreement, for not all Chinese
anti-imperialist nationalists accepted the need for such a wholesale
Westernization. Moreover, even among the more radical elements
conflict raged over which Western political theories and which

sociopolitical institutions were appropriate for China. Throughout the last decade of Manchu rule, and the early years of the republic, then, various elements of Western political and social thought were the subject of scrutiny and debate in China.

Curiously, in light of the ultimate course of Chinese history, Marxism elicited little response among Chinese intellectuals during the first decade and a half of the twentieth century. Only a very few items of Marxist literature were translated into Chinese before 1919. Translations of writings from other branches of socialist thought were also sparse. A Chinese Socialist Party was founded in 1911, and it tackled various educational projects during the following two or three years; it did not function as a real political party however, nor was it genuinely socialist, though it did help spread some socialist ideas among the most radical of Chinese intellectuals. Despite the party's work, and a vague sympathy with socialism in the most Westernized Chinese intellectual circles, it is probably fair to say that most Chinese regarded socialism as irrelevant to the Chinese scene. Even Sun Yat-sen, who talked about socialism as part of his program at least as early as 1905, conceived of it not in terms of immediate problems, but as a vague possibility in the indeterminate future. China had little industry, virtually no proletariat, and capitalism was utterly undeveloped in terms of the assumptions that lay behind the various schools of socialist thought. Most important, as stressed above, Chinese intellectuals were concerned primarily with the development of national power, not social revolution, and they did not clearly perceive the links between the two.

Anarchism was a separate intellectual current among young Chinese after the turn of the century. The movement was centered in Paris and Tokyo, where Chinese students came under the spell of brilliant French and Japanese anarchists, but a number of youths who stayed at home were persuaded by the writings of Bakunin and Kropotkin. In the early 1920s a young Chinese writer described his own conversion in lines that probably expressed the feelings of many young Chinese in Tokyo and Paris; Kropotkin's writings, he said, "gave me the ideal of love for mankind and for the world, instilled in my naive mind the faith that a society where everyone would be happy can arise with the sun tomorrow, that all evil could disappear at once."[2]

Despite anarchism's opposition to nationalism and elitism of all kinds, the leading anarchists cooperated closely with Sun Yat-sen and the United League. (Ultimately, they affiliated with the Kuomintang right wing.) The only apparent explanation for their readiness to compromise anarchistic principles is that they had personal confidence in Sun Yat-sen and they considered their short-range goal of overthrowing the Manchu Dynasty so vital that the cooperation with the League was deemed advisable. After the 1911 Revolution a number of anarchists returned to China, where they established a Society to Advance Morality. Arguing that social reform was necessary, and that it required the example of personal integrity and purity, they set up a system of self-denial that ranged from giving up prostitutes and gambling to abstaining from liquor and meat. Adherence to some or all of the restrictions depended upon one's seriousness and determination.

By 1915 there were a few small groups of students interested in the study of anarchism in some of China's major cities. The stress on personal cultivation had acquired a modest kind of faddism in student circles, and was associated with the anarchists, though in fact this concern for individual morality had deep roots in the Chinese tradition. The main stream of anarchist ideas still had few followers in China in the early years of the republic. The chief importance of anarchism was in familiarizing young intellectuals with some of the social and political concepts that would become of great interest and consequence a few years later.[3]

The nations that impressed the Chinese with their wealth and power were neither socialist nor anarchist; they were capitalist, and, in political terms, they used forms of representative bourgeois democracy. Moreover, the bulk of early translations that introduced the Chinese to Western political thought related to the parliamentary tradition. This preponderance of attention to the parliamentary process was not only because England, as the preeminent power of the time, was a natural model for the process, but also because the great pioneer Chinese translators were interested in things English. Yen Fu, the most important translator of the late nineteenth and early twentieth centuries, started his systematic analysis of the West in a naval school, where he had to learn English. He later spent time in England, and many of his most important translations were from the English liberal tradition. Yen himself came to advocate parliamentary government, though he later decided that China was not yet ready for such a system. His change of heart could not alter the impact of his translations, however, which stimulated interest in parliamentary democracy. Lin Shu was another pioneer translator, who specialized in novels. Of the 180 or so books he translated into Chinese, about two-thirds were from English literature, and these, too, subtly fostered interest in the English tradition.[4]

Reformers and revolutionaries encouraged the same train of thought. Liang Ch'i-ch'ao—reformer, scholar, and brilliant journalist—was the intellectual leader of progressive young Chinese during the decade before the 1911 revolution. His powerful, emotional writing directed many Chinese to nationalist and Western ideas. Liang opposed the notion of anti-Manchu revolution; he advocated instead a constitutional monarchy under the Manchus. Sun Yat-sen and the revolutionaries, on the other hand, argued that the monarchy should be overturned and replaced by a republic. The spokesmen of these two groups denounced one another with great vigor, yet the two intellectual approaches they advanced complemented one another to encourage Chinese to think in terms of some form of representative government.

Political circumstances within China also lent appeal to a representative system, as we have seen. The provincial elite, whether traditionalist or modernist, wanted to protect provincial interests, and a representative system seemed to offer a convenient means to that end. The new Chinese bourgeoisie that was coming into existence—industrialists, businessmen, professionals—also thought in terms of a representative system similar to that in the capitalist nations. After 1912, of course, the difficulties of making the republic work as republics were supposed to work inevitably made representative government a lively focus of interest for all politically conscious Chinese.

It is easier to identify the chief currents of Western political thought in China than to describe who accepted them, and to what degree. If we are to understand generalizations about the invasion of Western thought, ideas must be matched with numbers of people in specific social situations or with explicit manifestations of influence. Unfortunately, we have little quantitative data. Even so, it is possible to talk about various sectors of the Chinese population, at least in broad terms and it is of special interest to do so in connection with Confucianism. After several decades of "decline," what had happened to Confucianism and the Confucianists?

The dissolution of Confucianism had gone farther in some areas and classes than in others. Moreover, certain concepts, institutions, and values of Confucianism had come under very destructive attack, while others had suffered only minor damage. Thus it is difficult to generalize about the fate of Confucianism as a whole. Nevertheless, there is little doubt that Confucianism was still strong in many aspects of Chinese life on the eve of the May Fourth Movement. Up to that time the most conspicuous repudiation of Confucianism had been in terms of central political institutions and concepts. The monarchy had been eliminated, and with it the notion of the Mandate of Heaven and the idea that the monarch's virtue justified his rule. Although some conservative Chinese continued to view the monarchy as the best form of political organization, and despite two attempts to restore it during the early years of the republic, by 1917 the Confucian conception of monarchy seems to have had only the slightest support among politically sophisticated Chinese. The abolition of the civil-service examinations in 1905 had repudiated the principle of selecting officials on the basis of their mastery of Confucian classics, and by the beginning of the republic this reform had been generally accepted as necessary and reasonable; the Westernization process increasingly confirmed the irrelevance of the old system. By 1915 the Chinese had also discarded their old conception of foreign relations as the ritualized expression of China's cultural superiority.

In the nineteenth century a few merchants had begun to deal in Western or Western-style machine products. After the turn of the century, the new merchant-industrialist class expanded, particularly after the abolition of the examination system in 1905 eliminated the old road to wealth and influence and prompted even gentry families to embark openly on economic ventures they might earlier have avoided, or at least concealed. Confucian economic assumptions, in other words, were set aside as prerequisite to the march toward modern industrialized power. One clue to the scope and swiftness of Chinese economic expansion in the early decades of the twentieth century is the growth in the number of modern chambers of commerce, specifically developed by the new bourgeoisie and encouraged by the government. In Shansi, for example, there were 28 chambers of commerce in 1912 with a total membership of 4,220. By 1918 the number had grown to 104 with a membership of almost 8,000. Other provinces showed similar expansion, and by 1919 there were more than 1,100 chambers of commerce in China with a total membership of about 162,500.[5] They comprised the core of a modern urban business class that retained few Confucian economic values.

Chinese formal education, which had always meant the acquisition of Confucian learning in preparation for the examinations, had changed markedly by the beginning of the republic. After the turn of the century the number of students studying in foreign countries grew steadily, with the majority going to Japan. In China itself, more and more schools modified their curricula to include Western subjects like geography, world history, mathematics, and foreign languages. In many schools the Western elements were only superficial, especially before the Revolution of 1911, but in others a solid Western-style education was offered. After 1912 science became an important part of the middle- and high-school curricula. By 1916 perhaps as many as 10 million Chinese had in some way or other been introduced to Western learning; for some it was no more than a taste, but many acquired their entire education in Western-style institutions.

The challenge to Confucian norms of interpersonal relations during this period prior to the May Fourth Era was far less successful than attacks on Confucian political institutions and economic practices, probably because they were less clearly related to national power. The Confucian family system was still deeply entrenched in city and countryside, and among all classes of the population. The salient characteristics of the family at that time were similar to what they had been a century earlier: the father still ruled the family, owned the family property, made all the important decisions, and possibly had a concubine or two if he could afford them; males dominated females; the young still obeyed their elders; and marriages were arranged by parents without consulting the young people to be married. Only a handful of young intellectuals had denounced this system openly. A much larger number, probably a substantial portion of young people who had been exposed to West-ern-style education, were restive under familial restraints and had begun to think or talk about breaking out of the old mold; very few of them, however, had taken a strong, unequivocal stand against parental authority or the family system generally. The tensions and personal tragedies produced by these changing conditions have been movingly portrayed by Pa Chin in his celebrated novel *The Family.*

The emancipation of women had begun in these years, but it was still in its infancy. By the 1911 Revolution, women had partici-pated in the revolutionary movement, and even middle-class, mod-erate women had taken part in anti-imperialist mass meetings. A few had obtained an advanced education, and the most blatant manifestations of feminine inferiority—notably foot-binding—were beginning, but only beginning, to go out of style. Yet the number of women affected by these trends and measures was infinitesimal. There are scattered indications that the majority of girls from edu-cated urban families and many of the daughters of the rural gentry had begun to dream of independence and of the great outside world. But for most independence was still a vague, festering dream; few had moved to assert themselves.

Various other Confucian values also persisted unchanged or with some modification among young, Westernizing students as well as among their parents. Although the character of education and learn-ing was assuming a new dimension as Western subjects and Western modes of analysis increasingly displaced the moral categories of Confucian thought, the great prestige of learning that Confucian-ism had cultivated continued strong. The prestige of learning in-stilled by Confucianism is one of the reasons why student partici-pation in the vanguard of social and political movements would be so important. An undefined corollary of the prestige of learning, similarly rooted deep in the Chinese past, was a contempt for man-ual labor, and the assumption that those who engaged in it were somehow inferior to those who did not. Even study in Western countries did not extirpate that attitude, but it was particularly strong among the older generation, the parents of the student gen-eration. More subtle and difficult to measure was a cluster of Con-fucian values held by the parents of the students but hardly venerated by the young people—though they still colored their attitudes. These values, or attitudes, included a certain hostility, or feeling of superiority, toward merchants; a skepticism about law as the appropriate basis for social organization; and an appreciation of harmony and compromise. Moreover, whereas young students inclined toward emotional repudiation of the past, their parents still sought justification for their activities and aspirations in the depth of the Chinese tradition.

The challenges to Confucianism had little effect on the peasantry. For most practical purposes, Chinese peasant life continued in its ancient ways. The patriarchal family was still the basic rural economic unit, and the values of the family system continued to be held with no significant modification. Peasant life was marked by some deterioration of quality as disorder and poverty increased, but otherwise it was little changed from the late imperial era. Children were desired for the same age-old reasons, and when they came they were raised in the same age-old ways. The peasants still went to the same temples, tilled their fields in the same way, worried about the same gods and spirits, organized the same local institutions, and suffered the same exploitation.[6]

In sum, by about 1915 nationalism—a national state of mind— was important but still far from being countrywide in its scope. Western institutions and values had displaced Confucianism in major political institutions and in urban economic activity. But Confucianism still formed the bedrock of personal moral standards, though young intellectuals resented the restrictions these standards imposed upon their individual lives. In that context, there occurred a sudden and dramatic acceleration in the transformation of Chinese thought and values. This was the Intellectual Revolution, or the May Fourth Movement.

The May Fourth Movement

In 1915 Ch'en Tu-hsiu, a 35-year-old scholar and revolutionary, founded *Youth Magazine* (later renamed *New Youth*, by which name it is usually remembered). Ch'en's background was similar to that of many Westernizers of the time. He had a classical education, had passed at least one of the traditional civil-service examinations by the end of the nineteenth century, and then had turned against the Manchus and begun to study Western learning. During the first decade of the twentieth century, he had studied in both Japan and France, and participated in the publication of at least two revolutionary periodicals in China. Ch'en had taken part in the Revolution of 1911, and later in the brief 1913 revolt against Yuan Shih-k'ai, after which he fled to Japan. He returned to Shanghai in 1915 where he promptly set up his new publication.

The first issue was as bold as it was iconoclastic, and these traits remained characteristic of the journal. Ch'en called upon Chinese youth to exert themselves to save China by destroying obsolete and irrelevant institutions and values, and to select from among the ideas of mankind those that were fresh and vital and appropriate for China. In the issues that followed, Ch'en not only vigorously criticized Chinese history, tradition, and institutions, but introduced his readers to a wide range of Western thought. For example, among the many Western authors and intellectuals discussed at length in *New Youth*, or whose works were translated, were Turgenev, Wilde, Schopenhauer, Franklin, Maupassant, Dostoevski, Mill, Nietzsche, Ibsen, Tolstoi, and Bakunin.

A year after the founding of Ch'en's magazine, another innovative intellectual current appeared, this one at Peking University. *Peita*, as it was generally known, was then considered China's leading university, although most of its students seemed to view it more as a gateway to official position than a ladder to learning. It had a reputation for stuffiness, conservatism, and moral corruption. But in December, 1916, Ts'ai Yuan-p'ei, another classical scholar who turned to Western learning and to revolution in the late Ch'ing period, was appointed chancellor of *Peita*. Ts'ai immediately began to transform the university. He installed many of China's best-known and most creative intellectuals, and allowed free expression to all ideas and views, from the most radical to the most conservative. Ts'ai also brought in Ch'en Tu-hsiu as dean of the School of Letters, and many of the contributors to *New Youth* were members of the Peita faculty.

In 1917 and 1918 the *New Youth* and other progressive journals argued passionately for the reevaluation of Chinese tradition. They urged that the old family system be abolished and that the equality of all individuals in society, especially the equality of the sexes, become a reality in China. They asked for freedom of choice in marriage in place of parental arrangements, and they opposed the double standard of sexual morality. Old superstitions and religions were denounced, and scientific standards and methodology advocated. Writers called for a literary revolution, which meant the use of the vernacular instead of the literary Chinese that was standard for serious writing. It meant, too, an emphasis on humanism in literature in place of the formalism and traditionalism that then prevailed in the world of letters.

Chinese students responded enthusiastically to Ch'en and his colleagues. The circulation of *New Youth*—now printed in the vernacular—soared, and Peking University became the center of an extraordinarily active intellectual life, with experimentation and reform the dominant trends. Young people formed various organizations dedicated to study and reform, and interest in Western history, philosophy, political theory, and institutions became ardent and all-embracing. Chinese intellectuals dedicated themselves to the creation of a new culture, and, indeed, these years came to be labeled the New Culture Movement. In the midst of this ferment and enthusiasm, the May Fourth Incident occurred.

In 1914 Japan entered the First World War on the side of the Allies, and not long afterward it occupied the 200-square-mile territory of Kiaochow in the Chinese province of Shantung, territory that had been leased by Germany in 1898. The Chinese were indignant, understandably interpreting it as an attack upon China as well as an attack upon Germany, and they claimed that the territory should be restored to China. Japan would not agree, but the Chinese consoled themselves with the thought that the peace settlement at the end of the war would surely return Shantung to China, an expectation that seemed doubly certain when China, too, joined the Allied cause. But when Chinese negotiators finally began their work at Versailles, it turned out that England, France, and Italy had already signed secret treaties agreeing to Japan's claim to German rights in Shantung. Moreover, it also turned out that the warlord government in Peking had earlier virtually agreed to Japan's control of Shantung. As a consequence, the peace conference resolved to transfer to Japan all of Germany's former interests in Shantung, and this decision became a formal part of the Versailles peace treaty.

Chinese indignation over Japanese policies in China had been simmering throughout the war, fueled not only by the seizure of the Shantung concessions but by the Twenty-one Demands, political and economic privileges forced from China by Japan in 1915. When news of the Versailles decision reached China, that long-smoldering indignation burst into open fury, especially in the intellectual community. The Chinese were particularly angry over the fact that the warlord government in Peking had conceded Chinese interests in Shantung even before the war was over, and students vigorously denounced the pro-Japanese officials involved as traitors to China.

On May 4, 1919, about 3,000 students in Peking launched a mass demonstration to arouse the people against imperialism and to denounce the Chinese officials who had betrayed the country. At first the demonstration was peaceful, but turned violent when students invaded the home of one of the accused officials. Police arrived, a fight erupted between them and the students, and 32 youngsters were arrested and taken to prison. That was the May Fourth Incident.

The Peking students immediately began to organize with three objectives in mind: to arouse the nations' sympathy for their imprisoned comrades, to compel the government to refuse to sign the Versailles treaty, and to dismiss the pro-Japanese officials. They were successful in garnering support from many parts of the country. University and high-school students in numerous cities conducted local protests and began cooperating with other students on a nationwide basis. Students in many foreign schools, chiefly missionary, also participated—much to the consternation of foreign diplomats. Merchants and urban workers went on strike, and even the Shanghai gangsters cooperated. An outcry of national indignation on such a vast scale was unprecedented, and the warlord government was forced to yield. The arrested students were released, the three officials generally held responsible for the pro-Japanese policy resigned—and Chinese representatives did not sign the Treaty of Versailles.

The May Fourth Incident stimulated the cultural-intellectual ferment that had been nurtured during the preceding several years by *New Youth* and *Peita* circles. Intellectual leaders at *Peita* and elsewhere admired and supported the students in their anti-imperialist agitation, and the students espoused the new thought more enthusiastically than ever, convinced that only in cultural rejuvenation could they hope to create the national power required to resist imperialism. Students with moderate or conservative social views were also caught up in the anti-imperialist emotion, and were thrust among the more radical and iconoclastic youth who influenced them. Older intellectuals were also touched by the fervor of the time. Thus, although May Fourth Movement was a phrase that originally designated the incident on May 4 and its immediate consequences, Chow Tse-tsung, who wrote the definitive study of the movement, quite appropriately used it to designate the whole process of intensified intellectual change from about 1915 to the early 1920s, embracing what contemporaries called the new thought movement, new culture movement, and the literary revolution. This usage has become common.

The publishing industry revealed the sudden acceleration of Westernization and intellectual innovation. Before this time, few Western books were translated or published in China, and those few rarely included contemporary works. In fact, few books of any kind were published. Many newspapers were published, but they were overwhelmingly trivial and untrustworthy; most were subsidized by politicians or warlords. In 1917 well over 50 newspapers were published in Peking alone, though their average circulation was about 400 and they were maintained through political payoffs. There were no more than three "which any intelligent Chinese would read for information."[7] Chinese periodicals were also trivial and traditionalistic, with only a handful treating current problems.

An explosion of new publications followed the May Fourth Incident. Within six months some 400 new periodicals, written in the vernacular, appeared. The titles of many revealed the sense of rebirth that infused them: *The New Learning, The New Student, The New Life, The New Atmosphere, The New Man.* Most of them declared their intention to introduce new ideas and institutions to China in order to save the nation, and if the nation could have been saved by the quantity of new ideas, China would no longer have been in any danger. Their subjects were the social and natural sciences; political ideologies; Western customs of marriage, courtship, family practices, and other interpersonal relations; nontraditional educational philosophies; biographical material on Western thinkers; translations of foreign works; Western music, art, and literature; movements to liberate women, workers, peasants—any subject, in other words, that fell naturally under the widely declared aim to spread new thought. Many of these periodicals failed rather quickly, but some were viable. Moreover, long-established publications also changed to the use of the vernacular and shifted their editorial policies to accord with the new tide of iconoclasm and intellectual ferment. New books tumbled off the Chinese presses, including new translations of Western works, and a host of organizations mushroomed to promote intellectual and political causes.

One of these causes was Marxism. The Chinese had paid little attention to Marxism before this time, but as part of the general surge of interest in foreign thought during the May Fourth Era study groups were organized in Peking to discuss and analyze Marxism. The Russian Revolution stimulated interest in the subject, and in the spring of 1919 the influential *New Youth* published a special edition devoted to Marxism. During the rest of the year, and into 1920, a few intellectuals devoted themselves to the study of Marxist thought, and in the fall and early winter of 1920 small Communist organizations came into existence in several major cities. In the summer of 1921, representatives of these groups came together to found the Chinese Communist Party. It then consisted of 57 members, but it would grow steadily through the early 1920s.

The May Fourth Movement not only had an enormous cultural-intellectual effect; it had an effect as well on many other aspects of Chinese life. Its influence on the family, on labor, on the peasantry, on education, for instance, became increasingly apparent in the years that immediately followed. Many young Chinese tried to make their living patterns accord with their intellectual enthusiasms, particularly in the realm of personal relations. More and more young urban intellectuals refused to continue their traditional subservience to the family system; they insisted upon making their own life decisions, a stance exemplified by their rejection of parentally arranged marriages. One of the conspicuous themes in Chinese literature of the 1920s was the contrast between the happiness of an independent young person who insisted upon freedom of choice in a marriage partner and the sadness of another who submitted to his parents' choice. Many young women also rebelled. They bobbed their hair, went to school, and participated in the demonstrations and political activity. Like the men, they insisted on free choice in marriage. Women were not emancipated overnight—a provincial assemblyman in 1925 could still assert that coeducation would "degrade mankind to the level of beasts"[8]—but the May Fourth ferment constituted the most significant stimulus yet to the women's movement.

The modern labor movement also stemmed from the May Fourth Era. From late in the nineteenth century, foreigners had established modern industries in China, and a small proletariat came into existence. During World War I, when the Western powers were preoccupied in Europe, Chinese industrialists swiftly expanded their own enterprises, which further accelerated the growth of a working class. The May Fourth agitation led to the organization of workers for anti-imperialist purposes, which in turn quickly led to more conventional labor-union activity. In Canton, to give one example, the movement to boycott Japanese goods, which the students had organized, gradually melded into demands for improved conditions of labor and efforts to create a labor party. The students also organized a system of 10-man groups, and these units came to serve as an organizational model for laborers.

The May Fourth Movement gave a much less powerful, but still important, impulse to the organization of peasants. The peasants took little part in the stirring events of 1919, and most intellectuals gave them little thought. Yet there were suggestions that students "go to the peasantry," and some recognition of the need to organize peasants not only for their own protection but as a national political force. The leading leftist intellectual in particular, Li Ta-chao, recognized that China should not think of creating a strong, modern nation until the peasant was liberated from poverty and ignorance and the wall between peasants and intellectuals removed.

The May Fourth Era also affected educational practices. The vernacular rapidly became the medium of communication in all levels of school. Educators became more aware of the need for adult and vocational education, a need that had emerged even before 1919 and exemplified the growing fusion between urban intellectuals and Westernized business circles.

A new and vital Chinese literature began to appear, using the vernacular. It was humane, realistic, iconoclastic, and modeled on Western literary forms, but it expressed the problems and aspirations of modern China. As in so many modernizing societies, the new literature served a profoundly important educational function by introducing new values and new modes of behavior in dramatic, realistic, and comprehensible fashion.

For all these reasons, the May Fourth Movement was a significant impulse toward the modernization of China. Its most important feature was that it marked the coming of age of a new intellectual elite, albeit a fragmented one. The unanimity of anti-imperialist indignation engendered by the May Fourth Incident only temporarily concealed the differences that had developed among even the most Westernized intellectuals in the first fifteen years of the century. The rapid influx of Western thought after that time added even more raw material for intellectual and philosophical disputation. The May Fourth experience underscores the acute problems China faced at home and abroad, but with the introduction of so many new ideas, of such a variety of notions as to what should be done about these problems, it is not surprising that unanimity was an impossibility. Consequently, in the years after the May Fourth Incident a number of major intellectual disputes took place, revealing some of the divisions within the new intelligentsia.

Intellectuals in Conflict

Even at the height of the May Fourth Movement, basic intellectual differences were expressed in the proliferating periodical press. The most celebrated and revealing of these early conflicts was between Hu Shih and Li Ta-chao over the question of "problems versus isms."

Hu Shih was professor of philosophy at *Peita*. Nine years earlier, in 1910, after a mixed Chinese-Western education, Hu had gone to the United States as a young scholarship student. He had enrolled at Cornell where he hoped to study agriculture for the sake of his country, but soon switched to philosophy, which he found more suited to his tastes. He had received his B.A. in 1914 and gone to Columbia to continue his education under John Dewey. In 1917, with a Columbia Ph.D., Hu had returned to China a confirmed exponent of Dewey's experimental philosophy, which he found intellectually persuasive and personally congenial. Convinced that every problem must be specifically and clearly identified, and systematically resolved, Hu was disturbed during the May Fourth Movement by the uncritical enthusiasm of many intellectuals for various brands of Western thought. It was particularly the surging Chinese interest in socialism that prompted Hu in the summer of 1919 to argue that intellectuals should be wary of seductive isms—ostensibly quick and fundamental solutions to myriad social problems. Civilizations are not created that way, he argued, and in any event it is utterly deceptive to think that some doctrine devised to meet the needs of another time and another place could suddenly provide the means of resolving China's difficulties. The task for Chinese intellectuals was to study specific, individual social problems and in that way, a bit at a time, society could be understood and improved:

> From my personal observation, the future tendency of the New Thought should be to lay emphasis on the study of problems important to life and society, and to carry out the task of introducing academic theories through studies of these problems. . . . Liberation means the liberation of this or that system, of this or that idea, of this or that individual; it is liberation by inches and drops. Reform means the reform of this or that system, of this or that idea, of this or that individual; it is reform by inches and drops. The first step in the recreation of civilization is the study of this or that problem. Progress in the recreation of civilization lies in the solution of this or that problem.[9]

Hu's academism and moderation were unacceptable to the passionate young Li Ta-chao; Li was a revolutionary. He had studied political economy in a modern Tientsin school from 1907 to 1913, when he went to Japan. During his three years in that country, Li had studied a wide range of Western political thinkers, and also participated actively in the radical politics of the Chinese intellectual community in Japan. After returning to China in 1916, Li had assumed the editorship of a Peking daily. In 1918 he became librarian, and later professor, at Peking University. Activism was the keynote of Li's personality and of his politics: China could be saved if the Chinese would simply act with force and determination to save it. Li agreed with Hu Shih that social problems needed resolution and that they could be resolved, but he argued that the majority of people would have to work together actively to resolve them. To attain that kind of cooperation, individuals in society had to be able to see the connection between their own problems and the problems of society. And it was precisely in clarifying such connections that isms—comprehensive theoretical structures—could play a crucial role.

Hu Shih, by stressing the need to study specific problems, seemed to be arguing for close attention to the realities of China. Ironically, however, his views exemplified one form of alienation from Chinese life: the conception of Chinese problems in terms of foreign assumptions. Specific social problems cannot be resolved in a vacuum; they exist in a context of political and social institutions and values that dictate the general orientation which solutions must assume. The political emancipation of women, to take one example, assumes a viable political system in which that emancipation will be realized. The warlord republic in China did not constitute such a system; it was unstable, and did not operate according to the rules. Hu Shih's recommendations seem to have derived from his years of experience in the United States, and the influence upon him of John Dewey in particular. In the United States, problems could be isolated, studied, solutions recommended, and attempts made to implement the recommendations. Hu Shih wanted to use this rational and attractive approach in China, forgetting, as he had himself admonished Li Ta-chao not to, that what was relevant to one social situation might not be relevant to another. Hu Shih's assumptions were nonrevolutionary, and it was natural that he advocated working within the system to isolate and solve problems. To Li Ta-chao, however, the system itself was a major problem, and could only be eliminated by revolution. The issue of revolution was the critical underlying difference between them, and it foreshadowed a fundamental division among intellectuals.

The accelerated Westernization of China in the early 1920s, and the blanket repudiation of tradition it implied, provoked extensive controversy in which other basic divisions among Chinese intellectuals were revealed. Liang Ch'i-ch'ao struck the first note in a report expressing his disillusion with European civilization after World War I. In 1919 Liang and a group of other Chinese intellectuals visited Europe. On his return Liang wrote an article explaining that the depressing state of war-torn Europe had changed his views of the West—and of China. Liang thought that in Europe the human spirit was increasingly dominated by materialistic determinism. The authority of science had destroyed the traditional bases of man's moral life: religion was declining; philosophy was undermined; free will was denied by rigid scientific law; and, therefore, men no longer assumed responsibility for deciding good and evil. Many Europeans themselves acknowledged that their civilization was in decay. In fact, Liang and others had been much influenced in their changing views of the West by the writings of Western critics; Henri Bergson, in particular, appealed to Liang with his "creative evolution." Nevertheless, Liang thought that the best efforts of European thinkers would achieve little unless they received some support from the outside—and the humane values of the Chinese tradition, he concluded, were just what was needed. A synthesis of Chinese and Western cultural elements promised the only hope for those Europeans seeking salvation from the bankruptcy of a materialistic civilization. Liang did not advocate a mechanical restoration of Confucian institutions, but a critical-sympathetic examination of the Chinese tradition to find and refurbish its best values and attributes.

Liang's views were welcomed by a number of old-style conservatives, but, more important, they also stimulated some Western-educated Chinese to enter the lists against the West and in behalf of China. Liang Sou-ming, for example, had acquired a Western-style education in China, but he had never studied abroad. He had participated in the Revolution of 1911 as a member of the United League, but a few years later despaired of the republic, went into seclusion, and turned to the study of Buddhism. An article he wrote about Buddhism attracted the eye of Ts'ai Yuan-p'ei at the time he was building up Peking University, and he invited Liang to join the faculty as a lecturer in Indian and Buddhist philosophy.

The special feature of Liang Sou-ming's approach to life and culture was his emphasis on the distinctive character of the will. He viewed culture as the product of an endless interaction between individual wills—the sum of which constituted a kind of collective will—and environment, and thus concluded that cultures differ as wills differ. He saw three main types of will in the history of the world. These had produced three distinctive types of civilization, each of which was represented in the modern world. One was the aggressive will. It was suitable for an age when the demands of physical survival are primary, and make mastery over nature the prime concern of man. Contemporary Western civilization exemplified this kind of will. The second type was the accommodating will, which sought satisfaction not in altering the environment but in adapting to it. It was fitting for an age when man's material needs have been satisfied, and the aggressive behavior characteristic of the first type would only produce unnecessary social conflict. China typified that kind of civilization. The third type was the result of the action—or inaction—of the passive will, which neither struggles nor adapts but ignores the fact that there is conflict between man and his environment. It was characteristic of an age when man is preoccupied with understanding the abstrusities of his own nature. India represented that type of civilization in the modern world.

Of these three, the West produced conflict and India was the victim of its environment. Only China typified the happy balance, the way to harmony between men and between nature and man, despite China's delay in establishing control over nature. The argument was ingenious, and enabled Liang to attack the excessive Westernization of the May Fourth Movement, to attribute a kind of superiority to Chinese civilization, and at the same time to explain China's embarrassingly inferior physical strength compared with the forceful, aggressive West.

Liang also cited more specific reasons to exalt Chinese civilization and deprecate the West. He argued that the dominant characteristics of contemporary Western civilization were reliance on the use of reason and emphasis on the concept of self. These traits contrasted sharply with those of the Chinese, who had not sacrificed intuition to cold reason, and who had subordinated the self in other human relationships. The Western way had only produced a dehumanized mechanical civilization that was degrading and inhuman for all people, rich and poor alike. "The unnaturalness of life, its mechanical and barren tastelessness, is the same for all."[10] The West would have to move from the first to the second stage of civilization, from its dehumanized isolation to the warm humanity of the Chinese way. At the same time, Liang conceded, China would do well to introduce some science and democracy into its own life, but only if it could be done without sacrificing the spiritual, humane, and intuitive values that were the marks of Chinese superiority.

Early in 1923 Chang Chün-mai—Carsun Chang—delivered a lecture expressing similar views. His point of emphasis was different from that of either Liang Sou-ming or Liang Ch'i-ch'ao, but in a certain basic sense the message was the same: China has something spiritual and human that the West does not have and that cannot be attained through science.

Chang Chün-mai studied law and politics in Japan before the Revolution of 1911, and generally supported Liang Ch'i-ch'ao's proposals for a constitutional monarchy. After a short stint as a journalist following the revolution, he went to Europe where he studied at the University of Berlin and, for a brief period, in London. He returned to China in 1916, and three years later again went to Germany where he studied philosophy until 1922. Early in the following year Chang lectured at Tsing Hua University on the "Philosophy of Life." His lecture created a furor, and initiated a comprehensive debate about science and metaphysics that had clear implications for the discussion about comparative civilizations.

Chang argued that a philosophy of life is by its nature subjective, freely willed, intuitive, and not amenable to scientific analysis. Notions relating to right and wrong, to family and social relationships, religious beliefs, one's inner yearnings and hopes, attitudes toward social change, all are unique and individual, a synthesis of personal values and attitudes that cannot be analyzed into its component elements without losing its real nature and significance. Science, on the other hand, is exactly the opposite; it is objective, assumes uniformity in nature, and relies on systematic reasoning. As a consequence, science is relevant only to dead matter. Chang held what was virtually a mystical view of the impossibility of science's dealing with organic life. Science could be useful in physics, but of no use in history; it was relevant to chemistry, but law and psychology were inherently imprecise. In other words, in those areas most directly related to the spiritual dimension of man's life, science was useless. Science, therefore, could play no positive role in developing or understanding a philosophy of life.

But if so many areas of life are unknowable to science, how can they be apprehended, and understood? Through intuition, Chang seems to have accepted the views of the celebrated fifteenth-century philosopher Wang Yang-ming, who viewed intuitive knowledge—which he conceived as having a strong moral dimension—as the only real source of knowledge and of right action. Western civilization, by its preoccupation with science and materialism, did not use and benefit from intuition, and therefore it was not surprising that it produced a mechanistic and corrupt civilization. China, if it continued to be overly concerned with the quest for wealth and power might find itself in the same unfortunate position.

It was fitting that the first person to attempt a comprehensive rebuttal of Chang Chün-mai—and the whole pattern of criticism of science and Western civilization—was one of China's leading Westernized scientists, Ting Wen-chiang. Ting had been trained as a geologist in Europe, and later became professor of geology at Peking University. Though a proponent of Westernization, he had not been conspicuously iconoclastic during the May Fourth Movement. He had accompanied Liang Ch'i-ch'ao and Chang Chün-mai on the European trip after World War I, but had not shared their negative reactions. After Chang delivered his celebrated lecture, Ting stepped forward with a refutation in order, he explained, that Chinese youth would not be unduly swayed by what Ting considered an obsolete mystical view. Ting argued that only scientific knowledge is true knowledge, and that it embraces all of reality, which is knowable. The diversity of beliefs in the world did not attest to the fallibility of science, but to the insufficient spread of scientific knowledge. As science became increasingly understood and accepted, diversity of views would increasingly yield to the unity of truth.

Ting completely rejected the notion of intuitive knowledge; to him, it would render study and learning unnecessary and useless. His own epistemology proved to be suspect, however, even to his pro-science associates. Ting declared that scientific data is under-

stood by sense perceptions in the brain, but that the relation of
these perceptions to the material world is unclear. Ting explained
that those who accepted this epistemology were called "skeptical
idealists":

> Because they consider that sense apprehension is our only
> method of knowing physical bodies and that concepts of physical
> bodies are phenomena in the mind, they are called idealists. Be-
> cause they acknowledge that they do not know, and believe that
> men should not ask, whether or not there exist things outside the
> world of sense perception, or behind the surface of self conscious-
> ness, or what kinds of things physical bodies fundamentally are,
> they are called skeptical.[11]

Knowledge, in this view, is the arrangement one's mind gives to
sense data, although the reality behind the data is intrinsically unknowable. And reality cannot be divided, as Chang and others
would like to divide it, into what is knowable through science and
what is knowable through intuition; science is the only road to understanding whatever is knowable. Intuitive knowledge is an illusion. Science is the only reliable guide to a philosophy of life. The
shortcomings in Western civilization derived not from science but
from the insufficient use of science.

Hu Shih, Ch'en Tu-hsiu, Wu Chih-hui and others who spoke out
on behalf of science were disturbed by Ting's postulating a divorce
between material substance and mental phenomena. They thought
it might open the door to religion or mysticism—though Chang
Chün-mai and the other metaphysicians took no note of that aspect
of Ting's argument. Wu Chih-hui, an early anarchist and associate
of Sun Yat-sen, and Hu Shih focused much of their fire on the issue
of the "spiritual East" compared with the "materialistic West." Wu
offered the longest and most flamboyant argument, but Hu was perhaps more influential. Hu contended that material advancement was
the basis for spiritual quality. When man's material needs are fully
met, he has the time and energy to seek spiritual experiences and
satisfactions. Thus, Western civilization, which had moved effectively to meet the material necessities of human life, could not
properly be called a materialistic civilization. It was, Hu argued, the
very opposite: idealistic, indeed spiritual. Chinese civilization, on

the other hand, was characterized by poverty and by the fear of ignorance. How could one call this a spiritual civilization, and claim
it superior to the West? In actual fact, the passive acceptance of
what Fate brings, the quietism in the face of poverty, were not virtues of Chinese life, as asserted by those who claimed China had a
spiritual civilization; they were really the shortcomings of Chinese
life.

Both sides in this debate were expressed by Westernized Chinese, men who exemplified the new intellectual elite. But each par-
ticipant argued within the framework of a cosmology in which, as
in traditional Chinese orthodoxy, principles of nature, of social
organization, and of ethics were combined in a single harmonious
whole. This approach rendered compromise, or any modification of
views, highly unlikely. It was a natural approach for Chinese
thinkers, nonetheless, and perhaps the only one that their audience
would accept. As Charlotte Furth has pointed out:

> When faced with fundamental questions about nature, the aver-
> age Chinese intellectual of the early twentieth century, whether
> sympathetic toward science or not, thought that some form of
> speculative cosmology supplied the *kind* of answer required.
> Moreover, he believed that a philosophical question at some point
> had to involve a question about ethics, and he remained insensi-
> tive to the internal guidelines to thought provided by Western
> logical forms, unless these forms were interpretable in a strictly
> empirical fashion. This being the case, he tended to make the
> theories of science into systems of belief, using concepts sug-
> gested by those theories—he came to social Darwinism before he
> came to the science of biology, and he talked of the mechanistic
> universe before he examined the laws of mechanics.[12]

Divisions among Chinese intellectuals found expression not only
in debates about the nature of civilization and the role of science,
but in conflict over the proper role of the new literature in changing
China. Until the time of the May Fourth Movement, most writing
employed literary Chinese, quite different in form from the spoken
language and permeated with archaisms. Writing was highly for-
malistic, and some forms popular in the West—notably the novel—
were not considered respectable by the Chinese; the great Chinese
novels of the past had all been produced outside the mainstream of
Chinese orthodoxy, and few authors were willing to acknowledge

their creations. In 1917 Hu Shih and Ch'en Tu-hsiu challenged those old standards with an appeal that sparked a literary revolution. They called for writing that was simple, direct, in the vernacular, and with a humane sense of social responsibility. For two or three years, creative work in the vernacular was sparse, experimental, and of poor quality. But by the early 1920s, writers began to master the vernacular as a literary instrument, and also acquired greater familiarity with Western literary forms. A new literature emerged, and its character was just as much the subject of dispute as any other aspect of new thought, and the literary arena throughout the 1920s was crowded with shifting individuals and factions.

Two groups of writers exemplified the Westernizing thrust of the May Fourth Movement, although there were differences between them. The first to appear was the Literary Association formed by about a dozen young writers at the end of 1920. The publishing outlet for the group was *The Short Story Magazine,* a monthly that had existed for some years but which was transformed into the leading journal of new literature early in 1921; it was to hold a distinguished place in Chinese letters until its presses were destroyed by Japanese bombs in 1932. Writers of the Literary Association included many who became luminaries of modern Chinese literature: Shen Yen-ping, better known under his pseudonym, Mao Tun, one of the founders and the first editor of the rejuvenated *The Short Story Magazine;* Lu Hsün, a celebrated author not formally one of the group but generally in sympathy with its position; Chou Tso-jen, brother of Lu Hsün and a well-known scholar and essayist in his own right, author of the association's founding manifesto.

Writers of the Literary Association sought to foster a realistic and humane literature. As Mao Tun explained it:

> We believe that literature does not exist merely for the purpose of diverting melancholy people or for delighting the senses of those who try to escape from reality. Literature has the positive quality of stirring men's hearts. Especially in our time, we hope that literature can take upon itself the great responsibility of awakening the masses and giving them strength.[13]

Association writers also wanted to introduce a number of Western authors, and they translated some of their works in the pages of *The Short Story Magazine.* Among others, they were interested in Tol-

stoi, Turgenev, Gorki, Ibsen, Maupassant, all of whom exemplified
the kind of social realism that the leading writers of the Literary
Association admired. Because of their concern for social problems,
and their somewhat didactic aims, writers of the association have
often been described as wishing to create "literature for life's sake."

A few months after the formation of the Literary Association,
another group of young writers organized the Creation Society, with
its own periodical. Kuo Mo-jo and Yü Ta-fu were the best-known
members of the group, which quickly came to exercise great influence among modern-minded Chinese intellectuals. Creation Society
writers scorned the aims of the Literary Association, which seemed
to them grossly utilitarian, and espoused the romantic conception
of "art for art's sake." "Artists should not preoccupy themselves with
human problems," they argued. "The moment that they produce
works of art, their duty is fulfilled. They need not ask themselves if
their work is useful to others or not."[14]

The Creation Society writers did not long retain this disregard
for human problems, however. The continued chaos of warlord politics intensified their distress over domestic conditions, and the
shooting of Chinese by foreign-led police in Shanghai in 1925 in-
flamed anti-imperialist passions. At the same time, mounting Russian influence through literary translations, political propaganda,
and Russian aid to Chinese political groups all fostered the growth
of radicalism in the Chinese intellectual world. Creation Society
writers in particular responded to these stimuli, and shortly after
the middle of the decade were calling for the creation of revolutionary literature, a proletarian literature. For example, one of the
members of this group, Cheng Fang-wu, argued in 1927 that the
imminence of revolution confronted writers with only two alternatives, to be revolutionary or anti-revolutionary; there was no middle
road, and only revolutionary writers could retain their place in the
world of letters. Writers of the Literary Association, who had in the
first half of the decade been fighting the romantic disregard of
social problems on the part of the Creation Society, in the second
half argued against the dogmatism and nonliterary values they
claimed the Creation writers were bringing to literature in an attempt to make it revolutionary.

Despite their disagreements, the writers of the Literary Association and of the Creation Society were nontraditional. They all rejected the Chinese literary tradition, but in different ways, and they all used the vernacular. Other writers, however, deplored this literary Westernization, argued for more sympathetic attention to the Chinese tradition, and for continued use of the literary language. In 1922 Mei Kuang-ti, Wu Mi, and others founded *The Critical Review*, a monthly journal that was to last for more than five years in opposition to the chief currents of the literary revolution. Both Mei and Wu had been educated in the United States where they had studied under Irving Babbitt. Babbitt, a Harvard professor, was one of the preachers of a "new humanism," an elitist body of thought that scorned the notion that society could be improved through radical humanitarian reforms; neither iconoclasm nor revolution, but reliance on values tested by the past, including literary values, was the only way to a civilization of quality. *The Critical Review*, true to Babbitt's teachings, denounced the iconoclastic writers of the Literary Association and the Creation Society for ignoring the richness of the Chinese past, and also for knowing only most superficially the Western literature that they tried so slavishly to imitate. Mei and his associates also argued that the vernacular was by its nature changeable, and thus not the most appropriate vehicle to create a lasting literature. The vernacular had its uses, but so did the literary language. They therefore wrote in the literary language, although shorn of pedantic allusions and archaic rhetoric.

Even more conservative views were expressed in Chang Shih-chao's *The Tiger Weekly*. As a young man, Chang had participated in the anti-Manchu revolutionary movement, but had early turned away from radicalism. He had studied in Europe, worked as a journalist during the early years of the republic, and occupied several positions in warlord governments before 1925. In that year, he served briefly as Minister of Education in Tuan Ch'i-jui's government, and he also launched *The Tiger Weekly* to attack the new culture movement generally and the literary revolution in particular. Chang vigorously opposed the widespread adoption of Western ideas and institutions, and maintained that China's agrarian society required uniquely Chinese institutions because those copied from the industrialized West were totally inappropriate for Chinese conditions. *The Tiger Weekly* also denounced the use of the vernacular for literary purposes. "If one wants liveliness in literature," one contributor wrote, "there is nothing better than *wen yen* [literary Chinese]. The things in the world that are difficult to describe, the feelings of the human heart that are difficult to put into words, all those kinds of things cannot be adequately described with the words used in daily speech."[15]

The conservative spokesmen in all these debates were not obscurantists who blindly rushed against the clear tide of history in an attempt to save what was already irredeemably lost. Opposition to the use of the vernacular in writing, it is true, seems a particularly futile and short-sighted cause, but in other ways these men called attention to a profoundly important point: Chinese problems demanded Chinese solutions. When Liang Sou-ming, Chang Chünmai, and others spoke out against excessive Westernization, they were calling for more concern with the realities of Chinese life. Liang Sou-ming, for example, saw no reason why he should be called a traditionalist; he had studied the West, been temporarily attracted to it, and only later made his way back to elements of the Confucian tradition that seemed to him to be germane to the Chinese present. Clinging to tradition for its own sake was absurd, he thought, but he insisted that China should "send forth new shoots from an old root."[16] It was in that spirit that Liang turned to rural reconstruction in the late 1920s, and for some years focused his energies on practical measures for the economic and social development of the countryside. In that respect, however, Liang was unusual, almost unique. Most of the intellectuals were Westernizers, and moved farther and farther from the rural backbone of China—one reason social disintegration accelerated during and after the May Fourth Movement.

The Intellectual Revolution
and Social Disintegration

The Intellectual Revolution produced a clear shift in China's intellectual center of gravity. The rapid diffusion and acceptance of Western thought during the May Fourth Era, combined with the normal maturation of young intellectuals with Western-style education, and the inevitable withdrawal of the older generation, created a Chinese intelligentsia that was clearly and definitely non-Confucian. Views that only a few years earlier were on the radical periphery of respectability now occupied the center of China's intellectual stage. But this shift did not imply the universal acceptance of a new orthodoxy; as the preceding pages have shown, the new intellectuals divided over social, political, and philosophical questions. At the same time, they generally agreed about certain national needs: national unity, national power to resist imperialism, effective national government, the end of warlordism. But they did not agree about how to pursue even the goals they shared.

This transformation of the intellectuals marked an intensification of social disintegration, particularly because it set them so distinctly apart from the peasantry. The intellectual movement of the May Fourth Era was largely an urban phenomenon and hardly touched the peasantry. The peasants were not involved in the communications network—university classes and lectures, periodical and newspaper articles, translated books and essays, various other publications—by which new thought was spread and elaborated, and therefore they were little affected by the paroxysm of Westernization that the intellectuals experienced. The use of vernacular by the elite did not affect the illiteracy of the mass of the population; in fact, in one sense the vernacular was more alien than the literary language because it was so widely used to promote foreign ideas. As one intellectual leader declared, the vernacular had "become dressed in European cloth and the academism of Oxford, Cambridge and Columbia."[17] In any event, to use the vernacular, like the literary language, required an understanding of the Chinese characters, and those without that knowledge remained as illiterate as ever.

While the Intellectual Revolution widened the gap between intellectuals and peasantry, however, it also encouraged steps to bridge it; it intensified the disintegration of Chinese society, but it pointed the way to reintegration. Despite its iconoclastic and Westernizing thrust, it was at that time that modern—not traditionalistic—intellectuals began to realize that Chinese could not abandon their roots, that the Chinese past had something of value to contribute to the present. Moreover, earlier in the century intellectuals seem to have assumed that the peasants had little participatory role in shaping the new nation, except perhaps to man the armies. But the radical ideologies of the May Fourth Era encouraged the notion that the reintegration of the nation in modern form required the knowledgeable participation of the mass of the population.

During and following the May Fourth period, a number of intellectuals urged the necessity to "go to the people." Many of them, however, interpreted this idea in a highly elitist way that had little to do with the needs of the people themselves. Ku Chieh-kang, one of China's outstanding new historians of that time, declared that the people had an enormous capacity for enlightenment, but that to develop it would require the protracted guidance of the intellectual elite. Few intellectuals offered themselves for that task, and Ku concluded that it was because the gap between the masses and the elite was simply too great. Said Ku: "We educated ones are too far from the people; we consider ourselves cultured gentlemen and them as vulgar; we consider ourselves as aristocrats and revile them as mean people." No wonder, he complained, that the common people did not aspire to "our level."[18]

There was more than a touch of arrogance among the new elite, especially among the returned students. Because the new elite believed that Westernization was the only salvation for China, those who had studied in the West must, inevitably, be the "leaders and saviors of the nation," a notion that the returned students accepted without demur.* Some of the new generation of literary artists also seemed to consider themselves different from, superior to, and

* T'ao Hsi-shen, a journalist and scholar associated with the Kuomintang, recalled that returned students had a custom similar to that of traditional scholars. In the old days those who passed the examinations in the same year considered themselves bound together in a loose but nonetheless real fraternity, and one of the first questions any official or literatus would ask another was the year he had passed. The returned students did the same. When they met someone they would ask: "What year did you return?" The response was usually one of three types. If he had returned not long before, he would say when and the two would discuss their experiences cordially. If the person had returned a long time before, and was already of some eminence, he might answer curtly, "I returned before you were born." If the person, like T'ao himself, had never studied abroad, the response was usually confused. T'ao said he was always very awkward and embarrassed when he had to admit that he was not a returned student. Not until the 1930s could he answer the question with equanimity. (T'ao Hsi-sheng, *Ch'ao liu yü tien ti* [Tides and drops] [Taipei: Chuan-chi wen-hsüeh tsa-chih she, 1964], p. 76.)

more "capable of heightened emotional responses than are ordinary men."[19]

Ku Chieh-kang and others thought that the first step in getting the elite "to the people" to help them was to encourage the elite to study the people. Understanding would be the first step toward a partnership in which the elite would guide the peasantry to a new level of life. But Ku's own work showed the danger of such an approach, particularly when taken by academics. Ku studied Chinese folklore, an aspect of popular culture but one that was in no way tantamount to understanding the living needs of the peasantry—to say nothing of acting to meet them.

Many Chinese liberals typified this kind of academic obtuseness, including Hu Shih. It was ironic in Hu's case in view of his passionate exhortation to deal with specific problems. Hu and other liberals rejected the notion of revolution, advocated working within the existing political system to improve it, and to isolate and solve one specific problem after another. Yet in fact, aside from a few ineffective manifestos and statements, these intellectuals devoted themselves largely to academic research in ancient history or the criticism of ancient literature. This concern with antiquity was at least partly motivated by a desire to illuminate the relevance of Chinese history for the present, and to that extent to resist the wholesale Westernization that threatened to engulf Chinese intellectuals. It was thus important, but it had nothing to do with the lives of most Chinese, or with current politics; it was purely a matter of elite concern.

More radical intellectuals refused to accept the existing political structure because they thought it oppressive domestically and impotent vis-à-vis foreign imperialism. They sought to organize politically to overthrow warlord governments, involve the people in the transformation of their own lives, and to create a modern nation. It was in pursuit of these goals that the Chinese Communist Party was founded, and the Kuomintang reorganized, in the early 1920s. The relationship between these two parties was to dominate Chinese national politics until the end of the republican era, and to reflect in political and military policies some of the basic philosophical differences that divided the intellectuals in the wake of the May Fourth Incident.

V

Coalition and Conflict

THE CHINESE COMMUNIST PARTY was formally established in 1921; three years later the Kuomintang was reorganized to make it a stronger revolutionary party. The two parties agreed to cooperate to end warlord rule, unify the country, and check imperialism in China. They launched a great military campaign to destroy the warlords, and organized millions of workers and peasants as the basis for a new order. The contradictions between the philosophies and ultimate goals of the Communists and the Kuomintang, however, were simply too great for their coalition to last indefinitely, and the closer they came to success, the more each felt threatened by the other. As a result, before the coalition attained its goals it collapsed in a bloody conflict that marked the beginning of civil war.

The Kuomintang-Communist Coalition

Why should Marxism, virtually ignored in China during the first two decades of the century, suddenly become of sufficient interest to warrant establishment of a Communist Party? The answer lies in the combined influence of the May Fourth Movement and the Russian Revolution. The movement stimulated interest in diverse Western ideologies, including Marxism. Marxism found a sympathetic hearing among the May Fourth youth who had been radicalized by the iconoclasm of the age and by the agitation against the Versailles settlement of the Shantung question. This sympathy was intensified after March, 1920, when news reached China that the Soviet Union had unilaterally relinquished all of the privileges of the "unequal treaties" concluded between China and Czarist Russia. This declaration by the new Russian Communist regime seemed a concrete manifestation of Leninist hostility to imperialism, the most attractive element of the Marxist-Leninist package to anti-imperialistic young Chinese.

The May Fourth Movement fostered interest in other attractive ideologies, which gathered their own followings, but the intellectual prestige of Ch'en Tu-hsiu and Li Ta-chao, and the force of their leadership, added to the interest in Marxism. Li was the first Chinese intellectual leader to proclaim acceptance of Marxism. At the outset, his endorsement was based largely on his enthusiasm for the Russian Revolution, which he saw as a triumph for freedom and humanism and a start toward creating the basis for a synthesis of Eastern and Western civilizations. But as he studied Marxism, he found it surprisingly compatible with dialectical and revolutionary ideas he had developed on his own. Ch'en's early response to Marxism also focused on the Russian Revolution itself rather than on the ideology that inspired it; by 1920, however, he too had come to believe that Marxism was a practicable guide to revolution in China. Both Li and Ch'en were drawn not only by the anti-imperialist thrust of Leninism, but also by the hope that Marxism could guide China to rapid economic development.

Although interest in Marxist ideas was widespread, and though these ideas by the mid-twenties were exerting a powerful influence on the intellectual world, membership in the Chinese Communist Party grew slowly at the outset. It numbered only 200 or 300 by the beginning of 1923, and still did not exceed 1,000 by the spring of 1925. Only then did membership mushroom.

Ch'en Tu-hsiu took the first concrete steps toward the formal organization of the Chinese Communist Party. He was encouraged and assisted by Gregory Voitinsky, an agent of the Communist International, or Comintern, who had been in China since the spring of 1920. For nationalistic and ideological reasons, the Russians sought to promote revolution in China. At that time the Bolshevik leaders felt that the success and permanence of their own revolution depended upon the spread of revolution abroad. In addition, they felt that friendly relations with a new nationalist government that would presumably emerge from the Chinese revolution would confound attempts to encircle the Soviet Union by hostile capitalist powers. For these reasons, Voitinsky encouraged Ch'en to found a Communist Party and promised recognition and aid from the Comintern.

Russian efforts to find supporters and clients in China went beyond urging the organization of a Communist Party. Voitinsky and other Russian agents also talked with Sun Yat-sen, whose Kuomintang was then an enfeebled party. It had some prestige because of its pre-1911 revolutionary antecedents, and because it had maintained a government in Canton in opposition to the warlord government in Peking since 1917. However, it also relied on warlord support, its organization was flabby, its ideology amorphous, its goals ambiguous. Nevertheless, the Russians thought it promising. It had a revolutionary tradition, it had supported the labor movement in Kwangtung, and its leader, Sun Yat-sen, was clearly prepared to bend every effort to gain power. By late 1922 Sun was receptive to Russian overtures not only because of a vague sympathy with the Russian Revolution and frustration over lack of support from Western nations, but primarily because he needed some reliable aid in order to consolidate his base in Kwangtung and march from there to unify China.

Russian talks with Sun finally led to a formal understanding expressed in the Sun-Joffe Manifesto. This statement, issued in January, 1923, over the signatures of Sun and the Russian representative, Adolf Joffe, acknowledged that China was not ready for Communism, but that it urgently needed to be both united and independent, and that the Russians were prepared to aid Sun and his party in bringing these events to pass. In the autumn of 1923 Michael Borodin arrived in China to serve as Sun's special political adviser, and Russian aid, in the form of military and political advisers and various material, began to pour into China.

The Russians promptly initiated a thorough reorganization of the Kuomintang that was formally approved at the Kuomintang National Congress in January, 1924. Party organization was modeled

after that of the Russian Bolshevik Party to create a much higher
degree of centralization than had existed, and far more rigorous
and effective party discipline. The party accepted the principles of
democratic centralism, in which each level of organization obeyed
unquestionably the decisions of higher levels, and Sun Yat-sen, at
the apex of the party pyramid, was given extraordinary dictatorial
authority not common even to ordinary Communist organizations.

The reorganized party reaffirmed its commitment to the ideology
developed by Sun Yat-sen, although, under Russian prodding, anti-
imperialism was emphasized more strongly than ever. The core of
Sun's political ideology lay in his so-called Three Principles of the
People: nationalism, democracy, and people's livelihood, which Sun
had first formulated in 1905. As a corollary of party reorganization
during the first months of 1924, Sun undertook a series of lectures
to describe in detail the Three Principles as he had finally worked
them out through the years.

Sun's principle of nationalism had undergone the greatest
changes since its earliest formulation. Originally, it had been largely
synonymous with anti-Manchuism, and as an objective, therefore,
it had been realized in the 1911 Revolution. In the early 1920s Sun
began to revive the principle of nationalism, and in his 1924 lectures
presented it as a vigorous denunciation of imperialism in China. Sun
said that the Chinese nationalist spirit had long ago been destroyed
by the Manchus, and in its absence China had been subjected to
three destructive forces: stagnation of population in a world where
other nations were growing rapidly; political domination by foreigners; and economic exploitation by foreigners. To check these
forces, said Sun, China must create a new national solidarity on the
basis of its clans and families, refuse to buy foreign goods, and try
to limit foreign economic exploitation. If these countermeasures
were successful, the problem of population stagnation would take
care of itself. Running through Sun's lectures was criticism of those
who blindly copied the West without regard to Chinese conditions,
a position that evidently prompted him to advocate reviving China's
ancient morality and using China's ancient wisdom. As critical as
he was of blind copiers, however, he also argued that China must
learn from the West.

In discussing his principle of democracy, Sun reasoned that the twentieth century was the age of democracy, and that China should be up-to-date and part of that age. Many nations that had employed democratic systems for a long time, however, had not been very successful, Sun argued; therefore, he had worked out a new and better system of democracy in which the populace would turn over political power to intellectually superior individuals whom they would control through the rights of suffrage, recall, initiative, and referendum, and to whom they would entrust a government organized on the basis of a "five-power constitution" providing for executive, legislature, and judiciary branches of government, and also for censorate and civil-service examination branches.

Sun's five-power constitution was not to come into effect immediately. He conceived of the revolution in China in three phases: the military conquest of the country; a period of tutelage, during which the population would be trained to operate a constitutional government; and the realization of constitutional government.

Sun was especially vague about his third principle, the principle of livelihood. He identified it with socialism and with communism, but the comparisons among them were far from rigorous. Sun vigorously attempted to repudiate Marx, particularly on the need for class struggle; he wanted to improve the standard of living for the mass of the population through industrialization and economic modernization, but he wanted even more to avoid class warfare. To improve living standards without bloodshed, Sun advocated the regulation of capital, which he said could be achieved through state ownership and development of industries, and the reduction of the exploitative potentialities of land ownership, which he thought could be accomplished by funneling to the state the increase of land value produced by social improvements. Sun recommended the use of agricultural machinery, chemical fertilizers, and the overall improvement of agricultural technology to achieve greater productivity. He also believed that the peasants had to be liberated from confiscatory rents, and that improvements had to be made in the distribution of commodities to ameliorate their living conditions. In short, Sun postulated humane and progressive economic goals. Unfortunately, he developed no specific, practicable economic programs to achieve them.

The First Party Congress accepted Sun's Three Principles as the basis of party policy, and the manifesto of the congress summarized the principles with emphasis on their revolutionary and anti-imperialist aspects. The congress also approved the policy of Kuomintang-Communist cooperation by allowing Communists to join the Kuomintang—a step that had profound consequences. The Russians were largely responsible for establishing the coalition between the Kuomintang and the Chinese Communist Party. The Communist Party was in its infancy, and the Russians thought they could not count on it to initiate and carry through the kind of revolution they hoped would undercut imperialism in China. Moreover, the Russians considered that the socialist revolution in China was a long time off, that the revolution was in its bourgeois-democratic phase, and that the Kuomintang was the chief vehicle for the revolution during that phase. The Kuomintang, the Russians told the Chinese Communists, should not be viewed as the political party of the bourgeoisie, but as an alliance of revolutionary elements from all four major classes: peasantry, workers, intellectuals, and petty bourgeoisie. The Chinese Communist Party therefore should do nothing to disrupt the Kuomintang's efforts, but should support them. Because the Russians were advising and assisting both parties, their desire could not be ignored; the Chinese members of each party, however, had mixed views.

The Communist Party and the Kuomintang could both see that the combined power of warlordism and imperialism was so great that the unity of all revolutionary forces was obviously desirable. The Communists recognized that their party was still small and weak, and that it could profit from the contacts and reputation of the Kuomintang. Sun Yat-sen, on the other hand, appreciated the potential strength of the labor movement, on which the Communists had concentrated their organizational energies immediately after founding their party. Sun wanted all revolutionaries, of whatever stripe, under his leadership. It has been suggested that he specially wanted the Communists subject to the control of the Kuomintang as a means of precluding their independent development and the class warfare he thought that development would produce. Whether that was a key reason or not, there were clearly a number of arguments in favor of cooperation. But the real question was the form the cooperation should take. Sun Yat-sen, with Comintern agreement, wanted a coalition; he wanted the Communists to join the Kuomintang as individuals; he would not agree to the two parties functioning separately but in tandem, as a kind of united front.

Some Chinese Communist leaders also favored the policy of coalition. Li Ta-chao, for example, thought that international capitalism exploited all classes in China, and therefore all classes should unite to oppose it. Li was less inclined to look to a single revolutionary class, the proletariat, than to the entire nation, which he considered a "proletarian nation," all elements of which had to struggle together against imperialism. Mao Tse-tung, one of the founding members of the Communist Party, also supported the coalition policy. However, many Communists strenuously objected to joining the Kuomintang; they did not agree with the Russians' theoretical justification for the coalition. The Chinese argued that the Kuomintang was the party of the bourgeoisie; they might have added that the conception of a party as an amalgam of several classes was not very good Marxism. Some of the Chinese Communists also hoped that China would bypass capitalism on the way to socialism, and if that were possible—if there was to be no capitalist phase—the necessity for a bourgeois-democratic revolution did not exist. Moreover, in immediately practical terms, they feared that the new policy was tantamount to handing over to the Kuomintang the leadership of the labor movement, their chief social base. Some feared they would become "Kuomintangized." In fact, many thought that the new policy meant the end of the independent existence of the Chinese Communist Party. The Communist leadership had decided as early as 1922 that cooperation with the Kuomintang was desirable, but at that time it was thinking in terms of an alliance of two parties. When the Comintern agent pressed the policy of Communists joining the Kuomintang, there was so much opposition in the Communist Party Central Committee that it appeared the proposal would be defeated. The Comintern agent called upon the Chinese to adhere to international discipline, and they finally yielded. At the third congress of the Chinese Communist Party, in 1923, the policy was approved by one vote.

Many Kuomintang members also objected to permitting Communists to enter their party. Several prominent Kuomintang figures left the party in protest against the policy, and formed anti-Communist organizations to assure that Communist influence in no way adulterated the purity of Sun Yat-sen's thought and program. Thus, in both parties there were strong doubts about the wisdom of the coalition.

A basic contradiction threatened the coalition from the outset. Despite the Russian analysis of the mixed composition of the Kuomintang, it was fundamentally the party of the bourgeoisie. Though some of its leading spokesmen talked in fiery terms of world revolution, they did not speak for all members of the party, and they did not mean everything they said. The Kuomintang wanted to eliminate the warlords, abolish the unequal treaties, and begin to modernize the country under the guidance of the educated, propertied class. The Communists also opposed warlords and imperialism, but they envisaged ultimate power in the hands of the workers and peasants; they envisaged, in other words, a thoroughgoing social revolution. The ultimate aims of the two parties, of course, determined the methods each was inclined to use. The Communists wanted to overthrow the warlords and oust the imperialists through the organization of a social revolution, thus combining social and national goals. The Kuomintang wanted to achieve the first two objectives, but opposed class warfare. Conflict between the two parties was, therefore, inevitable.

The only way the coalition could have worked would have been for the Communists to renounce their goals and devote all their energies to the Kuomintang. Indeed, the fiction that they would was part of the rickety basis of the coalition. But if they had renounced their goals, what justification would there have been for the continued existence of the Communist Party? What could the party have looked forward to after the country was unified inasmuch as the Kuomintang's program called for a period of tutelage during which it would exercise a national dictatorship? The Communist Party, of course, did continue to exist because its members never intended to limit themselves to Kuomintang goals. And that policy, too, had its own iron logic: if they were to pursue Communist goals while members of the Kuomintang, they would be virtually compelled to try to dominate the Kuomintang.

Not surprisingly, the policy of Kuomintang-Communist coalition produced a good deal of controversy in the Comintern itself, where the blueprint for the Chinese revolution was being drawn. Some maintained that in order to oppose imperialism, cooperation with bourgeois democrats—revolution "from above"—was permissible, whereas others insisted that Communists should organize workers and peasants for revolution "from below." In the final analysis, both approaches were recommended: the Communists were to steer a course between revolution "from above" and "from below." This impossible juncture of opposite methods ran through Comintern policy and sometimes imparted to Comintern instructions and views a curious air of unreality.

The contradiction at the root of the Kuomintang-Communist coalition inevitably grew more acute as the two parties worked to develop their particular organizational and power interests. The Chinese Communists had resolved at the founding meeting of the party in 1921 that it should focus its efforts on the organization of industrial workers. It created the Chinese Labor Organizations Secretariat to promote labor activity, and from the summer of 1921 this secretariat concentrated on developing union organizations and strike action. After Communist members joined the Kuomintang, they continued to put their energies into the labor movement, and later into the peasant movement as well. Many Kuomintang people also participated in various aspects of this work, but by and large the mass movements became Communist strongholds of organization and influence.

The Kuomintang, on the other hand, gathered the chief strands of military power into its hands. Chiang Kai-shek, a young Kuomintang military officer, was made director of the Whampoa Military Academy, which was specifically created to turn out revolutionary officers for a revolutionary army. Many Communists served in the army as political officers, responsible for the political training of the troops, agitation, and propaganda. Evidently, the Communists thought they could control the army through their political officers, but in the long run it did not work out that way. Instead, a kind of practical division of labor emerged, with the Communists dominating in political work, particularly in mass movements, and the Kuomintang dominating in the armed forces.

Mass Movements

The May Fourth Movement initiated the modern labor movement in China. Traditionally, Chinese workers had organized in
craft guilds, which included employers as well as workers. In the
two or three years just before 1919, a few organizations exclusively
for workers appeared, but these were devoted to social activities,
mutual-aid projects, and educational programs, not to militant
trade-union work. Although there had been a surprising number of
strikes from about the turn of the century to 1919, they were brief
outbursts, irrepressible responses to harsh conditions, not organized-
labor actions.

In response to the May Fourth Incident, many workers participated in the demonstrations, the anti-Japanese boycott, and the
strikes held in protest against government repression. The traditional guilds helped organize and support this activity, but the success of the workers' response demonstrated the effectiveness of strike
tactics and stimulated more militant labor organization. As a result,
a number of new labor organizations sprang into existence in 1920
and 1921, including several genuinely working-class groups—groups
run by workers and willing to fight for worker interests. This labor
movement was most advanced in Shanghai and Canton, and its first
great achievement was the Hong Kong Seamen's Strike of 1922.

Hong Kong seamen had compelling grievances. After World
War I, prices had soared and wages had not. Moreover, the seamen
were victims of a vicious labor-contract racket whereby men could
get seamen jobs only by paying a fee to a recruiter, who then sometimes took a percentage of their pay for months. In 1921 certain
Hong Kong mutual-aid societies were reorganized into one genuine
union headed by a member of the Kuomintang and with Communists in key positions of leadership. In the fall of that year the new
seamen's union formally submitted a demand for higher wages and
other benefits, but received no reply. When two subsequent communications also went unanswered, the workers went on strike in
January, 1922.

By the end of January, about 30,000 seamen were on strike. Employers opened negotiations, but early talks were not fruitful and Hong Kong coolies and dockhands then went on strike in support of the seamen. The Hong Kong government turned to suppression: it closed the seamen's union office by force, arrested its leaders, seized its records. And the shippers tried to import strikebreakers from other ports. But the strike simply grew. By mid-February, 40,000 men were out, and workers in other ports cooperated to keep strikebreakers from going to Hong Kong. Late in February, virtually all Hong Kong workers walked off the job. Workers left printing plants, dairies, business offices, restaurants, hotels; even rickshaw pullers struck, and domestic servants. Faced with this massive demonstration of support for the strike, the shippers settled early in March. It was a stunning victory for the workers.

The success of the Hong Kong Seamen's Strike had several significant aspects. It spurred the growth of the labor movement; what Hong Kong seamen could do, others could also do if they created a similar organization. It revealed that nationalism and class consciousness were beginning to modify the regionalism and narrow loyalties that had earlier characterized the labor movement, as well as most other movements, in China. British ships went to Canton to buy food during the strike, but they found merchant food guilds unwilling to sell to them. These guilds were run by merchants, not workers, and their support of the Hong Kong seamen was prompted by anti-imperialist feelings coupled with sympathy for fellow Chinese. Moreover, though economic in its inception, the strike was used by both the Kuomintang and the Communists to spread anticapitalist and anti-imperialist propaganda, so that it acquired a strong, and effective, political coloration.

Through the remainder of 1922 the labor movement expanded with extraordinary speed, and many strikes were called. The Communists were active in organizing and leading this movement, but Jean Chesneaux, the leading Western scholar of the Chinese labor movement, insists that the organizational impulse came directly from the workers; the leaders simply helped guide and direct a movement that had spontaneously come into being.

The momentum achieved by the Chinese labor movement after the Hong Kong strike came to a bloody halt, however, in February, 1923. At the beginning of that month, 16 railwaymen's clubs amalgamated to form the Ching Han General Union. Wu P'ei-fu, the dominant northern warlord of that time, banned the conference at which the organization was to be founded. The delegates met anyway and after quickly and formally declaring the organization to be in existence, immediately dispersed. Nevertheless, some were arrested. The union responded by calling a general strike, and on the fourth day of the strike, February 7, 1923, Wu's troops responded by attacking the strikers, killing 35 and wounding many more. This brutal assault marked the beginning of a period of repression in the labor movement; a few labor organizations disappeared, and all reduced the level and militancy of their activity. Another consequence of February 7 violence was that it lessened the opposition of Communists to the policy of joining the Kuomintang; faced with the naked armed power of the warlords, their best hope seemed to lie in the development of a revolutionary army and the consolidation of a base at Canton that would include all revolutionary elements. For two years after the February 7 killings, there was something of a lull in the labor movement, particularly in central and north China where warlords ruled unopposed. On May 30, 1925, however, the lull came to a crashing end.

In the backround of the May Thirtieth Incident was a series of labor conflicts in Shanghai, particularly in Japanese-owned plants. Wages were low, and steadily rising prices made them worth even less. Moreover, warlords had repeatedly exacted huge sums from Shanghai, and most of this was ultimately taken from the pockets of the workers. Foreigners owned many plants in China, and Japan owned no less than 27 cotton mills in Shanghai alone. Working conditions were as bad in the foreign plants as they were in the Chinese, and in Japanese-owned factories it was not unusual for workers to suffer beatings at the hands of the Japanese staff. By early 1925 labor was restive, angered by low wages and brutality. Then on May 15 a fracas occurred between Chinese workers and supervisory personnel at a Japanese mill. The Japanese opened fire on the Chinese, killing one worker and wounding several others. In protest, a massive demonstration was held on May 30 involving several thousand people. A clash developed on Nanking Road between the demonstrators and the foreign-controlled police of the International Settlement; the police shot into the crowd, leaving 10 dead and more than 50 injured.

Not only the residents of Shanghai, but Chinese all over the country—indeed, all over the world—reacted to this shooting with furious indignation. It was the May Fourth Movement all over again, but this time the anger was deeper, centered in the working class, and characterized by broader support and more effective organization. On May 31 leaders of all strata and groups in the city decided upon a general strike and boycott of foreign goods, and the following day normal Shanghai activities slammed to a stop. Shops and banks closed, students stayed out of classes, and workers stayed off the job. By mid-June, more than 150,000 people were on strike in Shanghai, and in some two dozen other cities throughout China demonstrations and strikes erupted in protest against the Nanking Road Massacre, as the Shanghai shooting was called. In Hong Kong and Canton there began one of the longest general strikes and boycotts of foreign goods in all history; it lasted 16 months.

These great strikes were political in nature, not economic. True, economic demands were involved in the early discontent of workers in Shanghai plants, but the strike was primarily political when it finally came. It was a resounding cry of protest against imperialism in China, and it resulted in specific demands for freedom of speech and assembly, the withdrawal of foreign armed forces from Shanghai, and the abolition of extraterritoriality. The Canton-Hong Kong strike began in response to the May Thirtieth Incident with no demands of higher wages or better working conditions, though labor legislation was included in the political reforms the strikers demanded. It was a sympathy strike, and many sympathy strikes were called elsewhere in the country. As sympathy strikes they were, of course, also political, although some strikes took the opportunity to present economic demands. The May Thirtieth Movement thus emerged as an impressive demonstration of the power the Chinese people, acting in concert, could bring against imperialism. But it also revealed the conflict between nationalist and class interests.

The divergent interests of the Shanghai merchants and industrialists on the one hand, and the working class and students on the other, manifested themselves shortly after the general strike began. A joint committee of workers, merchants, and students was organized to formulate strike policy, but the General Chamber of Commerce of Shanghai stepped in to act as intermediary between the committee and the foreigners. The joint committee formulated the strike demands in the form of 17 points, and these were given to the chamber. The chamber, however, passed on only 13 demands to the diplomatic corps, omitting those calling for the right of workers to strike, the right of workers to organize trade unions, the abolition of extraterritoriality, and the control by Chinese of police in the International Settlement. As the general strike went on, Chinese businessmen increasingly complained of their losses, and on June 25, evidently with the reluctant consent of the joint committee, the Chinese merchants and industrialists reopened their businesses, though they continued to advocate the boycott of Japanese and British goods.

The foreigners now knew where the strikers' weak point lay: merchants and industrialists were not above putting their own interests first. When the strike began, Chinese workers had walked out of the electric power plant. It was located in the International Settlement, but served sectors of the Chinese city. Foreign volunteers had kept the electric plant operating, but they now informed the Chinese industrial users that service would be discontinued in early July. The Chinese mill owners and other industrialists, whose plants were operating full blast while their British and Japanese competitors were idle, were dismayed by this prospect, and when the electricity finally was turned off, they shifted to outright opposition to the strike.

Faced with this rift in the strike forces, with the unyielding position of the foreign powers in Shanghai, and with the establishment of martial law by warlord troops who administered Shanghai and who promised draconic punishment for anyone who tried to "create trouble," the strikers in August moved to bring the strike to a close. The original political goals of the strike were by and large dismissed, and the economic objectives of gains for the workers took their place. In August and September agreement was reached on the basis of these demands, and the strike movement came to an end in Shanghai, though some of the strikes it had spawned in other cities continued, notably in Canton and Hong Kong.

The May Thirtieth Movement was not a success in terms of the strike goals declared at the outset. Moreover, it revealed the limits imposed on anti-imperialist unity by the class contradictions between the workers and the bourgeoisie. It also demonstrated the threat that warlordism posed to the working-class movement; at the end of 1925 the Shanghai warlord closed down the General Labor Union, which remained underground until early 1927 when it reemerged in support of the Northern Expedition. Despite these setbacks, the membership of the Communist Party soared from about 1,000 to roughly 30,000 during the year following the May Thirtieth Incident, an increase attributed to the impression made by the Communist leadership during the strike.

Another mass movement also took hold during this period—among the peasantry. Like the labor movement, the peasant movement started shortly after the May Fourth Era. Its major growth, however, did not occur until 1926 and 1927. The Communists, in their orthodox preoccupation with the organization of labor, more or less ignored the peasantry in the first couple of years of the party's existence. After that, the party leadership took increasing note of peasant needs and eventually promulgated quite radical slogans aimed at the countryside. But the leadership's attention was not matched by practical work in the rural areas. Until 1926, the central headquarters of the party did not even include an organization to direct peasant movements. Accomplishments in peasant organization during these early years—and there were significant achievements—were those of more or less maverick individuals working independently at first, and later, from 1924, in the Peasant Department of the Kuomintang. The most notable peasant leader was P'eng P'ai.

P'eng P'ai, son of a landlord and evidently among the first members of the Communist Party, persuaded the peasants in his home district of Haifeng in Kwangtung Province to organize in order to protect their interests. By the beginning of 1923, he had organized the Haifeng Federation of Peasant Associations, which initiated progressive measures to improve peasant life: expansion of public education, improvement of sanitation, medical assistance, and attempts to reduce agricultural rents, among others. Despite opposition from the Kwangtung warlord of the moment, the pattern of peasant association developed by P'eng was readily adopted by peasants in other Kwangtung communities, and by the spring of 1923, the movement had grown sufficiently to justify the creation of the Kwangtung Provincial Peasant Association, and P'eng was named chairman. After the reorganization of the Kuomintang in 1924, P'eng was made secretary of the Peasant Department of the Kuomintang, and effectively fostered the creation and growth of peasant associations in Kuomintang-controlled territories. His policies became increasingly radical. By the end of 1925 the association's membership exceeded 600,000, and it was undertaking land expropriation, the forcible reduction of rents, and the execution of some landlords.

Kwangtung remained far in the lead in terms of the extent of peasant mobilization, though peasant organizations gradually came into existence in at least 15 other provinces. Except in Kwangtung, Hunan, and Honan, these organizations were on a very small scale. Warlord control inevitably restricted the growth of peasant associations, and not until the revolutionary armies moved northward would the peasant movement expand into a major force.

The Rise of Chiang Kai-shek

Involved as members of the Kuomintang were in the mass movements, the guiding spirit behind the movements was Communist. The Kuomintang, on the other hand, dominated the National Revolutionary Army, in which Chiang Kai-shek was a crucial figure.

Chiang, the son of a salt merchant, had decided early on a military career and studied in Japanese military schools from 1908 until 1911; while in Japan, he had also joined the United League. Chiang had returned to China when the Wuhan revolt broke out, and participated in the action around Shanghai; he went back to Japan shortly afterward, when friction between Yuan Shih-k'ai and the republicans showed the precarious character of the new political system. Chiang's career during the following decade is obscure at points, but it is clear that he continued to serve Sun Yat-sen loyally, and by the beginning of the 1920s was known and appreciated by Sun as an important and promising young follower. When Ch'en Chiung-ming drove Sun out of Canton in 1923, Chiang spent some days in close contact with the revolutionary leader and apparently impressed Sun with his outstanding loyalty and ability. But it was not this alone that prompted Sun to send Chiang to Moscow in late 1923 to study Soviet military systems. A recent study has shown that Chiang's Russian assignment was in response to his own importunate requests; in fact, he threatened to resign if he did not receive the assignment. Chiang was generally informed of the kind of military aid the Russians planned to provide, and he evidently wanted to be sure he would be in a favorable position to play a key managerial role in its use.[1] A visit to Moscow, to become the party's expert on the Russian military, would put him in just that position.

When Chiang returned, he quickly put his newfound indispensability to use. Named head of the Whampoa Military Academy, the new center to train revolutionary officers, he refused to take the post until a number of personnel and political questions were settled to his satisfaction; Chiang already distrusted the Russians and the Chinese Communists. Nonetheless, to many observers he seemed to be ardently leftist. Perhaps Chiang assumed this public stance because it was the policy of the Kuomintang to cooperate with the Russians and the Communists, and he did not feel that he was in a sufficiently powerful position to repudiate that policy. In any event, Chiang doubtless saw advantages in such a stance. He was quite frank about approving actions contrary to the party's principles if they would enhance the party's power, and he may well have applied this rule to his personal role as well.

Chiang proved to be extremely successful in uniting and inspiring the early classes of Whampoa cadets. He called upon them for patriotism and self-sacrifice, and for a commitment to the revolution and to the goals of the Kuomintang. He exhorted them to struggle to realize what Sun Yat-sen had described as the sole purpose of the Whampoa Academy: "creating a new revolutionary army for the salvation of China."[2] Because of his success at Whampoa and his apparent revolutionary fervor, and because his trip to Moscow had subtly identified him with the Soviet Union, the Russian advisers thought highly of Chiang. Stamped with the approval of the Russians and Sun Yat-sen alike, and in charge of training officers for the revolution, Chiang was a leading figure in Kuomintang circles by 1925. After the death of Sun Yat-sen, Chiang became one of the contenders for top party power.

Sun Yat-sen died in March, 1925. There were no firmly settled succession arrangements, and therefore a long struggle for party leadership ensued that ultimately became inextricably interwoven with the conflict between the Kuomintang Right and the Kuomintang Left and involved the whole issue of Kuomintang-Communist relations. It also had a powerful influence on the balance between civilian and military elements in the party.

The obvious candidates for party leadership were Wang Ching-wei, Hu Han-min, and Liao Chung-k'ai. The three men had been intimately associated with Sun after joining the United League almost immediately upon its founding in 1905. Wang Ching-wei was the most famous of the three because of his attempt to assassinate the Manchu Prince Regent in 1910. The attempt failed, and Wang was captured. He boldly proclaimed both his guilt and his commitment to the revolution. Perhaps awed by such candor, or more likely fearful of the effect Wang's execution might have on the tottering dynasty, the government only imprisoned him, and after the 1911 Revolution he walked out a national hero. Wang spent several of the following years in Europe, but returned in 1917 to work closely with Sun Yat-sen until the leader's death. His standing in the party was shown in the Kuomintang Congress of 1924, when he was elected second ranking member of the party's Central Executive Committee.

Hu Han-min was elected the first ranking member of the committee. Hu had devoted many years of hard work to Sun Yat-sen's cause. He had helped Sun set up several revolt attempts in south China in the years before 1911, and for a while was director of United League affairs in Southeast Asia. After the 1911 Revolution, Hu held a wide range of positions in the revolutionary party and in the governments it sponsored. He was consistently one of Sun's closest lieutenants.

Liao Chung-k'ai became known as the party's financial expert. He worked in various capacities on Kuomintang financial programs, and published explications of Sun's economic theories. Liao was somewhat more leftish than most of his associates. He argued in favor of developing China along socialist lines, he was enthusiastic about the Russian Revolution, and he was centrally involved in arranging for Russian assistance to the Kuomintang. After the Sun-Joffe Manifesto announcing the broad lines of Russian aid to the

Kuomintang, Liao and Joffe, in seclusion in Japan, hammered out the details of the arrangement. Liao also helped plan the 1924 reorganization of the party, and, after it was put into effect, was named to the Central Executive Committee. He was charged with handling worker and peasant affairs, and became party representative at Whampoa where he helped organize the system of political representatives in army units. By the time of Sun's death, Liao was generally considered the most prominent figure in the left wing of the Kuomintang, and the keystone of Kuomintang-Communist cooperation.

As pioneer revolutionary and a celebrated international figure, Sun Yat-sen had been the unchallenged head of the Kuomintang. In his own person he had held together a party that had several major factions. No single individual, however, could immediately replace Sun in that capacity, and so committee leadership was inaugurated, with the heads of the major factions holding committee positions. The revolutionary government in Canton was transformed into a "national" government; presumably this Nationalist Government, as it was called, would expand its functions as the revolution spread, ultimately embracing the entire nation. The government was led by a committee of 16, with Wang Ching-wei serving as the elected chairman—in effect head of the government. Hu Han-min, to the right of Wang, was named Foreign Minister, an exalted title with little substance inasmuch as the government had no relations with other countries. Liao Chung-k'ai, the leftist, was named Minister of Finance. In short, the left was somewhat stronger than the right, but Wang, somewhere left of center, was the only major figure acceptable to both extremes, as well as to the moderates. In that way, Wang assumed the leading position, but with his power still conditional upon support from the factions.

Two months after the Nationalist Government had been created, in August, 1925, assassins killed Liao Chung-k'ai. The murder has never been definitely solved, although a committee of inquiry at the time—including Chiang Kai-shek—believed that a cousin of Hu Han-min was responsible. The cousin fled, and Hu Han-min, though not personally implicated, had to retire from political life for a while.

With Liao dead, and Hu Han-min politically indisposed, Wang

Ching-wei appeared clearly to be the dominating figure. The left wing now gravitated around Wang, thus making him increasingly offensive to the conservatives on the right. In effect, Wang became the leader of the left wing, and the communists supported him as part of a tactic of allying with the left against the right. In November a group of 15 Kuomintang Right members of two leading party committees met at Western Hills, outside Peking, and declared their meeting to constitute a session of the Central Executive Committee. In that capacity, they decided that Borodin, chief Russian adviser to the Kuomintang, should be dismissed, that the Communists should be expelled from the Kuomintang, and that Wang Ching-wei should be suspended from the party for six months. The leaders in Canton denied that the Western Hills group constituted the quorum required for such actions, and, to settle the matter in a broader context, convened the Second National Congress of the Kuomintang.

The Second Party Congress opened in January, 1926, and its proceedings displayed unequivocally the predominance of the left in party affairs. The congress confirmed Wang Ching-wei's leadership, and elected more Communists to the top Kuomintang committees. About half of the Kuomintang departments were put under Communist or Kuomintang Left directors. Finally, the congress reaffirmed the party's commitment to the line laid down at the First Congress two years earlier: cooperation with the Soviet Union and collaboration with the Chinese Communist Party. The congress expelled two leaders of the Western Hills group and warned the others.

Not everybody, even on the left, was happy with these developments. The activity of the Western Hills group was only the most conspicuous of many signs that Kuomintang members were concerned over Communist inroads in their party. Even some of the Communist leaders deplored such blatant ascendancy of the left in the Kuomintang. Chang Kuo-t'ao, one of the founding members of the Communist Party, a leader in the labor movement, and a member of the Communist Party Central Committee, asserted in his autobiography that he argued with Russian and leftist leaders behind the scenes that a few more Kuomintang posts in Communist hands would not substantially increase real Communist power, but would certainly intensify Kuomintang resentment against the Communists and the Kuomintang left. Chang insisted that the Communists should work against the extreme rightists in the Kuomintang, but not alienate the moderates, and that such a policy required moderation from the Communists. Borodin rejected this argument and pushed to bring the Kuomintang Left and the Communists closer together to form a single group that would dominate the Kuomintang and the national government.

From Borodin's standpoint, the Second Congress was a smashing success. The left was clearly in the saddle, and, in fact, Communist influence and power in the Kuomintang was pervasive. Communists held about one-fifth of the Central Executive Committee seats and one-third of the seats on the Executive Committee's Standing Committee. Communists controlled the important Organization Department of the party, and the majority of members in provincial and municipal Kuomintang headquarters were Communists. The Propaganda Department was headed by Wang Ching-wei, an index of its importance, but Wang had so many tasks that the department was essentially run by his deputy, Mao Tse-tung. Communists held important posts in the Labor Department and Youth Department, among others, and a Communist headed the Peasant Department. They held many other positions, but those mentioned provide an indication of the extent to which they had penetrated the top echelons of the Kuomintang. When Borodin left for north China shortly after the Second Congress, he could leave with confidence that his allies and protégés had the Kuomintang very much in hand. But Borodin had badly misjudged one man: Chiang Kaishek.

On March 20, 1926, Chiang took several dramatic steps which revealed that the left was far less in control of the Kuomintang than appearances had indicated. On that day, alleging discovery of a Communist conspiracy against him, Chiang declared martial law in Canton, arrested Soviet advisers in the city and Communist political advisers in the party army, and closed trade union and strike committee headquarters. On the basis of this demonstration of strength, and pointing to the disproportionate power of the Communists in the Kuomintang, Chiang summoned a meeting of its Central Executive Committee to readjust party affairs.

Even before the meeting convened in May, Wang Ching-wei had left the country. Wang was ill at home when the March 20 coup occurred, and he promptly denounced Chiang as a counter-revolutionary. Wang, however, as he also did on later occasions, showed no capacity to respond effectively to strong, determined action. He took no practical steps to punish Chiang's usurpation of authority. On the contrary, he disappeared from sight for some days, then declared his intention to retire from politics, and departed for Hong Kong, and from there to France. Wang was the first major casualty of Chiang's coup. Overnight the balance of political power in the top ranks of the party shifted, and Chiang had taken a long step toward party leadership.

Chiang vigorously pursued his advantage when the Central Executive Committee met in May. The committee formally ousted Wang Ching-wei and installed one of Chiang's supporters as chairman, though Chiang himself assumed the position about a month later. It also approved resolutions incorporating Chiang's proposals to limit the influence of Communists in the Kuomintang. These resolutions included the following points: Communists in the Kuomintang must not criticize Sun Yat-sen or his ideas, and must accept his program wholeheartedly; no Communist can serve as chairman of the Central Executive Committee or as director of any Kuomintang department; Communist membership of Kuomintang committees must not exceed one-third of the total number of committeemen; Communists must submit to the Kuomintang Central Executive Committee a list of all their party members in the Kuomintang; the Communist Party Central Committee must present to the Kuomintang Central Executive Committee all orders to Communist Party members within the Kuomintang. Following this action, there was a reshuffling of personnel as Communists moved out of positions as department heads to make way for Kuomintang replacements.

While these steps were being taken, Chiang confused the Russian advisers and the Chinese Communists with a series of conciliatory statements. He apologized for the actions taken against the Russians on March 20, and explained them as a result of a misunderstanding on the part of his subordinates. He also said that he saw no reason for changing the nature of the Kuomintang's relations with the Soviet Union, and requested that the Soviet advisers continue their work as usual. And he restated his support of the policy of Kuomintang-Communist collaboration. That these statements represented Chiang's sincere views was made easier to believe by the fact that, in April, he emphatically denounced the right wing of the Kuomintang and dismissed several of its figures from important positions.

The March 20 coup brought profound changes in the collaborative relationship between the Communist Party and the Kuomintang, and to the overall balance of political forces in the revolutionary camp. It was, of course, a gross setback for Wang Ching-wei and a serious blow to the Kuomintang Left, which he led, particularly to the Communists in the Kuomintang. Wang was thought by many to be Sun Yat-sen's political heir, an assumption confirmed by his heading the government after Sun's death. But his weak response to Chiang's move—rhetorical denunciation and flight abroad—was the first of a long series of evasions that were to characterize the rest of his career. The limits on Communist membership of committees, and the other restrictions on leftists, were perhaps less important than the policy orientation these measures symbolized. Communists could contribute to the Kuomintang, but they would no longer be permitted to hold positions of real power within that party.

Chiang's coup was also a setback for the principle of civilian control of the military. The Kuomintang had gone to some pains to erect an organizational structure that would keep the army obedient to political leaders. In the government organized in mid-1925, the military council was subordinate to the political council. The system of political representatives in the army was another agency of party control over the military. After the coup, however, Chiang removed political representatives from the army (though later he replaced them with non-Communist political officers). It was obvious to all, then, that Chiang had unilaterally repudiated the political leadership of Wang Ching-wei and usurped the top position himself. Members of the Kuomintang Right, and many moderates who might have been expected to be most sensitive to implications of Chiang's moves, were silenced by the fact that he had checked the Communists, a consummation they had long devoutly wished.

By his coup, Chiang propelled himself into the powerful centrist position, between the extreme left and the extreme right. He took, in essence, the position that Wang Ching-wei had enjoyed before the assassination of Liao Chung-k'ai and derived similar advantages from it. It marked the beginning of a long period during which Chiang maintained his own dominance by balancing between rival factions and manipulating them.

As his soft words after the coup revealed, Chiang was not yet ready for a complete split with the Communists. The Kuomintang, having consolidated its southern base in late 1925 by gaining control over the provinces of Kwangtung and Kwangsi, was ready to launch a military campaign against the northern warlords in order to unify the country under party rule. For this campaign, the so-called Northern Expedition, Chiang wanted continued Russian military assistance and the cooperation of the Communists. He did not have a sufficiently strong economic base to allow himself to repudiate the left completely. Kwangtung merchants were already finding it difficult to support the Kuomintang army, and the continuation of the Canton-Hong Kong strike rendered the economic situation there precarious. For all these reasons, Chiang tried to retain Russian and Communist cooperation as he laid plans for the Northern Expedition. Some Chinese Communists, on the other hand, wanted to terminate the policy of Communist membership in the Kuomintang, to withdraw completely from it. Others wanted to try to seize control of the Kuomintang. In the end, however, the issue was resolved when the Comintern ruled that they should remain in the Kuomintang, so the Russians and Communists alike accepted Chiang's actions as gracefully as they could.

The Northern Expedition

The Kuomintang had long wanted to launch a Northern Expedition, a military campaign from the party's base in south China northward to Peking, conquering all the warlords along the way. On two occasions troops had actually started to march north, only to have changed circumstances necessitate aborting the undertaking almost immediately. The First Kuomintang Congress, in 1924, stipulated the elimination of the warlords as the party's first goal, which could only be achieved by a military compaign. Despite this long-held intention, there was disagreement about the Northern Expedition in 1926. Some Communist leaders, for example, opposed launching the expedition at that time, arguing that the revolutionary armies were not yet strong enough to engage the huge forces of the northern warlords. Borodin, who initially wanted to postpone the march, finally agreed to it, however, perhaps in return for Chiang's continued adherence to the policy of Kuomintang-Communist coalition. Early in June, the Kuomintang government formally named Chiang Kai-shek commander in chief of the Northern Expedition, and granted him virtually dictatorial powers over military, political, financial, and party affairs for the duration of the emergency.

The Northern Expedition officially began on July 9, 1926, though in fact military operations had begun a few weeks earlier when Kwangsi troops entered Hunan. Once under way, the National Revolutionary Army marched swiftly northward. Hunan was conquered by the end of July, and a month later the revolutionary forces were outside the walls of the Wuhan cities: Hankow, Hanyang, and Wuchang. Hankow and Hanyang were taken early in September, and Wuchang, after resisting siege for several weeks, finally fell on October 10. With Hunan and Hupei under control, Borodin thought that the Northern Expedition should continue northward along the Peking-Hankow Railway and join with Feng Yü-hsiang in attacking Chang Tso-lin; Feng, having just been defeated by Chang, was ready to cooperate with the Northern Expedition. Borodin reasoned that after the defeat of the Manchurian warlord, the revolutionary armies could then swing back southward along the coast to eliminate the last major enemy, Sun Ch'uan-fang, who dominated five provinces around the lower Yangtze. But Chiang Kai-shek rejected this plan, and moved directly against Sun and the rich provinces and financial centers of the east. The campaign against Sun went more slowly than the advance into Hunan and Hupei, partly because in the late phase of the fighting Sun obtained aid from Chang Tso-lin. However, by March, 1927, Sun Ch'uan-fang had been pushed out of the region, and the great cities of

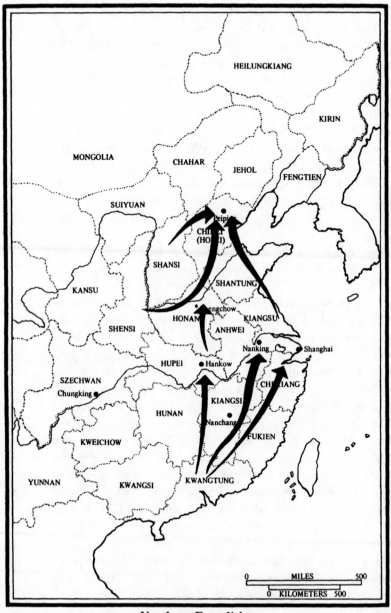

**Northern Expedition
1926–1928**

Nanking and Shanghai were in Chiang's hands. In less than a year, all of China south of the Yangtze had fallen under control of the revolutionary armies.

The Northern Expedition was no cakewalk; there was hard fighting at many points along the way. The rapidity of the march north was partly due to the effective fighting of the National Revolutionary Army, but it also derived from the fact that not all the warlords had to be defeated in war; some simply joined the Kuomintang and continued in their old commands but under a revolutionary designation. At the time, the revolutionaries deemed this policy reasonable; it assured reduced casualties and it expanded the revolutionary forces, thereby enhancing the possibility of victory over the chief warlords of the north. Yet by introducing warlords into the revolutionary army, with their power more or less intact, the groundwork for later trouble was laid.

The speed of the march north has also been attributed to the spontaneous uprisings of the masses who attacked the warlords and cleared the way for the revolutionary forces. Perhaps the earliest, and surely one of the most eloquent, expressions of this view is Harold Isaacs' superb account of those years, *The Tragedy of the Chinese Revolution:*

> The masses of ordinary people rose in a veritable tidal wave that swept the expeditionary armies to the banks of the Yangtze.
> The spontaneous rising of the people gave the Kuomintang armies little more to do, often, than occupy territory that had already been secured for them. The bands of political workers which went out in advance of the troops were able, with the slightest touch, to unleash forces which leveled all opposition.[3]

Many writers have echoed Isaacs' assertion.

More research is needed on the role of the masses during the Northern Expedition, but it appears that passages like Isaac's exaggerate it. In Shanghai, the workers did indeed take over the city before the arrival of the revolutionary army. Perhaps a few villages and towns were also seized before the army reached them. Elsewhere peasant unions and labor unions helped the army by providing transport, obtaining replacements for lost troops, supplying local intelligence. Also, the militance and vigor of the masses surely entered into the tactical considerations of a few warlords; the fear that their troops would defect was unquestionably one consideration that prompted certain warlords to join the National Revolutionary Army. The aid of the masses, therefore, was useful, but it hardly constituted an irresistible tidal wave, carrying all before it.

The fact of the matter seems to be not that the masses cleared the way for Chiang's army, but that the National Revolutionary Army cleared the way for an extraordinary development of the mass movement. T. C. Woo has explained that "as soon as the army cleared a district of the enemy," organization of party branches, labor unions, and peasant associations "went on with feverish speed."[4] Chang Kuo-t'ao recalls that the Hunan peasant movement "was developed right in the wake of the excellent opportunity afforded by the advance of the Northern Expeditionary Army."[5] Chen Ta is even more explicit:

> Prior to the arrival of the Kuomintang in the Wuhan center in the fall of 1926, the labor unions in that region were inactive and reactionary, because they had long been under the suppression of the military authorities, especially since the unsuccessful strike of the Peking-Hankow railway workers in 1923. But within three months after the Kuomintang government was established in September, 1926, about two hundred unions sprang up in Hankow, Hanyang, and Wuchang, following a series of prolonged and uncompromising strikes in the principal trades and industries there.[6]

This expansion of the mass movement after the Northern Expedition reached the Yangtze exacerbated the contradictions in the Kuomintang-Communist coalition and hastened its collapse.

The fall of 1926 to the spring of 1927 was a period of extraordinary growth and activity in the labor movement. Trade unions in and around Wuhan, for example, had a membership of about 100,000 in October, 1926; by the end of the year, only three months later, that number had grown to 300,000. During approximately the same period, 36 important strikes were called in the Wuhan area; the strikes were more politically than economically orientated. In the three weeks following the capture of Shanghai by the revolutionaries, 75 new unions were founded in that city, already a center of labor activity; moreover, a workers' militia was formed that numbered about 3,000 men, armed with weapons taken from police during the seizure of the city in March. By the beginning of 1927, the All China General Union, China's Communist-led national labor organization, was a powerful cohesive body with hundreds of thousands of industrial workers and more than a million handicraft workers and shop employees.[7]

The Northern Expedition also produced an explosive expansion of the peasant movement in Hunan and Hupei. On the eve of the Northern Expedition, perhaps 200,000 peasants were organized in Hunan. By December, 1926, a few months later, peasant associations had been organized in 54 of Hunan's 79 *hsien* (counties) and totaled more than 1,360,000 people; in February, 1927, membership had grown to more than two million. Some historians have estimated that by May it reached four and a half million—possibly an exaggeration, though without doubt the increase was phenomenal. In Hupei peasant unions also grew rapidly; the 280,000 members at the end of 1926 had soared to 800,000 by March of 1927 and reached more than two million by May. The total of organized peasants in all provinces by the spring of 1927 has been estimated at "not less than fifteen million."[8]

Both the labor and peasant unions asserted their burgeoning strength with force and vigor. Strikes proliferated in Wuhan, and wage demands finally produced a threat from employers that they, too, would go on strike unless unions moderated their positions. A similar situation occurred in Kwangtung, where the provincial civil commissioner insisted that the demands for higher wages and shorter hours had become "incompatible with the present stage of development of Chinese industry."[9] Shanghai was the chief example of labor strength, and both the old and the new unions produced a stream of demands. The peasants were even more aggressive. Peasants and landlords clashed frequently over such issues as reduction of rent and reduction of interest. Often these confrontations led to peasant refusal to pay rent and interest, and in some cases to a determination to seize the land. "Local bullies and evil gentry" were abused in various ways, from forcing them to parade through the streets wearing a dunce cap to outright execution.

In the cities of north China, the labor movement was much less developed because industry was sparse and warlord control was tighter. Labor agitation, therefore, was largely confined to central and south China. Northern peasants, however, created their own type of organization, called Red Spear Societies, in which they banded together to defend their localities and fight warlords. They were usually poorly armed, but on occasion they wreaked serious damage on inferior warlord armies.

The End of the Coalition

The expansion and militance of the mass movement frightened landlords, businessmen, and moderate and conservative politicians and military officers. Officers of the National Revolutionary Army, many of whom came from well-to-do rural families, found reports of rural disorder disquieting and ominous. And this fear of the mass movement nourished fear and suspicion of the Communist Party.

The burgeoning mass movement presented the Communists with a dilemma. If they encouraged the peasants, and provided them with leadership and support, it would doubtless bring to an end the Communist coalition with the Kuomintang, to whose members such radicalism was unacceptable. If, on the other hand, they tried to maintain the coalition, they would be in the awkward position of attempting to restrain a revolutionary movement that they had earlier encouraged. Advice from the Comintern was not very helpful because it advised doing both: "[support] all the economic demands of the peasant masses," but "stay in the Kuomintang and intensify . . . work in it."[10] But despite what Comintern directives said, the real thrust of Russian desires was to maintain the Kuomintang-Communist coalition, and to that end the Communists deplored peasant "excesses" and generally tried to hold the agrarian revolution in check.

Meanwhile, Chiang Kai-shek again came in conflict with the Kuomintang Left, which the Communists supported. After the capture of Wuhan in the fall of 1926, party leaders, including Chiang, decided to shift the Kuomintang Central Executive Committee from Canton to Wuhan to create a political center of gravity sufficiently strong to preclude unilateral action by T'ang Sheng-chih, the Hupei warlord recently turned revolutionary Kuomintang general. Also, a central rather than a southern location seemed more appropriate for a government that purported to govern the entire nation, and expected soon to have the power to do precisely that. In December a Joint Council composed of Communists and leftist Kuomintang members of the Kuomintang Central Executive Committee and the Nationalist Government was formed at Wuhan. It was to make preparations for the arrival of the government from the south, and to exercise governmental authority while the main body of the government was making the long move.

By the beginning of 1927, however, Chiang was having second thoughts about Wuhan as the revolutionary capital. T'ang Sheng-chih not only seemed to have a good deal of influence with the Joint Council, but had shown signs of hoping to replace him as commander in chief. The leftist political cast of the council made it suspect to Chiang in any event, and this feeling was strengthened by the fact that the council seemed to be uncooperative about providing money and supplies for his army. And if a left-dominated Joint Council, cozying up to a rival general, were not enough to deter the switch to Wuhan, it was also true that Hunan-Hupei was proving to be the heart of the booming mass movement. Whether or not the choice of Wuhan as a capital was originally related to plans to continue the Northern Expedition from Hankow north along the Peking-Hankow Railway as Borodin urged, Chiang moved east to attack Nanking and Shanghai before proceeding north. For all these reasons, he no longer wanted Wuhan as the seat of government, and argued that a much better capital would be Nanchang, in northern Kiangsi.

Through the first three months of 1927, Nanchang and Wuhan argued back and forth about the location of the capital as Chiang was moving against Sun Ch'uan-fang. In the meantime the leftism of the Wuhan government became ever more conspicuous,* and the

---

* The character of the Wuhan government is clearly shown by the public holidays it officially celebrated. Eleven were nationalist celebrations, including the anniversary of the 1911 Revolution and the death of Sun Yat-sen. Four were directly concerned with the labor movement, and the remaining seven commemorated notable events in the world Communist movement, including the death of Lenin, the proclamation of the Paris Commune, the birth of Karl Marx. (Jean Chesneaux, *The Chinese Labor Movement 1919–1927*, Stanford University Press, 1968, p. 331.)

mass movement in Hunan and Hupei ever more powerful. Chiang's old rival, Wang Ching-wei, had returned to China and, as leader of the Kuomintang Left, was the foremost figure in the Wuhan government. In some ways, the situation seemed to have reverted to what it had been a year earlier on the eve of Chiang's March 20 coup: the Kuomintang Left, supported and influenced by the Russians and the Communists, seemed to be dominating the government and promoting a revolution far more fundamental than others in the Kuomintang had ever envisaged. And now, in the spring of 1927, that revolution was beginning to boil as peasants took more and more aggressive action in the countryside.

Chiang Kai-shek had already begun during the Northern Expedition to take a strong anti-Communist stance. At the end of 1926 one of his closest advisers, Ch'en Kuo-fu, had organized an Anti-Bolshevik League in Kiangsi, and early in 1927 Chiang had denounced the aggressive attitude of the Chinese Communists and proposed to "put a stop to their activities."[11] In March he had executed several Communist labor leaders, and ordered the dissolution of at least two trade union councils. He had also reorganized the municipal governments of Nanchang and Kiukiang, to remove Wuhan sympathizers. In April, 1927, came the most explicit—and overwhelming—evidence of Chiang's anti-Communist position. For now, having occupied Nanking and Shanghai, Chiang was ready to move in force against the Communists. With military support from the staunchly anti-Communist Kwangsi Army, financial support from Shanghai bankers, and at the very least the moral support of the foreign powers, Chiang struck at the Communists and revolutionary organizations with devastating force.

In the dawning hours of April 12, 1927, bands of troops and groups of gangsters suddenly attacked working-class headquarters in all parts of Shanghai. The workers housed in or guarding the various buildings resisted, but were quickly killed or captured. Many of those seized were executed later in the day; by that night, several hundred had been killed. On the following day the slaughter of workers continued in Shanghai, and soon spread to other chief cities under Chiang's control. Ultimately, many hundreds—some reports say thousands—of workers lost their lives, and the working-class movement was shattered in most cities. The Communist Party was decimated and disorganized. The Wuhan government promptly branded Chiang a counterrevolutionary and stripped him of his offices. Chiang responded by setting up his own national government in Nanking on April 18, 1927.

As successful as Chiang's April 12 coup was, the Wuhan leftists were not without weapons to undermine it if they cared to use them. They still headed a peasant movement which, Isaacs argues, could have been used against the forces of Chiang Kai-shek. The Communists, however, were still fettered by the fact that their decisions were being made in Moscow, not Wuhan. Moreover, they were being made with grand disregard for conditions in China, but with acute concern for their repercussions on the conflict between Stalin and Trotsky then raging in the Soviet Union. Trotsky argued that the April catastrophe was a direct consequence of the mistaken analysis of the Kuomintang as a block of four classes, and that the only hope now was to unleash the Communist Party, to give it independence, and to begin swiftly to organize soviets as the vehicle by which the mass movement could protect and extend the gains of the revolution. Stalin, on the other hand, already claiming the kind of retrospective omniscience that he later used to justify all of his errors, asserted that events had proved the correctness of his line, and that the gathering of all the counterrevolutionaries at Nanking had purified the revolutionary movement now being led by the Kuomintang Left at Wuhan. All power must now go to the "revolutionary center" at Wuhan, Stalin argued, and the Chinese Communists must cooperate with and subordinate themselves to that center.

Russian policy throughout this period showed an astonishing confidence in the radicalism of the Kuomintang Left—and in its willingness to be manipulated by Russians. There was, of course, little basis for either belief, at least not in the spring of 1927. Wuhan did not have the boldness, or even the revolutionary intent, required for a "revolutionary center." Wang Ching-wei, a master of vacillation and verbiage, was no man to take the decisive steps necessary to transform that phrase into reality. T'ang Sheng-chih, the chief military support of the Wuhan regime, was not and had never been a revolutionary. Like many warlords, his allegiance to the National Revolutionary Army had been made to serve his private ends more than to contribute to a national movement. Further, Borodin and

M. N. Roy, a Comintern agent sent to China in February, 1927, were locked in disagreement over whether the Northern Expedition should be resumed or the agrarian revolution deepened. Doubtless, conflicting reports were sent to Moscow, forming a most unreliable basis for decisions made there, while Comintern directives did little to eliminate confusion among the Chinese Communists. Wuhan, in short, was in disarray.

If the Wuhan leaders were confused, the peasants were not. Increasingly, they took things into their own hands. In Hupei and especially in Hunan, they arbitrarily canceled outstanding loans and rents, fined and imprisoned landlords and local bullies who had abused peasants, set up rural cooperatives and initiated other local reforms, and in some places began to appropriate and divide the land. The Wuhan government deplored these "excesses" and tried in various ways to restrain the peasant movement, but it took guns to accomplish that.

Most of the Wuhan efforts at restraint were in the form of speeches and government decrees, which were unavailing. Then on May 21, the warlord army of T'ang Sheng-chih stepped in, ostensibly serving the Wuhan government. One of T'ang's commanders, Ho Chien, had argued strenuously against radical agrarian policies, especially the seizure of land, because in the army generally, and certainly in his units, "among the officers and troops there are a number whose families own land."[12] On May 19 Ho Chien issued a statement charging that the labor and peasant movements in Hunan were sabotaging the Northern Expedition, and two days later one of his subordinates, the commander of the garrison in Changsha, the capital of Hunan, led his troops against all the mass organizations in the city. As the commander later recalled: "At 11 P.M. we started to move; shortly afterwards more than twenty Communist-dominated organizations and schools, including the provincial headquarters of the General Labor Union and Peasant Association, were swept clean of Communists."[13] The soldiers wrecked the offices, and shot or arrested everyone they found in them. This sudden assault initiated a reign of terror in Changsha that swiftly spread across the province. Peasant associations were smashed, and many hundreds of peasants were slaughtered by soldiers. The Wuhan government responded by sending an investigator—T'ang Sheng-chih himself;

the impotence, the virtual irrelevance, of the Wuhan government could hardly have been clearer. Not surprisingly, T'ang reported that his subordinate's actions were "animated by a passion for justice."[14]

At the same time warlord troops were smashing the beginnings of peasant revolt, the executive committee of the Communist International was meeting in Moscow. Stalin's views dominated the meetings, were accepted as Comintern policy, and expressed in a celebrated telegram of instructions that reached Wuhan on June 1, 1927. It was a mind-boggling mishmash of policies so contradictory and impossible to implement that the Chinese Communist leaders, when they read it, did not know "whether to cry or to laugh."[15]

Stalin instructed that land be confiscated and redistributed to the peasants, but that land belonging to military officers should be left alone. Such an inconsistent and discriminative program would not only be superbly difficult to implement, but so many of the officers came from landed rural families that the Communists were likely to have little land to confiscate. The telegram also called for the Communist Party to restrain the peasants from direct and excessive action—a directive that overestimated the power of the party to control the peasants. More importantly, it was rendered irrelevant by the fact that warlord troops were already restraining the peasants with bullets. Presumably, it was this military repression that prompted Stalin's next point: the elimination of unreliable generals and the creation of a new revolutionary army composed of 20,000 Communists and 50,000 workers and peasants. Stalin also called for a special revolutionary court to be organized to try reactionary officers. Stalin neglected to say just how all his instructions were to be carried out, particularly in the face of T'ang Sheng-chih's armed power and the continuing Comintern orders to acknowledge the leadership of the Wuhan government and avoid ruptures with it. Finally, Stalin said that new worker and peasant elements should be placed on the Kuomintang central committees. Even Borodin and other Comintern representatives in China acknowledged that there was simply no way to implement these orders.

Stalin's telegram had important consequences nevertheless. Roy, the Comintern representative to whom it had been sent, showed it to Wang Ching-wei and allowed Wang to make a copy of it. Wang and other Kuomintang Left leaders to whom he showed the message had already started to have their doubts about continuing the alliance with the Communists. Isolated from the Kuomintang moderates and rightists now in Nanking, they were finding it more and more difficult to maintain some semblance of independence in operating the Wuhan government. Day by day Communist support became less welcome to Wang; it promised to smother him and it blocked reconciliation with Nanking. Stalin's telegram confirmed the doubts of Wang and other Wuhan leftists. The Kuomintang leaders may have been less impressed by the impossibility of Stalin's instructions than what the message revealed about his readiness to go far beyond the cooperation envisaged in the original Sun-Joffe statement. In any event, in mid-June it suddenly became necessary for the Kuomintang Left to resolve its doubts one way or the other: Feng Yü-hsiang called upon Wuhan to purge itself of the Communists and the Russians.

In their competition with the Nanking government, T'ang Sheng-chih and Wang Ching-wei had decided to continue the Northern Expedition against Chang Tso-lin's armies, join with Feng Yü-hsiang, and then deal with Chiang Kai-shek from a position of strength. Thus, at the beginning of May, Wuhan troops began advancing northward along the Peking-Hankow Railway toward Chengchow, the railroad junction in northern Honan. Chang Tso-lin's Manchurian troops fought fiercely, and the battle raged throughout the month of May, with the Wuhan forces gradually pushing northward. In the meantime Feng Yü-hsiang, who had been readying his army in the northwest, swept in from Sian and occupied Chengchow almost simultaneously with the Wuhan troops. Feng was able to retain control of the city, however, and as it was a critical railway junction and gateway to the north, he thus held the key to any further advance in north China. As a consequence, both Wuhan and Nanking vied for his favor. In mid-June, Feng met with Wang Ching-wei and other Wuhan leaders and almost immediately afterward with Chiang Kai-shek and his associates. He then announced his decision in a telegram to Wuhan suggesting that the Russian advisers be sent home, and that those Wuhan leaders who wished to go abroad for a rest should do so. The remainder of the Wuhan group could join the Nanking government. Feng had joined the anti-Communist crusade, and Wuhan now followed suit.

Feng's ultimatum marked the end of the Wuhan government. Borodin and the other Russian advisers started their long journey home, the Kuomintang Left was purged of Communists, and the anti-Communist campaign—which had been launched in mid-May by the Wuhan warlord's minions—now received the sanction of official policy. The capitulation of the Kuomintang Leftists removed the chief obstacle in the way of reunification of the Kuomintang, though several months of jockeying and negotiating among Kuomintang generals and politicians were required before the matter was settled. Wang Ching-wei confessed that "it was I, not Comrade Chiang, who was really wrong. . . . When I look at the situation more objectively, I would like to criticize myself rather than comrade Chiang. I am saying this with all the sincerity at my command."[16] On this self-abasing note, Wang once more departed for Europe. Chiang Kai-shek assumed the positions of commander in chief of the Nationalist Army, chairman of the Kuomintang Central Executive Committee, and chairman of the Military Affairs Commission. He then turned his attention to unfinished business, the Northern Expedition.

For almost a year, while party conflicts raged, the campaign against the northern warlords had languished. Chiang ordered a general offensive to begin on April 9, 1928, and led his own army into southeastern Shantung. At the same time, Feng Yü-hsiang and Yen Hsi-shan, both recent converts to the National Revolutionary Army, attacked in different areas. Chang Tso-lin's forces put up serious resistance at a few points, but the revolutionary advance was swift. In just two months, Peking fell. For all practical purposes, the Northern Expedition was over—and China, it appeared, was unified.

Consequences

A great deal of dispute has taken place about the so-called Revolution of 1925–1927, with the Kuomintang-Communist conflict at its core, and about the role of the Russians. The passions generated directly and indirectly at that time have been nourished by the emotions stirred by the later stages of the Chinese civil war. Thus, writers who treat the tumultuous events of the mid-1920s have been generous in apportioning praise and blame. Yet, in the final analysis, shorn of details and partisan rhetoric, the essential situation was fairly simple: The Russians used the Comintern to guide the Chinese revolution for their own ends, and made decisions without due regard for Chinese conditions, or, ironically, for Marxist ideology. The Chinese Communists, like disciplined Communist revolutionaries, tried to obey the Comintern, but they also tried, like revolutionary Communists, to promote social revolution. It was impossible to do both for very long, because sponsorship of agrarian revolution alienated the Kuomintang, precisely what the Comintern did not want. Russian and Chinese Communists alike got into convoluted theoretical discussions trying to resolve this matter, but the logic of the situation was perfectly obvious to the Kuomintang. The Kuomintang had always been essentially a party of the middle class, the socialist overtones of Sun Yat-sen's program notwithstanding, and to it the Communist vision of China's future was frightening and repugnant. When the Russian Communist influence, together with the burgeoning mass movement, became so powerful as to threaten to transform the Kuomintang or destroy it, party members had only two choices. They could yield, in which case the party would cease to exist in the form and with the aims it originally had, or they could fight. They chose to fight, and Chiang Kai-shek led the attack.

Chiang's victory meant that he and the Kuomintang had won the opportunity to reintegrate China according to their own prescriptions. The story of their efforts to do so is part of the history of the following two decades, which will be discussed in later chapters. Suffice it to say here, then, that Chiang's reintegration policies were foreshadowed by his policies during the second half of the Northern Expedition, after his break with the Communists.

The two phases of the Northern Expedition—to the Yangtze, and from the Yangtze to Peking—differed profoundly. The first phase was a genuinely revolutionary march. The army's successes stimulated mass involvement, mass involvement contributed to the army's victories, and the whole process began to alter long-standing social relations between workers and employers, peasants and landlords, army and people, Chinese and foreigners, and to fulfill urgent peasant needs that had been intensified by warlord disruption of the rural economy and power structure. The seizure of Shanghai, the citadel of Chinese capitalism and the symbol of imperialism in China, by the workers of that city was a perfectly appropriate revolutionary climax to the first stage. But before basic social changes had gone very far, or acquired any roots, they were suppressed by Chiang Kai-shek. From that point on, from the April dawn attack on Shanghai workers, the Northern Expedition was not so much a revolutionary process as it was simply a war. Social mobilization in the first half of the Northern Expedition turned to military mobilization in the last half. Indeed, the campaign from the Yangtze to Peking was very similar to other warlord wars of the era. It aimed at, and accomplished, precisely what Wu P'ei-fu had much earlier tried to achieve, and with the same weapons: unification by force imposed by an agglomeration of warlord units.

The number of warlord units in the National Revolutionary Army ultimately far outnumbered the original components of the army. These militarists had various political ideas, goals, and attitudes, from radical progressive to reactionary traditionalist, and all of them mixed with personal and regional preoccupations. The absorption of so many diverse interests into the Kuomintang, and the assignment of important government positions to them, inevitably weakened Kuomintang unity and perhaps adulterated Kuomintang nationalism.

Moreover, warlord participation in the Kuomintang strengthened what had already emerged as an ominous trend two or three years earlier, the preponderance of the military wing of the party. The Kuomintang military had proved to be the only element in the party strong enough and disciplined enough to counter the growth of Communist influence, and Kuomintang politicians therefore had yielded to the military in order to put down the Communists. With the admission to party leadership of such powerful warlords as Feng Yü-hsiang and Yen Hsi-shan, there was less prospect than ever that civilians could recapture control of the party and the government.

Finally, Chiang's victory blunted the sharp anti-imperialist policy that had characterized the Kuomintang since 1924. By the middle of the 1920s, the foreign powers in China were clearly on the defensive. As early as 1902 they had agreed that the "unequal treaties" would be modified as soon as conditions allowed, but nothing was done, although the issue was raised on several subsequent occasions. After the May Thirtieth Incident, however, the passion of Chinese antiforeignism prompted the foreign powers to action. All the chief nations involved indicated willingness to alter and eventually eliminate treaty stipulations about the Chinese tariff and extraterritoriality, the two issues the Chinese most resented. But they wanted to effect any changes through negotiation, not by China's unilateral repudiation of the treaties. J. V. A. MacMurray, the American minister to China, explained that there were two schools of thought in China, the evolutionary and the revolutionary. The foreigners would be quite willing to give up their privileges to the evolutionary, but opposed the revolutionary, which was fostered by the Russian Communists. MacMurray did not say so, but his opposition to the militant anti-imperialists—the revolutionary school—was no doubt based on their promise to expropriate all foreign interests in China, whereas the evolutionary school would negotiate, and negotiations opened the possibility to gain concessions in return for concessions yielded.

Unquestionably, the chief focus of foreign fears in China was "the red hand of Bolshevism." Some foreigners in China, exemplified best by the editors of the *North China Herald*, a British daily in Shanghai, considered that the nationalist movement was a creature of Moscow agents, and was "ruthless and immoral beyond the worst excesses of the Boxers."[17] Others took a less frenetic view, and acknowledged that there was much justice in the demands of Chinese nationalists; however, they, too, hoped that the movement would shed its most radical fringe.

The worst fears of the foreigners seemed to be realized early in 1927. Chinese mobs attacked the British concessions in the cities of Kiukiang and Hankow, and literally took them over. The British, who had already made a policy decision to yield to Chinese nationalist demands where practicable, formally returned the concessions to the Chinese, much to the disgust of many old China hands who feared that such palpable weakness would encourage the Chinese to take even more intolerable actions. On March 24, 1927, the Nanking Incident seemed to confirm these dour predictions. While troops of the National Revolutionary Army were entering Nanking and warlord troops were fleeing, a group of soldiers attacked the Nanking foreign community. Six foreigners were killed, a number wounded, and foreign businesses and homes were looted. There seemed no doubt that troops of the Northern Expedition were responsible, and foreign officials concluded that they had been under orders from their superiors, that the attacks were part of a purposeful plan. Foreign governments ultimately accounted for this plan by attributing it to radical Communists in the Kuomintang bent on trying to entangle Chiang Kai-shek with the foreign powers in China. Once they had accepted this excuse for the incident, the foreign governments involved hesitated to respond vigorously to the incident for fear of embarrassing Chiang. For example, the Japanese foreign minister, "believing that Chiang Kai-shek would be both willing and able to maintain order, thought it would be a mistake for any of the Powers to take oppressive measures at the present time as this would merely assist the enemies of Chiang Kai-shek and enable the radicals amongst the Cantonese to get control of the Cantonese Government and army."[18]

By the time of the Nanking Incident, the split within the Kuomintang had become apparent even to foreigners, and they increasingly hoped that Chiang's wing would be evolutionary, not revolutionary, and that it would repudiate the Russian-sponsored Wuhan government. There were good reasons for thinking that Chiang's wing would follow this course. The Kuomintang had never taken a strongly anti-imperialist line until the 1924 party reorganization, which had been planned by the Russians. If Chiang's wing was turning against the Russians, as his April coup indicated, the party might return to its original, moderate foreign policy. Moreover, with the party split, Chiang would need some foreign aid of his own to counter the Russian backing of his rival in Wuhan. In addition, Chiang's bourgeois supporters got along well with the foreigners; they were certainly not Communists. The Shanghai money men who financed Chiang against the Kuomintang Left were men who talked the same language as the foreigners, who had the same general values and attitudes. They could be expected to negotiate the return of foreign privileges, not demand them arbitrarily, and they might even be slow to demolish the entire treaty structure. This hope was by no means far-fetched because some extremely Westernized Chinese thought the treaty system was quite justified by Chinese backwardness. Ting Wen-chiang, for instance, a scientist, official, and businessman, took this view because he looked at the treaty system with Western assumptions. It will be recalled, also, that after the May Thirtieth Incident the Shanghai Chamber of Commerce objected to the demand of Chinese strikers that Chinese police have authority in the International Settlement instead of foreign officers; it was not that these merchants were "running dogs of the imperialists" as much as it was that they appreciated the business value of the Western way of doing things.

Both the foreigners and the Chinese bourgeoisie, therefore, were reassured by Chiang's policy toward the mass organizations after his split with the Communists. Chiang demolished the labor movement. He systematically smashed labor organizations, executed many union leaders, and "reorganized" unions, which meant in effect that he rendered them impotent. Peasant unions were also dissolved. From a membership as high as 15 million in the spring of 1927, peasant organizations had virtually ceased to exist by the end of the year—a dissolution that perhaps says as much about the real strength of the unions and the degree of the members' political consciousness as it does about Chiang's suppression. The Kuomintang told workers and peasants that the party would look after their interests, so they did not have to organize and struggle independently. Ironically, it was Wang Ching-wei himself, the erstwhile radical of Wuhan, who late in 1927 explained that "the welfare of the Chinese peasants cannot be improved unless the general situation in China is improved," and that the workers can be liberated only "after the successful conclusion of our national revolution."[19] Thus workers and peasants should simply support the Kuomintang, which would take care of their needs in due time.

The Northern Expedition, then, did not completely attain the immediate goals that emerged from the May Fourth Movement, and that were explicitly accepted by the Kuomintang in 1924: elimination of warlordism and the repudiation of imperialism. Nevertheless, progress had been made. At least many of the warlords were now in the Kuomintang and pledged to work for nationalist goals and principles. The imperialist powers had also pledged to relinquish their special privileges in China. And the Kuomintang headed a national government pledged to build a modern nation. All that was left was to translate those pledges into reality.

Warlordism in the Nanking Decade

WITH THE COMPLETION of the Northern Expedition, the Nanking government faced a staggering task: the reintegration of Chinese society in a national and modern form. Of all the obstacles in the way of attaining that goal, none was more formidable than the continued existence of warlords and warlord politics. The Northern Expedition had not achieved its major aim: the unification of China under a nationalistic central government through the elimination of warlord power. On the contrary, warlords still controlled more of China than did Nanking during the early years of the Nanking decade (1928–1937). Despite Nanking's successes in warfare against the most assertive of the militarists during the first few years after 1928, important elements of warlord power continued to exist to the very end of the republican era in 1949.

Wars with the Central Government

Post-1928 warlordism derived partly from the oragnization of the National Revolutionary Army, which had been formed in 1925 by bringing together several regional armies that, despite their cooperation, remained substantially independent. Of even greater moment was the fact that during the Northern Expedition warlords were permitted to join the Kuomintang and continue in command of their troops. All they had to do was to declare their support for the rev-olution. Such opportunistic converts found it easier to switch than fight, but they remained wary of any diminution of their real power. The army that completed the Northern Expedition, there-fore, was itself shot through with warlords, warlord power, and warlord attitudes.

When the dust settled after the Northern Expedition, five mili-tary factions each controlled a cluster of provinces. A half dozen or more provinces stood alone, not part of any group, but not effec-tively under central government authority either. Chiang Kai-shek controlled the lower Yangtze Valley, including Nanking, the great financial center of Shanghai, and the provinces of Chekiang, Anh-wei, Kiangsu, and Kiangsi. Feng Yü-hsiang's sphere consisted of Kansu, Honan, Shensi, and, in theory, Shantung; Japanese troops had moved into Shantung during the Northern Expedition on the grounds that they had to protect their interests in Tsinan, and they prevented Feng from exercising real power in that province. Yen Hsi-shan continued to rule his old province of Shansi, as he had done since 1912, and he was now also preeminent in Suiyuan and Hopei.* Chang Hsüeh-liang dominated the three provinces of Man-churia, although at the end of 1928 he turned the management of Manchuria's foreign relations over to the Nanking government. The Kwangsi faction, led by Li Tsung-jen and Pai Ch'ung-hsi, ruled Kwangsi, had strong influence in Kwangtung, and had extensive power in Hunan and Hupei through Li's position as Chairman of the Wuhan Branch Political Council. The independent provinces that were not part of larger spheres were in the west and north: Yunnan, Kweichow, Szechwan, Chahar, Ninghsia, Sikang, Tsinghai, and Sinkiang. Within the regional clusters of warlord power, as well as in the single independent provinces, minor warlords continued to pursue their own interests. In the years immediately following the Northern Expedition, several armed conflicts broke out between the regional militarists and the new national government.

The first crisis erupted in 1929, when the Kwangsi warlords tried to expand and consolidate their domain by acquiring domi-

---

* The province of Chihli, in which Peking is located, was renamed Hopei in 1928. Peking was renamed Peiping, but in 1949 the People's Republic of China changed it back to Peking.

nance in Hunan, the province that lay between their base in Kwangsi and their central China enclave around Wuhan. Chiang Kai-shek's troops promptly attacked, and after a short campaign forced Kwangsi power out of central China. Chiang appointed a reliable follower to be governor of Hupei, but had to compromise with Hunan provincial interests in deciding the governorship of that province.

Almost immediately afterwards a confrontation occurred between Chiang and Feng Yü-hsiang, when Chiang appointed one of his own men to accept the return of Shantung from the departing Japanese. Feng's other provinces were exhausted and depleted by long years of war, and he had counted on gaining access to the sea, and foreign supplies, through Shantung. He therefore prepared to fight the government, but just as the shooting seemed about to begin Chiang Kai-shek bribed two of Feng's commanders to defect with some 100,000 of Feng's best troops. Yen Hsi-shan knew that if Feng were eliminated he alone would face Chiang Kai-shek in north China, and his own autonomy in Shansi would become precarious. He therefore offered Feng a haven in Shansi, and the two warlords became allies.

In the meantime, some left-wing members of the Kuomintang formed a political faction called the Reorganizationists. They feared that Chiang Kai-shek had dictatorial aspirations, and they wanted to force his resignation and to return Wang Ching-wei to leadership in the party and the government. Both the Reorganizationists and the northern warlords were hostile to Chiang, but they were not natural allies. Yen and Feng were essentially seeking the kind of regional independence that was incompatible with any genuinely national government, whereas the Reorganizationists were chiefly concerned with Chiang's administration of the government, and perhaps their own position in it.

Their differences kept the two groups apart in 1929 while each undertook independent military action against Chiang. When these actions failed, the Reorganizationists and the northern warlords joined forces, and in the summer of 1930 organized a rebel government in Peiping. Yen Hsi-shan was named head of state, and Feng, Wang Ching-wei, and others became members of the State Council. But even as Yen took the oath of office, his cause was falling apart. In extraordinarily stubborn and fierce fighting, the Nanking troops steadily pushed the rebel armies back, and in mid-September Chang Hsüeh-liang, whose support both sides had been entreating, announced his solidarity with Chiang Kai-shek. From that time, it was all downhill for the rebels, and by early October Chiang had defeated his enemies.

A quarter of a million casualties made the battle against the northern rebels the bloodiest war of the republican era to that time. Chiang's armies suffered 30,000 killed and twice that number wounded; the Yen-Feng casualties numbered 150,000. Property damage was enormous. The four-month war was the last paroxysm of the large-scale warlord conflict. Occasional clashes did occur, but from that time on Nanking and the warlords settled down more or less to a situation of mutual tolerance. The warlords gave nominal allegiance to Nanking, and the central government used or threatened force to exact obedience only in times of crisis, as when faced with open rebellion. This modus vivendi apparently accorded with a policy decision of the Nanking authorities; as a government leader explained in 1933, Nanking would no longer try to unify the country by force, but would consolidate the few provinces under its direct control and try to extend its influence gradually to the other regions of China.[1]

The military facts of life dictated that policy. From the beginning of the 1930s, Chiang Kai-shek was engaged in a difficult war with the Communists, and could ill afford another major struggle with the warlords at the same time. Further, any such conflict might aggravate China's weakness and disunity, and encourage foreign aggression. Japan's seizure of Manchuria in 1931, followed by nibbling aggression in north China, demonstrated the seriousness of that threat.

In the mid- and late-1930s, warlord fear of communism, the intensification of Japanese incursions, and the success of Chiang Kaishek's political and military maneuvers all served to reduce warlord autonomy. In 1934 the Communists were forced out of the base they had created in south-central China, and began their epical Long March through western China before ending in Shensi. When the Communists entered warlord provinces, the warlords accepted the armies that Chiang sent to help them. With his own troops in a provincial capital, Chiang tried to initiate financial and construction programs to link the province closer to Nanking; and when the Nanking forces left, they took some provincial troops with them whenever possible and left some central government soldiers behind. In that fashion, Nanking increased its influence in several provinces, notably Hunan, Kweichow, Yunnan, and Szechwan. Also, as the Japanese threat grew after 1936, some provincial leaders were willing to close ranks with the central government to resist the invaders, and others found their followers clamoring for resistance to Japan. Thus, by 1938 China was blessed with a greater solidarity and unity than it had known for some decades. But until that time, provincialism and warlordism flourished, and a substratum of provincial autonomy persisted even throughout the anti-Japanese war.

Independent Provinces

Provinces in the far west and southwest enjoyed the most complete autonomy. Their distance from the political and cultural centers of the country meant that they were the least integrated territorially. Their large non-Chinese populations and, in some cases, their relatively recent incorporation into China, meant that their political integration was also extremely weak at the best of times. But provinces in eastern China also retained substantial independence. A brief survey of some of the major provinces in all parts of the country will show that territorial integration only slowly developed under Chiang Kai-shek's government, and was far from strong even at the end of the Nanking decade.

Shansi. Control of this important province in north China had been one of the issues in the confrontation between Chiang Kai-shek and the coalition of Yen Hsi-shan and Feng Yü-hsiang in 1930. After Chiang defeated the warlord alliance, he removed Feng from command of his troops. For practical purposes, this terminated Feng's career as a warlord, for he had never been able to establish firm roots in a specific region. Yen Hsi-shan presented Chiang with a more difficult problem. Yen had governed Shansi from 1912, and had created the provincial power structure from the villages up. Any attempt to restructure that system from the outside might produce disintegration and turmoil that would open the door to the competition of ambitious minor warlords or, even worse, to radicals. Chiang therefore named one of Yen's subordinates as head of the province, and left the provincial administration essentially unchanged. In the meantime Yen, who had fled to Manchuria, watched for a chance to regain his province.

The Japanese invasion of Manchuria in late 1931 provided Yen with his opportunity. Shansi students demonstrated to protest Nanking's refusal to take military action against Japan, and Kuomintang agents shot into the demonstrators. The resultant fury drove the Kuomintang men from the province, and in the ensuing confusion Yen Hsi-shan returned, his former subordinates rallied to him, and he again gained control. The politically conscious elements of the population of Shansi generally approved. As in so many Chinese provinces, local patriotism was stronger than national patriotism. Even those critical of Yen would respond, when asked about the alternative of rule by Chiang's government: "God forbid! We want a Shansi man for Shansi."[2]

Chiang acquiesced in Yen's return to power, and Yen, in turn, announced his fealty to the central government. In subsequent years, Yen did not participate in anti-Chiang movements, and the public relations between the two men were generally cordial. But there was no doubt that Yen ran Shansi. In 1932, he launched a 10-year plan for economic reconstruction of Shansi. This plan envisaged the development of provincial industry; the expansion and modernization of education, with particular emphasis on technological and scientific training; the increase of both mining and agricultural productivity; and the limitation of the rural gentry's power by siphoning off some of its wealth through taxes and by urging officials and the population generally not to tolerate gentry exploitation.

It is difficult to weigh the successes and failures of Yen's efforts in any meaningful way. Without question, this industrialization program bore some fruit. The output of Shansi coal doubled, and Yen built a railroad across the province to facilitate its transportation— and that of agricultural products. Light industry expanded with the construction of enterprises such as a tannery, a paper mill, a brick factory, and match and cigarette factories. Some heavy industry was also created, including a large cement factory and several hydro-electric installations. On the other hand, the cotton textile industry, which Yen was particularly eager to develop, was virtually driven to the ground by cheap Japanese textile imports. Other local products were also undercut by the Japanese to the detriment of Yen's developing industries.

Yen also proved unable to cure agriculture's ills. He failed because his investment focus was on industry and he put too few resources into agricultural development. Moreover, Yen was unable to curb the powers of the provincial gentry, who successfully blocked virtually every measure aimed at basic reform in the countryside. As far as the majority of Shansi peasants were concerned, things got no better; they continued, as always, to "marry early, work incredibly hard, and then die having lived out their tortured and muddled lives without any hope for the future."[3]

The character of the bureaucracy also hindered reconstruction measures. Inefficiency, nepotism, and corruption permeated the government, and, in some measure at least, was fostered by the example of Yen himself, who salted away huge sums for his personal use. By 1937, Yen's program had yielded some results, but was still far from the great goals he had talked about at the outset.

Shansi was directly in the path of Japanese expansion in north China. As a result, Yen's relations with the central government after 1935 became closer as Japan's aggressive intentions became clearer. When Japan finally invaded in force in the summer of 1937, Yen accepted from Chiang Kai-shek appointment as commander of the Second War Zone, which consisted of Shansi, Suiyuan, Chahar, and part of Shensi. The Japanese promptly invaded Shansi, and Yen's troops put up a fierce resistance—on some occasions. On others, they made a terrible showing. By early 1938 Yen had to flee the province, though he later recovered a small chunk of territory in the southwestern corner and controlled it during the rest of the war.

In the early years of the war, Yen was not alone in battling the Japanese in Shansi. The Chinese Communists also entered the province to fight the invaders, and wherever they went their social reforms and their popular army gained much goodwill among the people. Indeed, the Communist influence initiated a social revolution in the Shansi countryside, and Yen Hsi-shan became increasingly worried, resentful, and hostile. By the beginning of the 1940s Yen was holding talks with the Japanese about possible cooperation against the Communists. Ultimately, Yen and the Japanese did stop fighting each other, and by 1944 Yen was fighting the Chinese Communists, allegedly with Japanese help.

After Japan's surrender in 1945, Yen used Japanese troops in Shansi to continue fighting against the Communists. The Shansi countryside quickly went over to the Communist side, however, though the capital city, Taiyuan, resisted bitterly, with Japanese soldiers carrying a major share of the fighting. Taiyuan held out until the spring of 1949, when it, too, fell to the Communists. Shortly before, Yen had fled to Nanking, and not long afterward went with the rest of the Kuomintang elite to Taiwan.

Shantung. Shantung was another northern province to remain largely outside Chiang Kai-shek's control. From the end of the Northern Expedition until the spring of 1929, Shantung was dominated by the Japanese. Chiang had promised jurisdiction of the province to Feng Yü-hsiang, but reneged on that promise when the Japanese departed. Chiang's deception was one of the causes of the war between his armies and those of Feng and Yen Hsi-shan. When that war ended in 1930, Chiang assigned one of Feng's former officers, whose defection had been instrumental in Feng's defeat, to the governorship of Shantung. That officer was Han Fu-chü.

Han governed Shantung, at the head of his 75,000-man army, until 1938. Like all provincial warlords, he gave nominal allegiance to the central government, and even sent more of the provincial revenues to Nanking than had earlier administrations. But his allegiance had its limits. Han obeyed only those directives of Nanking's that he cared to, and the central government, not willing to press him, rarely tried to intervene in Shantung affairs.

Han sponsored character-building programs, particularly for officials of the province, and promoted some economic modernization, particularly in transportation and communications. But his major efforts were devoted to rural reconstruction along more or less traditional lines. Han brought into the province Liang Sou-ming, the well-known intellectual who a few years earlier had argued so forcefully against excessive Westernization and on behalf of the unique qualities of Chinese civilization. Liang organized and led the rural reconstruction movement in Shantung, launching educational programs designed to raise the quality of rural life and encouraging the emergence of local leaders. He also set up marketing, credit, and other cooperative societies for the benefit of the peasants. These societies evidently did constructive work, though in the long run Liang's program did not solve any of the basic problems of the Shantung peasantry.

A striking manifestation of Shantung's autonomy, and of Han's attitude toward the central government, occurred in early 1934 when he asked the United States for military aid to Shantung in anticipation of a Japanese attack. Han promised that he would not use the weapons and material against the central government, although he conceded that he did not care much for Chiang Kai-shek. He told an American representative that he had no money to pay for such military aid, but offered the United States concessions in Shantung mines and industries, bases along the Shantung coast for American war vessels, and airfields for American aircraft. Han insisted that the central government was not able and not inclined to help Shantung in case of a Japanese attack, and said that Nanking had made it clear to him that defense of the province was his problem.[4] The United States refused Han's request.

When the Japanese finally invaded Shantung in 1937, Han's army offered far less effective resistance than anyone had expected. His troops steadily retreated before the Japanese despite a direct order from Chiang Kai-shek not to withdraw further. As a consequence, Chiang commanded Li Tsung-jen, who was organizing an anti-Japanese army south of Shantung, to arrest Han. After a secret court-martial, in which he was charged with dereliction of duty and a number of other crimes, Han was executed in January, 1938. Shantung, of course, went under Japanese control until the end of the war.

Fukien. Another coastal province, Fukien, was fragmented into small militarist areas. The provincial government's effective authority was extremely limited because a number of "provincial defense armies" divided most of the province among them, and ruled their respective areas without interference. In 1933 Fukien became the scene of the most dramatic and ambitious revolt against Nanking since Feng Yü-hsiang and Yen Hsi-shan attacked the government in 1929–1930.[5]

In mid-1932 Chiang Kai-shek ordered the Nineteenth Route Army to Fukien to fight the Communists in the western portion of the province and in Kiangsi. A few months later, he named the commander of the army to head the province, and provincial government became for all practical purposes a 19th Route Army responsibility. The army—widely celebrated for its gallant defense of Shanghai against a Japanese assault early in 1932—swiftly brought the independent provincial armed forces under control, and fought a few inconclusive battles with the Communists. But the army leaders soon concluded that political struggle was even more necessary than military, and they launched a series of social reforms in Fukien. Their social ideas were heavily influenced by close personal contacts with liberal democratic and socialist politicians from the old leftist Wuhan government of 1927. The social and political goals of these politicians, the personal ambitions of some of the top provincial leadership, and despair over Chiang Kai-shek's dictatorial policies all motivated the provincial government to initiate a revolt in late 1933. In November provincial leaders declared Fukien to be independent, and proclaimed the establishment of the People's Revolutionary Government. The chief target of the rebellion was Chiang Kai-shek, whom the rebels denounced for neglect of the popular welfare, failure to implement democracy, and inadequate responses to Japanese encroachments on China. The new government announced a strongly anti-imperialist stance, and a radical social program that included nationalization of the land.

The rebel leaders expected that powerful allies would immediately come to their support, an expectation partly rooted in the widespread discontent that Chiang Kai-shek's policies had fostered. But more specifically, the rebel leaders had negotiated with a number of warlords, and believed they had their backing. They had communicated with the warlords of Kwangsi and Kwangtung, with Feng Yü-hsiang, Yen Hsi-shan, and Han Fu-chü, among others, and some of these warlords told the Fukien rebels they would join the revolution when it came. The Fukien leaders also concluded an alliance with the Kiangsi Communists.

As it turned out, only one militarist came out on behalf of the Fukien rebels—a commander in far-off Ninghsia who declared himself in January, 1934, when the Fukien rebellion was already collapsing. There were several reasons why the rebels received so little support, despite the dissatisfaction with the Kuomintang and hostility to Chiang Kai-shek in all quarters. Chiang sent personal representatives to each of the leading warlords to admonish, persuade, and bribe handsomely. Mutual distrust among warlords had always kept them from uniting against Chiang, and this distrust was as rampant as ever in 1933. The radicalism of the Fukien government's social policies also alienated some of the warlords. A month or so after the revolt began, when it was apparent that no support was coming from the rest of the nation, the Fukien leadership moderated its social policies to make them more widely acceptable, but it was too late. The Fukien leaders then made the mistake of allying themselves with the Communists; they received no effective help from them, and the existence of the alliance alienated others. It was also alleged that Fukien leaders were cooperating with Japan. It was a rumor that seems to have been without foundation—one that was perhaps fabricated by the Nanking government—but it probably hindered the development of support for the rebels.

In the end, the Nineteenth Route Army had to face Chiang's armies alone, and there was simply no contest. The Nineteenth contained many green troops—replacements for men lost at Shanghai the year before—and none of the soldiers really had his heart on fighting the government at a time when everyone feared Japanese aggression. The rebel leaders were divided and uncertain about strategy and tactics, whereas Chiang moved swiftly and boldly. He regularly received precise intelligence about Fukien's plans and circumstances because the assistant chief of staff of the Fukien forces was a Nanking spy. With that information, and using an effective combination of air power and ground troops, Chiang defeated the rebels with little difficulty and brought the revolt to an end by the middle of January, 1934. Chiang installed a trusted officer to head the province, and Fukien fell into the government column.

Kwangtung. Directly south of Fukien is Kwangtung, a province in which distinctive cultural traits had combined with distance from

Peking to foster powerful provincial loyalties. Ch'en Chi-t'ang dominated Kwangtung during almost the entire Nanking decade. Ch'en
was a native of the province, and had risen through the Kwangtung
armed forces from platoon leader to army commander during the
1920s. Although he claimed revolutionary respectability based on
participation in Kuomintang military operations as early as 1922, he
was first of all a military man with his eye on the main chance, and
his social ideas were definitely not revolutionary. Ch'en came into
effective command of the Kwangtung military forces and of the
provincial government in 1929. Almost immediately he began to expand and consolidate his independent power. Early in the 1930s he
joined with the leaders of neighboring Kwangsi to institutionalize
their autonomy by organizing the Southwest Political Council and
the Southwest Executive Committee of the Kuomintang, in essence
a declaration of regional independence. The two provinces shared
a common aversion to Nanking and Chiang Kai-shek, but they remained independent of each other; the Southwest Political Council
was a regional coalition, not a regional government.

Ch'en Chi-t'ang expanded his military forces substantially, and
created a provincial air force. In 1933 he embarked on a provincial
program of economic development that involved building more provincial roads, improving Canton's public utilities, and, particularly,
constructing a network of sugar mills. He pursued a traditionalistic
social policy: he sponsored a Neo-Confucianist movement, urged
the study of Chinese classics in the school system, and prohibited
women from wearing short-sleeved dresses, or similarly revealing
garments. All the while, Ch'en maintained formal relations with
the Nanking government, but was in essence autonomous.

Through the early 1930s, Chiang Kai-shek made no determined
effort to bring Kwangtung and Kwangsi under the control of his
government. Both provinces jealously guarded their independence,
but neither had joined military campaigns against the government.
Moreover, the Communists had carved out their own state, the
Soviet Republic of China, on the Hunan-Kiangsi border, and this to
some extent formed a barrier between Nanking and the autonomous
provinces in the south. But in 1934 the Communists fled to the
northwest, and Chiang extended his control south to the borders
of Kwangtung. At the same time, increasing pressure from Japan

dictated the need for greater internal unity. Therefore Chiang acted
to bring the two southern provinces into line.

Chiang first attempted to negotiate. When the southern leaders
rejected his overtures, Chiang arrayed a half million men in a great
arc stretching through Fukien, Kiangsi, Hunan, Kweichow, and
Yunnan. The Kwangtung-Kwangsi armies seized the initiative, and
attacked through Hunan in June, 1936, but the war ended almost as
soon as it began. Some of Ch'en Chi-t'ang's forces defected to
Chiang, including virtually the entire Kwangtung air force. Ch'en
retired and left Kwangtung, and for the first time in almost a decade
Nanking's authority was genuinely effective in the province.

Kwangsi. The leaders of Kwangsi shared Ch'en Chi-t'ang's concern for independence from Chiang Kai-shek's government, but
differed greatly in social philosophy. During the closing months of
1925, three men—Li Tsung-jen, Pai Ch'ung-hsi, and Huang Shao-
hung—succeeded in expelling or subduing other militarists in
Kwangsi and uniting the province under their control. A year
earlier, they had joined the Kuomintang, so their victory in Kwangsi
brought the province into the ranks of the revolution. However, the
Kwangsi leaders did not relinquish to the party any authority over
their province. In fact, as we have seen, they extended their influence into central China during and after the Northern Expedition,
though they were forced back to Kwangsi in 1929. Not long after
that, Huang Shao-hung left Kwangsi to join the Nanking government, and was succeeded by another Huang, Huang Hsu-ch'u, who
became governor of Kwangsi. From this time on, the Kwangsi leaders concentrated on the development of their own province, and
succeeded in effecting many improvements. To the extent that the
term "warlord" implies antisocial, selfish, and destructive policies, it
is not relevant to Kwangsi leaders during this period, although the
term's denotation of political and military independence is completely appropriate.

Kwangsi authorities described their program as the "three self
policy," which meant self-government, self-sufficiency, and self-
defense. It was an authoritarian and spartan system pervaded by a
military spirit and military institutions. Indeed, the key institution
in the province was the militia, although its organization in Kwangsi

went far beyond what is normally understood by that term. Every able-bodied man between 18 and 45 was subject to conscription, and those not drafted had to join the militia, which was tightly organized and well-trained. Most important, it was integrated with the local political and educational systems. In each village, for instance, one individual acted as village head, militia chief, and head of the school. The higher political units, such as the township or the *hsien* (county), were similarly integrated with larger militia units. Under such an organizational plan, a massive civilian army was available when needed, and, in the meantime, the local units served to preserve order and to form a generally disciplined society.[6]

The regular army units in Kwangsi were also modernized and thoroughly trained. Provincial arsenals were created, and in at least one of them German munitions experts were employed. A modern air force of 50 to 60 planes was established, and an airplane assembly plant built.[7] The Kwangsi population had long enjoyed a reputation as tough fighters, and with modern training and equipment the provincial army constituted an extremely formidable fighting unit.

The policies dictated by the self-sufficiency section of the "three-self policy" consisted largely of schemes for cooperative efforts at reforestation, the planting of tung trees to develop the production and export of tung oil, instruction in improved agricultural methods, the establishment of village granaries, and the organization of corvee labor for government projects. There was evidently some attempt to limit rural rents, although it is not clear how thoroughly this effort was implemented; a thorough survey of Kwangsi agriculture in 1936 revealed that rural poverty was still extreme.

At least the Kwangsi peasant did not have his poverty flaunted by corrupt and self-indulgent bureaucrats. Officials were expected to wear gray homespun uniforms: silk clothes and Western-style cloths were prohibited. Regulations laid down severe punishments for officials guilty of corruption, and these seem to have been reasonably well implemented. Moreover, although the Kwangsi leadership was in many ways socially conservative, there was none of the traditionalism that was so prominent, for example, in Ch'en Chi-t'ang's Kwangtung. Hu Shih, who visited south China in 1935, wrote that his first powerful impression of Kwangsi was the absence of any "superstitious hankering after the past" such as he had seen elsewhere.[8]

Kwangsi's reconstruction program won much praise throughout the country, and Li, Pai, and Huang gained reputations as progressive and effective administrators. Visitors found that conditions in Kwangsi, though undeniably austere in some respects, compared favorably with most other provinces when all things were considered. To Hu Shih, it was a militarized province in the very best sense: the people were willing to fight for the province, and for the country, they were in excellent physical condition, and they respected their leaders. Hu also praised the air of frugality that permeated the province, and the degree of industry, order, peace, and security.

After Ch'en Chi-t'ang's flight marked the collapse of the Kwangtung half of the Kwangtung-Kwangsi coalition, Kwangsi armies stopped their campaign against Nanking, withdrew to their own province, and prepared for a hard fight. Chiang Kai-shek offered to negotiate, however, and the Kwangsi leaders recognized that this was their only sensible alternative. In September the two sides came to an agreement whereby Pai Ch'ung-hsi joined the national government as a member of the Military Affairs Commission, and Li Tsung-jen and Huang Hsu-ch'u remained in official posts in Kwangsi. Chiang sent his own officials to handle important financial positions in the province, so Kwangsi became more genuinely subordinate to the national government.

Hunan. Just to the north of Kwangsi is Hunan, which had a more limited independence than the southernmost provinces, but which nevertheless retained substantial autonomy through the Nanking decade under the leadership of Ho Chien. Ho was a native Hunanese whose career had been entirely in the Hunan military forces, where he had served various leaders. Ho was not one of Chiang's men, and his appointment to head the province illustrates the kind of compromise that Chiang had to make in a number of instances. Presumably, if Chiang had tried to put one of his own men in charge of Hunan in 1929, at the time he defeated the Kwangsi Clique's attempt to expand into that province, he would have sparked opposition among provincial leaders at just the time he was preparing to face Feng Yü-hsiang and Yen Hsi-shan. Chiang therefore approved Ho, who was acceptable to Hunanese militarists and politicians, and who had the additional virtue of being a proven anti-Communist in a province where Communists were active. It was one of Ho's units, it will be recalled, that attacked the mass movement in Changsha in 1927 to initiate armed counterrevolution against Wuhan and the mass organizations. In 1930, Ho would again demonstrate his anti-Communism in a dramatic fashion by the execution of Mao Tse-tung's wife. With these qualifications, Ho headed Hunan from 1929 to 1937, when the national emergency produced by war with Japan enabled Chiang Kai-shek to appoint a trusted subordinate to the Hunan governorship.

Until that time, Ho kept a fairly tight rein on his province. Virtually all provincial officials were Hunanese, and most received their appointments through personal contacts. Ho was jealous of his provincial revenues, of course, and was reported to have kept large sums that should have gone to the national government. Ho administered his province in the classic warlord fashion. He wasted much money on military equipment, including airplanes, nominally in order to fight the Communists but partly to assure his own strength vis-à-vis Nanking. He did, nevertheless, campaign against Communists in his province, and he rigorously enforced the *pao-chia* system, the system of collective responsibility for order in the villages that had been used by the monarchy. He generally emphasized the value of ancient Chinese culture and of the traditional virtues. Among other things, he established a center for national military skills, including various techniques of old-fashioned fighting with knives and spears to foster a spirit of militarism and pride.

Szechwan. Szechwan has always been something of a world unto itself. A huge, wealthy region, cut off from the rest of China by topography and distance, Szechwan could exist in splendid isolation more easily than most other provinces. During the republican years up to 1928, Szechwan warlords had occasionally been involved in national political and military activities, but only in a somewhat peripheral way; Szechwan itself was the great prize, and enough of a prize for most Szechwan warlords. From the beginning of the warlord period following Yuan Shih-k'ai's death, Szechwan was divided into a number of nearly autonomous regions, called garrison areas, each dominated by a warlord; a half dozen or so warlords of comparable strength vied with one another year after year. Their incessant fighting—one analyst has counted 477 locals wars in Szechwan between 1912 and 1935—created a situation of incredible disorder and confusion, and the end of the Northern Expedition hardly created a pause in these internecine struggles.

Szechwan ostensibly accepted the authority of the Nanking government, but in fact the "principal result of the Nationalist triumph was to open an eight-year period during which Szechwan militarists became stronger and more independent than provincial military rulers had been in the previous fifteen years."[9] There were not even systematic communications between Szechwan and the national government, and Nanking's influence in the province was virtually nonexistent. In 1932 the only agencies of the central government that functioned in Szechwan were the Post and Telegraph Administration, the Maritime Customs Service, the Salt Inspectorate, and a branch of the Bank of China. The Maritime Customs revenues, obtained under foreign supervision, were the only monies collected in the province that found their way to Nanking.

Simultaneous military and economic crises in 1934 began to undermine Szechwan's capacity to maintain its aloofness from Nanking. The long years of incredible tax exploitation, the extensive printing of money, and the sharp decline in trade because of exorbitant taxation, all conspired to produce an economic crisis in Szechwan. At the same time, Communist troops entered the province and began to carve out some territory for themselves among the local warlord garrison areas. In the face of these huge problems, Liu Hsiang, one of the leading Szechwan warlords, went to Nanking for assistance. Chiang appointed Liu governor of the province, and promised financial support for a campaign against the Communists. He directed Liu to set up a genuinely provincial government, and sent a staff of Nanking officers to advise the Szechwanese and to act as liaison with the central government. Chiang's efforts, however, were far from sufficient to bring Nanking's authority effectively to Szechwan; for two years Chiang and Liu engaged in a quiet tug of war, Chiang trying to extend his authority in the province, and Liu trying to block Chiang and attain dominance over the other Szechwan militarists. Not until 1937, in face of the Japanese threat, did Chiang finally force the issue. Liu Hsiang turned over his mint and airplanes to Nanking and agreed to incorporate the Szechwan armies into the national army. But the province was too large, and warlord fragmentation too thorough, to allow Chiang to bring it rapidly under genuine control.

In late 1938 the entire national government moved inland to Chungking, and that Szechwanese city began to overshadow the provincial capital, Chengtu. The move provided the national government with an unparalleled opportunity to extend its sway in Szechwan. Chiang Kai-shek himself assumed the governorship of the province for a short time, and then appointed his own man to the post. He also managed to send some of the Szechwanese provincial troops out of the province to the war front. Both moves substantially increased Chiang's influence in the province, but it was far from complete, nevertheless. Local warlords continued to dominate portions of the province throughout the war; in fact, on more than one occasion they asked American diplomats for arms and military training. Ostensibly, their reason for seeking such aid was to improve their capacity to fight Japan, but the Americans understood it to be primarily for the purpose of improving their strength vis-à-vis the central government.

Sinkiang. The major Chinese province least integrated into the national whole was Sinkiang—a vast, remote, and sparsely populated region that had been part of Chinese empires at various times for 2,000 years or more. Not until 1884, however, had it become a province. It was ethnically and culturally distinct, with a large majority of various non-Chinese peoples, most of whom were Muslims. Sinkiang's distance from the chief centers of Chinese power and culture, under conditions of primitive communication and transportation, made it difficult for Chinese leaders to bind it to the rest of the country. On the other hand, its location as the crossroads between China, Russia, India, Mongolia, and the southwest made it a strategically vital area. The existence of many peoples, some of whom were indistinguishable from groups across the border in Russia, also offered outside nations a convenient lever for stirring up trouble.

Between 1912 and 1928 Sinkiang was under the administration of governor Yang Tseng-hsin, who acknowledged the authority of the Peking government but paid no attention to it. He even concluded agreements with the Russians, in grand disregard of Peking's diplomatic relations with the Soviet Union. Yang's administration was corrupt, autocratic, and backward. The intellectual movements and innovative trends that roiled through China's great cities in those years hardly touched Yang's province; "for Sinkiang, time stood still."[10]

Yang was assassinated in July, 1928, just a month after the National Revolutionary Army entered Peking. His successor, Chin Shu-jen, was more corrupt than Yang, but less efficient and even less concerned to obey Nanking. He alienated virtually every important group in the province, and in 1933 all elements simply rose up and threw him out.

After Chin fled, the strongest militarist in the province, Sheng Shih-ts'ai, seized power, and Chiang Kai-shek's government confirmed him as head of Sinkiang. But Sheng also had little to do with Nanking. Instead, he immediately adopted a policy of close rapport with the Soviet Union, which in terms of economic importance and communications facilities was closer than the heartland of China. The Soviets provided Sheng with various kinds of technical aid and, on more than one occasion, with military support against rebels.

During this pro-Soviet period, Sheng initiated some genuine reforms, the most conspicuous of which was an enlightened nationalities policy that allowed the non-Chinese people in the province considerable leeway in pursuing their own identity and interests. Uighurs and Kazakhs were appointed to high positions in their own districts, and all non-Chinese nationalities were allowed to develop educational programs in their own languages in their own schools. Non-Chinese students were sent to the Soviet Union for advanced training. Provincial newspapers were published in several languages, and "cultural associations" began to function among various national groups. With Soviet aid, Sheng also undertook other constructive measures, including the stabilization of the provincial currency, the construction of roads and telephone lines, and the establishment of about 20 factories. For a time, it seemed that Sheng might even stop corruption in government, but that proved to be a mirage; Sheng himself put aside a fortune.

At the beginning of the 1940s, Sheng suddenly dropped his pro-

Soviet policy and turned to Chiang Kai-shek's government in Chung-king. Probably the reason for the switch was that the apparent success of the Nazi invasion of the Soviet Union convinced Sheng that he was allied with a loser, that the power of the Soviet Union was being destroyed, and that, obviously, no more aid would be coming from the Russians. Sheng wanted to pursue an independent policy in Sinkiang, but he did not want to stand all alone either; indeed, he recognized that in the long haul he would not be permitted to stand competely alone. He turned to the Kuomintang, demanded that Soviet technicians withdraw from Sinkiang, and executed a number of Chinese Communists, including Mao Tse-tung's brother. Moreover, his general political line shifted sharply to the right. His former tolerance of the non-Chinese peoples in Sinkiang gave way to a repressive policy, and he arrested not only Communists, but liberal Chinese. When the Russian counteroffensive demonstrated that Sheng had made a mistake, he tried to swing back to his earlier pro-Soviet stance, but the Russians would have none of it. He then had no support in any quarter, and Chiang Kai-shek removed him from office in 1944.

In the five years from the fall of Sheng to the victory of the Chinese Communists over the Kuomintang, a series of Kuomintang-appointed governors attempted to control Sinkiang. However, quarrels among Kuomintang factions had echoes in Sinkiang, which, combined with agitation among the minority peoples, kept the situation unstabilized until the Communist victory led Sinkiang to declare its adherence to the People's Republic of China.

Other Provinces. The instances of warlord independence discussed above are the most important; they are not, however, the only ones. When Chiang forced Feng Yü-hsiang into retirement in 1930, he was able to install his own appointee as governor of Feng's former province, Honan, and gradually pull the province into his own orbit. Chiang was less successful with Shensi, which became the headquarters for the Chinese Communists after the Long March. Kweichow was virtually independent until 1935, when Chiang's troops entered the province in pursuit of fleeing Communists; after that, the Nanking government appointed the provincial governors and retained essential authority. The Yunnan warlord, Lung Yun, kept his remote province outside of Nanking's control until the end of the war against Japan, when Nanking troops finally seized him and sent the Yunnanese army out of the province. The sparsely settled new provinces in the west—Ninghsia, Tsinghai, Sikang (which did not even have a provincial government before 1935)— played a negligible role in national politics at that time.

Persistence of Warlord Political Behavior

In view of the continuation of warlord power under the Kuomintang government, it is not surprising that the natural characteristics of warlord politics also flourished. For example, many independent governors put relatives and close friends into provincial and local offices, particularly sensitive and important posts.[11] Personal relations also continued to be a major ingredient in the cohesion of armies. In the spring of 1938, to give one example, the central government wanted to form two armies from the Twenty-ninth Army, and Ch'in Te-ch'un was asked to take command of one of the newly formed units. Ch'in declined, however, because most of the officers had been trained by another officer and he was the only person who could command them effectively.[12] Li Tsung-jen, serving as commanding officer of the Fifth War Zone from 1937 to 1943, found it extremely difficult to control his units, except those that had been trained personally by him. The most unmanageable, Li said, were the units of the "central army," because they would obey only Chiang Kai-shek himself.[13]

Money was the life blood of independence. In 1929 the Minister of Finance of the Nanking government reported that the revenues from Hunan, Hupei, Kwangtung, Kwangsi, Shensi, Kansu, Honan, Shansi, Suiyuan, Szechwan, Yunnan, Kweichow, and the three provinces of Manchuria, were entirely appropriated by the provincial authorities. There was improvement in subsequent years, but provincial leaders continued to cling stubbornly to provincial funds. H. H. Kung, who served several stints as Minister of Finance, recalled that in 1941 he was still struggling to limit the authority of the provinces in the matter of tax collection and retention.[14]

Just as during the pre-1929 warlord period, the warlord quest for money was hard on the peasantry. The land tax was not formally increased, but surtaxes were piled high on the basic tax, and the taxes were collected in advance, which meant double or triple taxes. Surtaxes exceeded the land tax by 26 times in Kiangsu, 3.8 times in Chekiang, 86 times in Hupei, and 9.5 times in Kiangsi. These provinces formed the base of Chiang Kai-shek's power, and the figures are from 1934, five years after the founding of the Nanking government. In Szechwan the situation varied from one minor warlord's area to another, but in one area in 1934 taxes had been collected 74 years in advance, four other areas collected it 50 years or more in advance, and in no case was it collected less than 22 years in advance.[15]

The refusal to turn central government monies over to the central government reflected a low level of national consciousness and patriotism that was another persistent characteristic of warlordism, despite much variation among individual warlords. Chang Fa-k'uei, when trying to figure out how to avoid yielding to Chiang Kai-shek and the national government in 1929, concluded that "the greatest danger was lack of chaos, lack of opportunity for the Fourth Division [Chang's army] to develop in the midst of chaos. Chaos ensured our survival."[16] Many warlords would not even cooperate for anti-Communist ends, although they were generally anti-Communist. For example, once Communist troops left a province, its provincial authorities ignored them; they became the worry of the rulers in the next province. This lack of concern for political principles showed up conspicuously when the anti-Japanese war came, and a number of petty warlords went over to the Japanese side for money.

Finally, the remnants of warlordism together with the dominance of the military within the Kuomintang made the military utterly superior to civilians in social and political matters throughout China. In the 1927–1937 decade, 70 men served as provincial governors, of whom 59 were military.[17] Even in personal relations, the military took precedence over civilians in virtually all respects. An American scholar in China in 1947–1948 witnessed many episodes in which "literary men were forced to defer to army officers, often in the most crude and embarrassing ways." On one occasion, he recalled, a district magistrate "acted as the virtual body servant of a general."[18]

Why was Chiang Kai-shek unable to eliminate warlord power? The short answer is that he did not have enough time to destroy warlordism by the methods he employed. The only way to have overthrown the warlords quickly would have been through military force. But military campaigns would have been expensive—and the outcome uncertain, particularly if several of the warlords joined together against him. Such alliances could happen, as the Yen-Feng coalition and the Southwest Political Council showed. Moreover, wars against the warlords could have produced opportunities for the growth of Communism, which Chiang considered by far the more dangerous enemy; at the very least, warlord conflict would have prevented Chiang's mobilizing all his resources against the Communists. Warlord strife might also have tempted the Japanese to further aggression against China.

With immediate military action ruled out, Chiang could only maneuver slowly, seizing every opportunity to subvert warlord power and increase the influence of the Nanking government in the provinces through gradual economic, political, and military changes. That alternative was precisely what Chiang chose. Whenever provincial forces challenged the central authority, Chiang immediately marshaled superior military strength to put them down, as in the case of the Fukien rebellion. But otherwise he was willing to wait because he felt he had no feasible alternative.

Chiang's inability to eliminate the warlords was symptomatic of the profound weakness of the Kuomintang government generally. The destruction of warlordism was more than a military problem. To give but one specific example, the extirpation of autonomous provincial military power implied the disbandment of at least portions of the provincial armies; there were simply too many men under arms. But unless disbandment were accompanied by effective programs for the employment of the soldiers involved, it would only produce the raw material for new bandit gangs and the seeds for a new phase of warlordism. When troops in Szechwan heard about government plans to reduce the size of their armed forces, they fled with their rifles: soldiers became bandits. Senior officers, who had been in the army so long that it had become their only

career, also opposed disbandment. Li Tsung-jen, who surely understood the problem as well as anyone alive, wrote that

> when an officer attained the rank of a major general, he would
> have become a professional soldier, and could not be used in any
> other category. If such officers were forced to retire and appropri-
> ate new jobs could not be found for them, those with troops un-
> der their command would not accept orders and the central gov-
> ernment would be in an embarrassing position.[19]

Warlord power might have been undercut by widespread local
reforms, by organizing the population in new economic and political
groupings. But to approach the problem in that fashion meant to
change the entire structure of rural power, and it was Chiang's aim
to preserve that structure. The ultimate explanation of warlordism
during the Nanking decade therefore lies in an examination of the
Nanking government as a whole.

Integration in the Nanking Decade

"The great need of society in China is an integrating force" Chiang Kai-shek wrote in the early 1930s.[1] He was quite right, and he had hoped that the Kuomintang would be that force. But the Kuomintang did not fill that need during the Nanking decade. Not only did it prove unable to liquidate the vestiges of independent military power in the provinces, but in political, economic, and intellectual terms as well, the Kuomintang failed to create the new unity that the nation so desperately required.

Government, Politics, Ideology

The end of the Northern Expedition, in Sun Yat-sen's revolutionary scheme, marked the end of the military phase of the Chinese revolution and the beginning of the period of political tutelage, during which the single-party government of the Kuomintang would train the population to operate constitutional government. Sun envisioned tutelage as taking only a few years, but in fact it formally continued until the eve of the Communist victory in China. Sun had described the steps by which the country would proceed from party tutelage to constitutional self-government, although, as in so much of his writing, areas of ambiguity and, perhaps, impracticality are apparent. Essentially, the government under the

Kuomintang was to appoint trained men to assist provincial districts in developing their local government agencies and institutions until they were capable of self-government in accord with the principles of the revolution. When all the districts of a province had attained the self-government stage, the province itself would then be considered self-governing. This process was to continue until all provinces had reached that status and the nation was a functioning democracy.

Sun said little about the awkward stage when some provinces and districts had attained self-government and the others were still under tutelage, but it made little difference in the long run because his plan was never implemented. The Kuomintang took no realistic measures to train people in self-government, which would have eliminated the justification for its own monopoly of political power. Instead, it immediately established a five-power government, which Sun had envisaged not as a beginning, but as an end, of the tutelage process.

The five-power government, as noted in Chapter V, consisted of five major branches, or yuan: executive, legislature, judiciary, examination, and censorate (or control). The first three were in theory roughly analogous to their counterparts in the United States. The Examination Yuan, inspired by the traditional Chinese civil-service system, was set up to examine candidates for government positions and administer the civil service. The Control Yuan, suggested by the censorate in the old Chinese bureaucracy, was designed to keep a wary and supervisory eye on the rest of the government, impeaching corrupt and ineffective officials, auditing finances, proposing administrative improvements, and so forth.

The five-power government never functioned very well. Its authority was compromised at the outset by the essential independence of so many provinces, which in some instances prevented the central authorities from even acquiring statistics for national planning. Government was based more on personal relations than upon institutions; from the beginning of the republican era, laws, formal institutional responsibilities, constitutions, were in substantial measure irrelevant to the realities of Chinese political life. They continued to be irrelevant during the entire Nanking decade. The government suffered from the old principles of squeeze, bureaucratism, nepotism—and also from Chiang Kai-shek's quest for dictatorial power.

The work of the Examination Yuan illustrates clearly some of the administrative shortcomings of the Nanking government. The functions of this yuan included responsibility for cleaning up the bureaucracy, which was shot through with corruption and incompetence after so many years of warlordism. The Examination Yuan would presumably discharge incompetent officials, recruit new ones after conducting tests, and thus create a capable and honest body of officials at all levels. In practice, however, it performed none of these activities. Most incumbents from the warlord period were allowed to remain, and most new appointments were made on the basis of personal connections, bribery, nepotism, or political favoritism of some sort. By 1938 less than 4 percent of the officials in the national government had obtained their posts through the examination system. Indeed, four years earlier the overwhelming majority of incumbents had already been confirmed in their posts, and "the extra-legal route to office had won the day."[2] A government with so little control over its own officials could not have much integrative force.

The top levels of the administration also suffered from multiple, overlapping appointments, and much shuffling around of positions, so that it lacked consistency or sustained administrative vigor. For example, a survey of 176 members of the Nationalist Government and the Kuomintang Central Executive Committee revealed that they averaged five positions per person, any one of which might require full attention. At the same time, officials moved from one office to another so rapidly as to preclude effective administration in any one. In the ten years after 1928, there were a dozen Ministers of the Interior, averaging eight months in office per man.[3]

Probably the most important feature of the five-power government was that it was virtually all on a national level, with little relevance or effective authority at the local level. Where the provinces were nearly independent, the central government had almost no access to the localities. But even in the provinces controlled by the central government, formal government pretty much stopped at the *hsien* level, with average populations of about a quarter of a million people. Below that level, power was wielded by local elites—the "local gentry."

Chiang tried to tighten control over the localities by reinstituting the *pao-chia* system. This system, which dated back to the Sung Dynasty, organized families in multiples of 10, all members of which were collectively responsible for one another's behavior. Ten households formed a *chia*, and 10 *chia* constituted a *pao*. The real purpose of the *pao-chia* system as employed by the Kuomintang was to prevent the spread of Communism in the countryside; anyone harboring a Communist endangered all members of his *pao* and *chia*. In addition, the heads of the *pao* and the *chia* had to be approved by the government; in a sense, they became extensions of the bureaucracy. The revived *pao-chia* system, however, failed; it did not limit the spread of Communism nor did it strengthen central control over localities. C. K. Yang, after studying in detail the problem of central control of the localities during the republican period, summed up his impressions in these words:

> Our conclusion is that the national government failed to substantially alter the traditional decentralized pattern of local government in which the village political life operated largely by its own local power structure and was but weakly integrated into the system of central authority. One reason for the failure was the variance between formal law and local mores. Lack of interest and knowledge in formal government on the part of the responsible personnel was another; the heads of *pao* and *chia* units were generally untrained in government affairs, and they received no remuneration for their services; many heads of pao units were illiterate peasants, and the others barely literate, incapable of reading elaborate government documents, the essential communication links in the operation of an extensive system of central authority.[4]

Intense political repression on the part of the government also weakened it by fostering resentment and dissipating support. The chief goal of government seemed to be to hang on to power, and it increasingly used harsh repression to attain that goal. Assassinations, illegal arrests, summary executions became commonplace. Censorship was extremely heavy. Between 1929 and 1936, some 450 literary works and nearly 700 publications in the social sciences were banned. A total of about 1,800 books and journals were proscribed during the Nanking decade, in addition to a host of newspaper items. When several prominent liberals and leftists formed the Chinese League for the Protection of Civil Rights in 1933, the government crushed it swiftly by assassinating the secretary of the league. Inevitably, such repression spawned indignation, alienation, and bitterness.[5]

The central government was also weak because, in a sense, it was irrelevant. For one reason, personal relations rather than government institutions determined much of what actually got done; for another, Chiang Kai-shek moved more and more toward a position as unchallenged dictator. Although Chiang emerged as a prominent leader in the mid-twenties, he did not immediately acquire autocratic powers over the party and the government. From 1928 to 1931 he ruled in cooperation with Hu Han-min and the party's right wing, and from 1932 to 1935 he and Wang Ching-wei worked together in leading the party. Whereas Chiang needed one or another of these men to keep the party intact during those years, it was not feasible for anyone to rule without Chiang Kai-shek, who controlled the army and had strong financial backing. Chiang by the mid-thirties had become the indispensable man.

Chiang shrewdly exploited and strengthened his position until he ultimately outdistanced all his competitors. The formal recognition of his arrival at the apex of power occurred in 1938 when he was elected the Kuomintang's *Tsung-ts'ai*, the Leader, or General Director. In this capacity, Chiang had an absolute veto over decisions of the party's Central Executive Committee and suspensive veto over decisions of the party congress. His word was now party law, and national law, too, as long as the party controlled the government.

Doubtless, the single most important fact in Chiang's rise to supremacy was his military position. In any political context it would have been important, but it was crucial in the face of warlord autonomy, the persistent challenge of the Communists, and the Japanese encroachments on China. Chiang's military primacy derived not only from his formal position as head of the government armies, but from his work as first director of the Whampoa Military

Academy in the mid-1920s. In that capacity he established ties of friendship and leadership with academy instructors and students that were to bind them to Chiang for the next two decades as they rose to leadership positions in the army. These bonds created what became known as the Whampoa Clique. The clique had no defined structure, nor a specific ideology, but the network of loyalties that held it together was nonetheless real and effective in helping to maintain Chiang's military and political leadership.

As the Whampoa Clique was taking form, Chiang began to acquire a grip on the Kuomintang party organization. In 1926, shortly after being named commander in chief of the National Revolutionary Army, Chiang recommended a close friend and protégé, Ch'en Kuo-fu, to head the Organization Department of the party. Two years later, Ch'en's brother, Ch'en Li-fu, assumed direction of the party security agency, and in 1932 succeeded his brother as head of the Organization Department. These were critical positions. The department established party branches, selected delegates to party congresses, determined executive committees below the central level, and in many ways directly and indirectly controlled party membership and activity. A leading Chinese student of politics in China has asserted unequivocally that "whoever controls the Organization Department controls the party."[6] The security agency was primarily responsible for the internal stability and safety of the party, and for keeping dissenters, but especially Communists, from penetrating the party, the party army, and the party government. The Ch'en brothers did not hold the same positions through the rest of the republican period, but they continued to dominate the Organization Department and the internal security apparatus, and used that power in the service of Chiang Kai-shek. The power bloc headed by the Ch'en brothers was known as the Organization Clique or, more commonly, the CC Clique, a named derived from either the brothers' surname or the Central Club in Nanking. Whatever its origins, it became a synonym for reactionary social policies and commitment to the interests of Chiang Kai-shek.

In addition to such support in the military and the party, Chiang also cultivated a following among politicians and bureaucrats from the central and provincial administrations, many with industrial interests and contacts. This grouping, often called the Political Study

Group or Clique, was less organized and less united than the CC Clique, and perhaps even than the Whampoa Clique, and had neither structure nor ideology. It was an association of men with common interests and personal relations that was already taking shape in 1917 or so, and it came under Chiang's influence on the eve of the Northern Expedition.

Thus Chiang had a more or less cohesive body of support in the military, in the party, and among influential bureaucrat-politicians. These three groups were sometimes in opposition to one another, but were all loyal to Chiang. Chiang drew support from their loyalty, but he also used the differences among them to his own advantage by balancing one faction against another.

Early in the 1930s there emerged from the somewhat amorphous Whampoa Clique a highly organized and strongly ideological group that later came to be known as the Blue Shirt Society. From the time the Whampoa Academy was founded in 1926, efforts had been made to unite Whampoa officers for political, especially anti-Communist, purposes. In late 1931 and early 1932, some Whampoa graduates, with Chiang Kai-shek's encouragement, created a tightly controlled, secret political organization along Fascist lines. It supported Chiang Kai-shek as the supreme leader, whose will was to be obeyed without question. Those who opposed the state, the party, the leader, and Sun Yat-sen's Three Principles of the People, were to be liquidated. The Blue Shirts assumed responsibility for eliminating such "politically undesirable elements," and shot and imprisoned politicians and intellectuals without bothering about judicial procedures.

With the Blue Shirts acting as Chiang's personal police force and terrorist organization, and with powerful networks in the party, the army, and among politicians and bureaucrats supporting him, Chiang had acquired complete control over the Kuomintang and the national government long before it was formally acknowledged in 1938. Simultaneously, the health and vigor of the Kuomintang as a national political organization steadily declined, partly a cause and partly a consequence of Chiang's rise to dictatorial status.

The formal decision-making organs—the Party Congress and the Central Executive Committee, and even the Standing Committee of the Central Executive Committee—all grew in size until they could no longer function effectively, and became little more than unwieldy rubber stamps. The party had always been a congeries of factions, held together by the leadership of Sun Yat-sen. Under Chiang the factionalism continued, though new alignments of factions emerged; besides the three cliques mentioned above, regional and personal groupings also developed. For example, under Sun men from Kwangtung had particular influence in the party, but under Chiang the political center of gravity moved to Kiangsu and, especially, to Chiang's own province of Chekiang.

The decline of the party's organization rendered it ineffective as a vehicle for national political integration. Moreover, in relation to the vastness of China's area and population, the party remained small; by 1935, excluding army members, who were automatically listed as party members, probably less than half a million people were in the Kuomintang. Five years after the end of the Northern Expedition, less than half of the provinces had established regular party committees. Less than 18 percent of the counties in the country had party branches, and most of these were clustered in the Yangtze Valley. In other words, party organizational strength went only as far as Chiang's bayonets. Consequently, the Kuomintang's organization was geographically limited, and was particularly weak in the rural communities of China. "The agrarian community," as one historian has put it, "remained relatively outside of the domain of the Kuomintang."[7]

The party was neither inspired nor dedicated. The party purge at the time of the split with the Communists in 1927 had eliminated many of the most progressive activists, and taught everyone that it was safer not to advocate any remedy for the nation's ills that was in the slightest way "radical," and that therefore might be considered Communistic. The purge thus encouraged opportunistic time-servers, and discouraged those committed to action for national welfare.[8] As early as 1930, Chiang Kai-shek himself acknowledged that "not only is it impossible to find a single party headquarters which administers to and works for the welfare of the people, but all are stigmatized for the most reprehensible practices, such as corruption, bribery and scrambling for power."[9] Chiang hoped that the Kuomintang ideology would help correct this situation, but the party's ideology was not adequate for such a task.

Ideology plays a crucial role in the reintegration of a society that has fallen apart. It provides a basis for understanding what has happened, and what must be done. That is, it defines social and political conditions and phenomena so that everyone understands them in essentially the same way. In China, for example, a valid political ideology had to be able to account for the nation's weakness in the face of imperialism, for the failure of the early republic, and for the dominance of the warlords. Ideology also defines the broad goals toward which a society should move, and the general route to travel in order to achieve them. It provides leaders with direction and purpose, and helps assure followers that their leaders know what they are doing; it serves as both plan and inspiration. Ideology is the chief device for integrating the elite, who can then lead the rest of the nation toward integration within an ideological framework. Ideology legitimizes the political system, and thus transforms bald power into moral and legal authority, a particularly important function for a newly established political order. In all these ways, ideology is essential to national integration; indeed, it is sometimes called the "integrative myth."

To exercise these functions, an ideology must be intellectually persuasive; to a substantial number of persons, it must seem reasonable, logical, intelligently conceived, and compatible with admirable human values. It must also seem relevant to the social context to which it is being applied. But most important, it must demonstrate effectiveness as a guide to action. At least, the authority that an ideology promotes must demonstrate by its deeds that it has the right and the capacity to rule, even if those deeds do not adhere strictly to the ideology's prescriptions. One way or another, action must confirm ideology, especially in a newly established regime where the authority that ideology justifies has not yet acquired the sanctions of history and achievement. A new regime and its ideology are on probation, and it is action that proves their relevance and logic. Intellectuals and the masses probably view ideology in somewhat different ways, but for both its realization in action is crucial. In China from the 1920s to the 1940s, intellectuals wanted this action to take the form of realizing the goals promoted by the May Fourth Era: national unification and national power associated with modernization and social progress;

for the peasant masses, it had to be a reasonably humane and just form of government. In these terms, the ideology of the Kuomintang did not qualify.

Kuomintang ideology contained several strands that were not completely consistent with one another. Some elements, largely derived from Sun Yat-sen, had a generally progressive thrust, despite Sun's sometimes sloppy analysis. Other elements, contributed by Chiang Kai-shek, not only displayed specious reasoning, but were retrogressive. Most important, the progressive aspects of Kuomintang ideology seldom found expression in effective action programs.

Officially, the core of Kuomintang ideology was the thought of Sun Yat-sen as expressed in works he had written over the years, but particularly as formulated in his lectures on the Three Principles of the People. Sun's analysis of nationalism, democracy, and people's livelihood was rambling, unsophisticated, imprecise, sometimes simplistic. It could hardly inspire Chinese intellectuals. Nevertheless, in general it had a clear relevance to Chinese conditions: imperialism did dominate China politically and exploit China economically, the Chinese did suffer from poverty and need improvement in the conditions of livelihood, and national unity was necessary if China was to have an effective government and improve its foreign standing. With a supporting framework of effective programs, Sun's thought could well have retained persuasive force. But national unity was not attained, and little was done to improve the quality of the peasant's life. Democracy had not been achieved, and the "period of tutelage" was marked by very little tutoring. The Three Principles were formally enshrined as the sacred dogma of the party and the government, but nobody seemed to pay much genuine attention to them.

When Chiang Kai-shek became leader of the party in the 1930s, his own social philosophy quite naturally became part of Kuomintang ideology—and it was not completely consistent with Sun's Three Principles. Chiang had always had a strong Confucian strain. Even while director of the Whampoa Military Academy, Chiang used as a textbook collections of maxims deriving from the Confucian statesmen who suppressed the Taiping Rebellion in the mid-nineteenth century. After his split with the Communists, this

Confucian orientation was expressed ever more clearly through the agencies of the government that Chiang came to dominate. Army officers were urged to study the Four Books, the central Confucian classics, and in the early 1930s a "Read the Classics" movement was launched for all Chinese. In the same years, Chiang's government increasingly fostered a cult of Tseng Kuo-fan, the leading anti-Taiping statesman, a noted Confucian scholar, and the architect of the *T'ung chih* Restoration, the program to create social stability under the restored Manchu government in the wake of the Taiping Rebellion. Tseng's works were republished in vast numbers, his writings were used in schools, and Tseng was generally held up as a model of statesmanship and personal integrity.

Chiang could point to Sun's admonition to revive China's ancient morality and use China's wisdom as justification for his return to tradition, but Chiang's latter-day Confucianism was very different from that of Sun's Three Principles. Sun's philosophy was far more receptive than Chiang's to the notion of basic social change. Chiang emulated the policies of the *T'ung-chih* Restoration because they were aimed at the same goal Chiang held, the restoration of social stability after turmoil, without engendering or allowing social revolution. Chiang's emphasis on the role of personal morality had the same purpose. Social betterment through the improvement of personal morality has usually been a policy that served the status quo.

Chiang also strongly inclined toward Fascism. The Blue Shirts were instilled with Fascist principles, and it is in Chiang's connection with the Blue Shirts that his Fascist ideas were most obvious. Chiang and the Blue Shirts abhorred democracy; it was infatuation with democracy, Chiang declared, that had produced in China "a chaotic and irretrievable situation." In place of democracy, what was needed was total reliance on a single leader, and total abnegation of the individual. In a speech delivered in September, 1933, Chiang declared:

> The most important point of fascism is absolute trust in a sagely, able leader. Aside from complete trust in one person, there is no other leader or ism. Therefore, within the organization, although there are cadre, council members, and executives, there is no conflict among them; there is only the trust in the one leader.

The leader has final decision in all matters. . . . I believe that unless everyone has absolute trust in one man, we cannot reconstruct the nation and we cannot complete the revolution.[10]

Neither the Fascism of the Blue Shirts nor Chiang's attempts to revivify Confucianism produced the social stability and disciplined individual behavior that Chiang sought. Therefore, when faced in 1934 with the task of assuring the loyalty of areas in south central China just recovered from the Communists, Chiang initiated a new program that added its own twist to Kuomintang ideology: the New Life Movement.

Chiang's Confucian views provided much of the facade for the New Life Movement. Christianity played a part, particularly the character-building programs of the YMCA, but Chiang's ideas about the effect of military discipline on individual and group characteristics, elements of the Japanese warrior code, and Fascist ideas derived from Western Europe formed the heart of the movement. Out of all these elements, Chiang formulated a program that was designed to create a virtuous and disciplined population behaving in an exemplary and socially conscientious fashion. Chiang's own words revealed the Fascist overtone of the movement: its purpose, he said, was "to thoroughly militarize the lives of the citizens of the entire nation so that they can cultivate courage and swiftness, the endurance of suffering and a tolerance for hard work, and especially the habit and ability of unified action, so that they will at any time sacrifice for the nation."[11] Chiang told the executive committee of the New Life Movement that China needed an "integrating force," that "our own national party has in many places lost public respect and cannot function as the needed force," and it was this end he hoped the movement would serve.[12]

The New Life Movement packaged Confucian morality into four virtues that were so ambiguous they could be used to exhort and rationalize a wide range of behavior. As a more specific guide, the movement formulated 96 detailed rules to govern personal behavior. People were told to maintain proper posture when sitting, to eat quietly, to form orderly lines for tickets and other public services. By eliciting such disciplined behavior, Chiang hoped to nourish a disciplined inner man just as similar rules are employed for similar purposes in military academies the world over. How-

ever, the movement had little force or effect. Although designed for rural areas recaptured from Communist control, it soon centered in the cities where sophisticated Chinese, considering it retrogressive and irrelevant, ignored it as best they could. That Kuomintang and government officials continued to behave in a grossly immoral fashion in their public lives also brought scorn on the movement.*
After a year or two, with few results achieved, the New Life Movement was turned over to Madame Chiang, to become her personal project.

Chiang Kai-shek's most comprehensive statement of his conception of China's problems came in *China's Destiny*, a book he published in 1943. Its most conspicuous feature was the absence of any serious analysis of China's problems, or any persuasive proposals to remedy them. Chiang repeatedly and insistently argued that the unequal treaties with foreign powers were the cause of virtually all of China's difficulties; they were the destructive agents that disrupted an exemplary society and corrupted the Chinese people. The remedy, of course, was the abolition of the treaties (which finally occurred on the eve of the book's publication). Psychological reconstruction of the Chinese people, Chiang wrote, would be undertaken through educational programs that would generate the restoration of China's ancient values and virtues. All reconstruction would be undertaken under the leadership of the Kuomintang, for "the destiny of China rests entirely with the Kuomintang."[13]

In sum, Kuomintang ideology did not present a persuasive or enlightening analysis of China's problems, nor a convincing method of solving them. Sun Yat-sen's analysis was simplistic and uneven. Chiang attributed most of China's ills to foreigners, thus by implication reducing the urgency of domestic change. His wish to return to tradition had the same effect. It was seen as a

---

* Some of the independent provinces paid lip service to the New Life Movement, although they did nothing about it. Some simply rejected it as absurd. Huang Hsu-ch'u, governor of Kwangsi from 1932 to 1937, said: "As far as Chiang's New Life Movement and his return to tradition were concerned, Chiang ignored the most important value of traditional China—justice; he paid no attention to it. Thus in Kwangsi those movements were simply ignored. And in Kwangsi, too, we did not teach the classics in the schools." (Interview with Huang Hsu-ch'u, April 4, 1967.)

long step backward by those who realized that in the nineteenth-century Confucianism had already shown its incapacity to meet the needs of China in the modern world. To those intellectuals who still harbored the May Fourth spirit, Kuomintang ideology of the 1930s seemed alien, and counter to the direction in which China had been moving for several decades. The Fascist elements of Chiang's ideology were not inherently repugnant even to many erstwhile liberals; Fascism at that time, before Hitler, had not yet unequivocally demonstrated its inhumane and retrogressive qualities. It was thought by many to be progressive and suitable for Chinese conditions, which, presumably, had already shown the irrelevance and impracticality of democracy. But the chief appeal of a Fascist dictatorship was effective government on behalf of the people. The Kuomintang government demonstrated neither the ability to rule effectively or to meet the needs of the masses. It was as a guide to practical action that Kuomintang ideology most conspicuously failed.

Economic Modernization

The economic achievements of the Nanking government in the decade before 1937 have provoked a good deal of controversy. Some argue that Kuomintang accomplishments "wrought under Chiang Kai-shek's leadership a transformation with few parallels in history," whereas others see "little more than the continuance of economic stagnation."[14] Evidence exists to support both views; Nanking's economic performance had a dual character, and both aspects related to the problem of national integration. Some growth in the modern sector of the economy did occur and it did contribute slightly to territorial integration, but the traditional rural economy continued unchanged and Chinese society remained divided between a vast traditionalistic peasantry and a small Westernized urban elite, itself fragmented by philosophical and political differences.

One of Nanking's first tasks was to bring order to the currency system, which had long been in confusion. Provincial currency was a product of provincial independence, and a great assortment of money circulated during the heyday of warlordism. The tael itself, the silver standard unit, was confusing. Tael was a measurement of silver bullion consisting of a specific weight of silver of specific quality. The specifics varied from region to region; the tael had no standard or stable relationship with coinage units. By 1935 the Nanking government had successfully outlawed the tael, and had also created a standard currency that was the only legal tender throughout the country. At about the same time, a new weights and measures law came into use, although standardization was largely ineffective at the local level.

Another government accomplishment was the centralization of tax collection agencies and procedures. Likin, the tax on internal trade that had long burdened foreigners and Chinese alike, was abolished, thus removing one obstacle to trade. By the eve of the Sino-Japanese War, all taxing agencies had come under the jurisdiction of one of three government units: the Customs Administration, the Salt Administration; and the Internal Revenue Administration, which taxed a wide range of consumer items from coal and tobacco to alcohol and flour. Administrative efficiencies, increased import duties, and other tax measures produced a dramatic rise in revenues from these various tax sources.

Even so, the Nanking revenue structure suffered from some fundamental shortcomings. Many provinces held back national revenues. Furthermore, the government agreed in 1929 that the basic tax in China, the land tax, would go to the provinces. This concession was yielding the inevitable, inasmuch as the government could not control the provinces anyway, but it meant that major national revenues were legally siphoned off into provincial coffers, some of which were managed by men with little concern for the fate of the nation. In addition, the taxes under the Salt and Internal Revenue administrations, which produced about half the national revenue, bore most heavily on the masses, those least able to pay, whereas many wealthy Chinese, who paid virtually no direct taxes, were not bothered by the taxes on commodities. There was no progressive taxation in China until the introduction of an income tax in 1936, but the income tax was a dead letter from the outset.

Despite the increase in national revenues, the government every year spent substantially more money than it took in. There were two major reasons for the red ink: foreign debts and military expenditures. The Nanking government inherited an enormous foreign debt when it came to power. One foreign expert has judged the Chinese debt structure in 1928 as "probably the most complicated in the world," involving old indemnities, various loans contracted by the monarchy, and a welter of obligations incurred after 1911.[15] The immensity of this burden is manifested in the Nanking government's first fiscal year debt payments: it required half of all revenues. Debt payments averaged about 33 percent of government expenditures until 1937. Attempts by foreigners and the Kuomintang government to effect a general settlement of foreign loans foundered on the enormity and complexity of the task, and on the many interests involved. Thus through the 1930s the Nanking government struggled with piecemeal settlements, trying to pay off arrears.

The government also laid out huge sums each year for military purposes. This category absorbed an average of 41 percent of the budget from 1928 to 1937. To pay for its guns, bullets, and planes, the government borrowed heavily by issuing bonds that paid investors a high rate of interest. In 1932 and again in 1936 the government could not meet its internal debt obligations, and had to arrange for reorganization of the debt. In effect, taxes wrung from the poor on purchases of such necessities as salt and flour ended up in the pockets of the rich when they collected the interest on their bonds.

The government could point to achievements in transportation and communications, such as highways, railways, and telegraph and telephone facilities. The first modern motor road in China was built in 1913, by the Hunan provincial government. Like almost all other projects in China in subsequent years, road building was in the hands of provincial authorities, and construction was sporadic, uncertain, and unsystematic. Nevertheless the total national mileage grew steadily. In the first years of the Nanking government, road building continued to be a somewhat haphazard and uncoordinated affair, but in 1932 a Bureau of Roads was created to centralize the planning and construction of highways, after which road building proceeded fairly rapidly. By December, 1936, a bit under 15,000 miles of new highway had been constructed. About half of this construction was in the four lower Yangtze provinces controlled by Chiang Kai-shek. The total road mileage in the nation in 1936 was slightly more than 68,000, about a quarter of which was paved. When the Japanese invasion forced the Kuomintang government into the southwest, more roads were built in that region, but at the end of the war with Japan in 1945 there were still only about 80,000 miles of highway in China.

By the 1911 Revolution, China had about 5,800 miles of railway line. Twenty years later, that figure had grown to roughly 9,000 miles, a third or so of which was in Manchuria. During the 1930s about 3,000 additional miles of track were laid in south and central China. Of course, with the outbreak of war with Japan in 1937 many railroads fell under Japanese control.

Nanking's accomplishments in expanding both roads and railways were not as economically important as they might have been, because they were constructed in large part for military, not economic, purposes. Their construction contributed little to the rural population; in fact, they were to many a source of oppression. As the British commercial counselor in China described it:

> Military and strategic, rather than economic, reasons have prompted most of this [roads] development. . . . Undertaken often with the assistance of forced labor, built on land which has been in many cases confiscated from the peasant owners without compensation, and along routes already served by railways or waterways, their use forbidden, in some cases, to barrows and carts carrying produce, and allowed only to motor-bus companies which have purchased a monopoly, there is no doubt that the immediate result of their construction has been to place further burdens on local industry and agriculture.[16]

Similar considerations, he pointed out, determined railway construction.

The Nanking government also increased the number of telegraph and telephone facilities, improved the postal system, and expanded inland waterway routes. Before the beginning of the war in 1937, a very modest civil airline system also came into existence, involving 30 airplanes of various size and manufacture flying over routes that totaled about 8,500 miles. In the first five years of the war, an additional 5,700 miles of air routes were established. During the war the government also organized a number of major transportation lines employing animal and human transport; in 1941 these networks carried just about twice the cargo moved by airplanes.

John K. Chang makes a cogent case for a surprisingly fast increase in the industrial growth rate throughout the entire republican period, a question he has investigated in detail.[17] Using output figures for 15 commodities for which data are relatively complete, Chang has found that industrial growth was extremely rapid from 1912 to 1920, a period when the removal of European competition due to World War I gave Chinese producers a fairly free hand in the domestic markets. But even after 1920, industry continued to expand uninterruptedly until the Sino-Japanese War, with greatest emphasis on the production of consumer goods until the early 1930s, at which time military pressures shunted industrial production toward ferrous metals, electric power, and other strategic and capital goods. Chang estimates the overall rate of industrial expansion in China Proper to have been about 6 percent a year during the 1926–1936 period; if Manchuria, under Japanese control for half the decade, were to be included, the annual figure would be substantially larger.

These impressive figures notwithstanding, the impact of industrial growth on the Chinese economy as a whole was weak, as Chang points out. There were several reasons why its effect was minimal. Modern industry was heavily concentrated in the coastal provinces, and particularly in treaty ports; before the beginning of the Sino-Japanese War, modern factory industry was all but unknown in the interior provinces. Foreign capital dominated many production activities, resulting in the export of many products from China that might have served as stimulants on other sectors of the economy. Coal and iron were examples. Factory industry was largely consumer-goods industry, and it served primarily China's large Westernized cities. Many of the factories were quite small; indeed, the entire modern industrial sector of the economy was small, despite the growth that had taken place. In 1933, for example, it accounted for only 3.4 per cent of the net domestic product. Total employment in factory industry, mining, and utilities numbered no more than 2 million, or 4 percent of the nonagricultural labor force. At no time before 1949 would industry produce more than 10 percent of the gross national product, and that percentage includes traditional handicrafts as well as modern industry. A critical factor in industry's weak impact on the Chinese economy was the role of agriculture, China's overwhelmingly dominant economic activity. As long as a poor peasant economy dominated the countryside, there was little market for industrial goods. As Albert Feuerwerker has noted, "The fundamental problem of Chinese industry was the weakness of demand.[18] Comprehensive modernization of agriculture would have stimulated industry; a massive attempt to provide chemical fertilizers, mechanical equipment, motor vehicles, and the other tools of modern agriculture would necessarily have involved industrial growth, but only the first faltering steps were taken in that direction during the Nanking decade.

China has always been primarily an agricultural nation. The vast majority of Chinese are supported by the land, and the Chinese social system and Chinese values have been shaped by that transcendent fact. But China is also a huge country of many parts, and the problem for the historian is to find generalizations that can encompass its size and diversity. For example, not only was there political regionalism during the Nanking decade, but certain economic practices, conditions, and customs were regionally defined. Important differences marked off the wheat-growing north from the rice-growing south; the eastern seaboard, with its Westernized cities, from the western hinterland where foreign influences were sparse and faint. And within those regions were many variations in such vital matters as landlord-tenant relations and conditions of rural tenancy.

For some years it was thought that agricultural conditions deteriorated during the late nineteenth and early twentieth century as China itself deteriorated territorially and socially. Recent scholars, however, have concluded that life in the countryside remained remarkably stable throughout that time. Yet there is little disagreement about conditions after 1930; Chinese and foreign scholars, then and now, have acknowledged the suffering of the peasantry and recognized the causes of it, which include warlord and government exploitation, civil war, high rents, uncertain tenure for some, high taxes, lack of cheap credit, and agricultural depression.

Some of the hardships imposed upon the peasantry by warlords —seizure of farm carts and animals, forced labor, civil disorder, unremittingly rapacious taxation—have been discussed above. Direct war-induced exploitation probably decreased after 1931, when the incidence of major wars declined, but extortionary taxation continued. As we have noted, myriad surtaxes came to be the norm, and were notably heavy in the areas controlled by the central government. The peasants continued to be subjected to forced labor by the central as well as the provincial governments. During the early 1930s, the normal difficulties of peasant life were intensified by extraordinary problems. In 1931 floods devastated large areas in five provinces of central China, and the government did virtually nothing to lessen the peasants' misery. The first half of the decade also brought severe agricultural depression, which produced "intolerable rural suffering.[19]

It is especially hazardous to generalize about tenancy, for there was extremely wide variation in the extent and character of land-rent conditions. Tenancy was much greater in south China than in the north, and not all tenants were impoverished by any means. In most regions the amount of land a family could use profitably depended upon the number of workers in the family; some who owned their own land could rent additional acreage, and even a rich peasant might rent land and hire laborers to help him till it. Nevertheless, testimony abounds regarding harsh and exploitative conditions of tenancy, with absentee landlords the chief villains.

In the proximity of cities, absentee ownership developed from two sources: urban capitalists and new emigrants from the rural areas. The capitalists sometimes invested in land, and put the collection of their rents into the hands of agents. The landlord-tenant relationship in the heyday of Confucianism should not be romanticized, but nonetheless the social consciousness Confucianism inculcated, and the pressure of public opinion in the community in which one lived, exerted a moderating influence on landlords that did not affect rental agents during the republican period. Yet it is impossible to judge how widespread this kind of absentee ownership was, and its extent may have been exaggerated. Many emigrants from the village to the city were able to accumulate a bit of money and use it to buy land in their villages. In a few villages, at least, a surprising portion of the land was owned by such individuals, although one suspects that absentee ownership of this type was not nationally significant.

Absentee landlords have been denounced as the worst exploiters in the countryside, but regardless of place or landlord, the normal conditions of land rental were onerous. Ordinary rents were high and allowed the tenant virtually no leeway to cover the cost of emergencies or meet important expenses. At the best of times, the poor peasant lived at the margin of subsistence—and not much was required to push him over.

The peasant often needed extra funds to fulfill social obligations dictated by tradition and custom, notably those associated with weddings, funerals, and other landmarks in the life of the Chinese family. The only source of rural credit generally available was the local moneylender, pawnbroker, or merchant-usurer, at rates ranging from 2 to about 5 per cent per month. The moneylender in one lower Yangtze rural community was called Sze, the Skin Tearer, which expressed the community's view of him. A Communist officer who participated in bringing revolution to many villages asserted that the peasants generally despised usurers more than anyone else. But they were forced to have recourse to them. Statistics gathered in the 1938–1947 period show that at least half of the rural population throughout the entire country was constantly in debt.[20]

The Nanking government commissioned studies and formulated plans to resolve these harsh problems of the countryside. Notable progress was registered: better strains of rice and wheat were developed; improvements were made in the techniques of animal husbandry; a better understanding of insect control was obtained; and other technical gains were achieved. These were important developments; in fact, they were absolutely essential to the *economic* problems of the rural areas because only modern agricultural technology could shatter the circle of rural poverty by increasing agricultural productivity, reducing the demand for rural labor, expanding the domestic market, and stimulating industry. Even so, not enough was accomplished, particularly in persuading local government to foster technological innovation systematically in the countryside. Nobody took the new information and techniques to the man in the field; the government failed to organize an efficient agricultural-extension system.

In the absence of a technological revolution, the peasant needed help in coping with rents, taxes, credits, and in creating a tolerable standard of rural life. The government did not succeed in providing it. In 1930 a land law was promulgated that included a provision to limit rents to 37½ per cent of the harvest, which would have eased the peasant's burden considerably. But the law was never enforced. Rents amounting to 50 per cent of the harvest were commonplace; 60 per cent was not rare. Several newly created modern banks elaborated paper programs designed to provide credit facilities for the peasantry, but somehow they never gave any significant help to small landholders, much less to tenants. Government-encouraged agricultural cooperatives were no more successful. Between 1933 and 1935, only 1 per cent of all agricultural credit was extended by cooperatives, and this amount was given to only 5 per cent of the peasants borrowing. The remainder borrowed from traditional sources: usurers, pawnbrokers, and landlords.[21]

Nanking's failure to deal effectively with the land problem was nowhere more glaringly revealed than in Kiangsi, where the Communists had set up their Soviet Republic in 1931 and instituted far-reaching agrarian reforms. Several foreign experts visited Kiangsi in 1933 and concluded that the tenancy system and the lack of cheap rural credit were the chief causes of unrest in the province. They recommended that reforms be implemented in the non-Communist areas and in the Communist regions as soon as they were recaptured. In 1934 the Communists fled from central China, and the erstwhile soviet regions fell into Kuomintang hands. But when one of the experts returned in 1936, he found that no reforms had been instituted by the Nationalist Government and that the old landlord order had been restored. An American scholar in China at that time noted that the Kuomintang had pursued a policy of "masterly inaction" as the land relations that had existed before the Communists had become entrenched in Kiangsi were restored.[22]

Throughout China in the Nanking decade peasants continued to plant traditional crops with traditional farming implements. Farm tools in use in north China were similar to those sketched in a Chinese agricultural handbook of the fourteenth and fifteenth centuries. Peasants in the immediate vicinity of urban manufacturing centers became slightly less self-sufficient, and the expansion of roads allowed peasants in a few areas to bypass standard markets and go straight to the city. But such phenomena were peripheral, variations on a basic theme that was virtually unchanged. The standard marketing area still constituted the basic rural unit; agricultural technology remained essentially traditional; and the Chinese peasant still "ate bitterness" as nature, landlords, soldiers, and officials all seemed to be trying to push him over the brink. As one member and supporter of the Nanking government has acknowledged: "By 1937 there had been little change in the overall rural situation."[23]

Long before it had attained national power, the Kuomintang had recognized the urgency of rural reform, and after 1928 many influential foreigners and Chinese exhorted the government to take realistic action. Why was so little done, in spite of the plans, studies, and laws that directly and indirectly underlined the need for action?

Again it is necessary to emphasize the persistence of warlordism. The Nanking government's capacity to effect change in the countryside was limited by the autonomy of so many provinces. Just how difficult it was for the government to deal effectively with the peasantry is illustrated by its inability to collect agricultural taxes. And as the collection of those taxes had to be left to the provinces, so to the provinces was left the initiative for rural reform. Some provinces did take such initiative—Kwangsi, for example.

Other circumstances also help explain the absence of rural reform in government-controlled provinces, as well as the lack of more vigorous attempts to deal with this critical problem even in warlord provinces. The character of government personnel was an important factor. Once the party purge had eliminated or silenced those members of the party interested in reform, opportunism and self-serving became the hallmarks of the Kuomintang and the Kuomintang government. To espouse reforms was to risk being identified with Communism. The Kuomintang's fear of Communism was itself a factor. It drove the party to conservatism. Instead of stimulating it to initiate reforms that might simultaneously gain peasant support, deprive the Communists of their appeal, and solve human problems for millions of peasants, the Nanking government's fear of Communism led it to seek support among those social groups who had their own reasons to fear Communism: merchants, industrialists, and, in the countryside, landlords and other members of the rural gentry.

The gentry was yet another factor. When the American minister to China urged Chiang Kai-shek's brother-in-law and adviser to institute genuine reform in agrarian communities, he found that the government thought "the strength of the rural communities rested upon the old gentry, and that at all costs the power of the gentry should be restored."[24] Chiang Kai-shek believed that the local gentry constituted the key to social stability and its members the strongest defenders against radicalism. After the Taiping Rebellion in the mid-nineteenth century, Chinese leaders tried to restore social tranquillity by strengthening the local gentry, and in the 1930s Chiang consciously and purposefully emulated that pattern.

Taken as a whole, the gentry opposed virtually every measure that might have improved the peasant's life. For example, an American missionary who was personally assured of Madame Chiang Kai-shek's backing in a program of rural reconstruction purposefully avoided including provisions for mass education because experience had shown him that "literacy programs tended to arouse the immediate opposition of the gentry."[25] Similar considerations prompted other rural reformers to decry peasant filth, ignorance, and poverty, yet formulate only programs that scrupulously avoided any fundamental overhaul of the social structure.

Perhaps the key factor in explaining the failure of the Nanking government to effect rural reform was that the government was essentially urban oriented. The Kuomintang was the party of the bourgeoisie, who were simply not informed about and not very interested in the problems of the countryside. There was a cultural abyss between the Westernized party and government in the cities, on the one hand, and the peasantry and even the rural gentry, on the other hand. Educational and social changes illustrated this culture gap very clearly.

Educational and Social Change

Like virtually every other aspect of Chinese life, the educational system had been disrupted by warlordism. After 1912, education ministers succeeded one another in whirlwind fashion. The entire educational system was reorganized twice before the advent of Kuomintang power, and curricula and textbooks underwent several modifications. The Kuomintang put still more changes into effect. Immediately after it came to power, the party formally decided to use education as an instrument of national integration. School books were infused with nationalistic content and were written in the vernacular. The schools were viewed as the major force in eliminating dialectical barriers through the use of the national language—essentially the northern dialect—as the standard medium of instruction. The Nanking government also introduced a centralized educational administration to determine standards and programs for all levels of schooling. But education under the Kuomintang government did not exert the integrative influence envisaged for it.

The limited educational facilities that were available existed in only a few areas. Of the 103 institutions of higher learning operating in 1934, 32 were located in Shanghai and Peiping, alone; most of the remaining 71 were also in urban centers, whereas some provinces had not a single college or university. During the same year, 1934, secondary education was accessible to 213 of every 10,000 people in Shanghai, but in such provinces as Shensi, Kweichow, and Kansu only 4 out of every 10,000 had the opportunity for secondary instruction. Seventy out of every 1,000 residents of Shansi had primary schools available, but only 7 out of every 1,000 residents of Hupei enjoyed that opportunity, and in other provinces the percentage was even less. Thus, in national terms, educational opportunities were geographically unequal and, in most places, inadequate.[26]

As these figures imply, rural education was most neglected. The number of schools and teachers in rural areas was extremely small, and the quality of those few was low. The expense of attending city schools, and of any kind of institution of higher education, effectively barred youngsters of most peasant families from enrolling.

Elementary and secondary education remained under the control of local authorities, although they were supposed to carry out central government directives with regard to such matters as curricula and teacher qualifications. The government aspired to create a four-year compulsory-education program, but could not muster the financial or other resources to realize this goal. In 1935 it launched a crash program to give one year of primary schooling to a substantial portion of school-age children over the course of the following five years. School enrollment did jump from about 13 million to 23 million in the next two years, but the program collapsed with the outbreak of war in 1937. The utterly inadequate scope of primary education was one of the most serious of China's educational shortcomings.

Neglect of primary education was a problem emphasized by a team of foreign educational experts who surveyed Chinese education in 1931 under the auspices of the League of Nations. The team's report discussed many aspects of Chinese education and made various recommendations for its improvement, but its central theme, to which all quantitative aspects were subordinate, argued that Chinese education at all levels was insufficiently Chinese. It copied foreign models, primarily American models, with little regard for the different conditions existing in China and the United States. The experts repeatedly stressed the dangers inherent in mechanically imitating foreign approaches and philosophies.

The universities, where many returned students taught, were particularly denationalized. Many professors used foreign textbooks, studied foreign problems, used foreign illustrations. "It is not unknown, for example, for a professor of agricultural science to be well-informed as to the conditions and methods of other parts of the world, but to find it difficult to apply his knowledge to those of China," the report declared.[27] At the university level, this preoccupation with foreign ideas and phenomena had an obvious corollary: students did not aspire to go out and work on China's real problems, but, instead, to find some official position in one of China's main urban centers. Indeed, despite China's obvious needs for talent in all phases of material reconstruction, most university students still had a literary bias; they studied literature, law, political science, for these were "appropriate" subjects for a Chinese intellectual, in accord with Chinese tradition and with their own aspirations for officialdom.

The tone and example set by the universities extended throughout the educational system. Not only were the majority of secondary schools organized on the basis of foreign models, but a large proportion of them were founded by foreigners, most of whom were missionaries. In art, needlework, and music classes, Chinese children were taught to avoid traditional Chinese motifs, and to copy Western models. One visitor to Chinese schools recalled: "How often have I lingered outside a classroom trying to identify the cacophony coming from inside and later discovered that it was 'Broadway Melody' or the 'theme song' from some film or other."[28] The League of Nations experts concluded:

> The result of all these conditions is the creation and development in China of schools and educational institutions not conducted on a strict system and not suitable to the needs and conditions of the country. The result is a favoring of schools of higher standard, generally rising far above the condition of the impoverished country whilst the primary and vocational instruction most indispensable for the people is neglected. There is also the lack of social ideals within the schools, an abstract kind of instruction not directly connected with surrounding life and the necessities of the country's rebirth usually obtaining. This creates an enormous abyss between the masses of the Chinese people, plunged in illiteracy, and not understanding the needs of their country, and the intelligentsia educated in luxurious schools and indifferent to the wants of the masses. Such an educational system is highly injurious to the masses and dangerous, because a carefully educated social elite not closely connected with general needs may become transformed into an unproductive clique enclosed within the narrow bounds of its own interests.[29]

The government tried to take steps to meet the situation described by the League of Nations' report, but it is difficult to say just how much was accomplished. Little was done to expand primary education until 1935; as described above, a special program was then launched that brought a large number of additional youngsters to special and part-time schools until the entire program broke down in the war with Japan. In higher education the government tried to discourage the study of literary subjects and to stimulate the study of those that were technical and "practical." This policy did produce a shift in university class enrollments in favor of scientific and technical studies; by 1935 roughly half of the students were enrolled in "practical subjects." Nevertheless, even a very friendly observer noted that on the eve of the war with Japan college students, including those who had majored in "practical" subjects, were still clustered in the few great cities along the eastern seaboard, and still had their eyes focused on official positions. It was a rare individual who tried to put his skills to use in engineering or scientific fields, and rarer still was the person who took his talents to the hinterland.

The eruption of war in the middle of 1937, and the rapid Japanese conquest of coastal areas in the months immediately following, changed the educational situation drastically. Within two years from the start of the war, 77 of China's institutions of higher learning were literally uprooted and moved many hundreds of miles into the interior. For the first time, university-trained Chinese intellectuals went in large numbers into the Chinese rural areas. Moreover, under the pressure of war needs, Chinese education turned more rapidly in the direction of practical studies. New courses were introduced in such fields as health administration and public health, paper manufacturing, and social scientists engaged in highly practical studies of Chinese communities and peoples in the regions into which the universities had moved. The exigencies of war brought Chinese intellectuals into contact with their own people.

Not only were there changes in the educational system during the Nanking period, there were social changes as well. The adoption of Western values and social institutions spread during the Nanking decade, but primarily in the cities, just as during the May Fourth Era with its New Culture Movement. The Intellectual Revolution, the family revolution, the revolution in the position of women, and other basic changes in long-held Chinese values were all concentrated in urban centers. There are innumerable witnesses to the backwardness and lack of basic social change in the country-side. This persistence of old ways can be illustrated with the central institution of traditional China, the family.

Like other aspects of change in China, changing ideas about the family began to appear in the late nineteenth and early twentieth centuries. But it was the New Culture Movement and the May Fourth Movement that triggered the family revolution. Young intellectuals deplored China's weakness against the "wolf and tiger" powers of imperialism, and attributed China's impotence to Confucianism. They rejected the Chinese past generally, but fastened upon the family system and arranged marriage in particular as the most hated symbols and the most onerous aspects of the Confucian tradition. Chinese literature of the 1920s frequently dealt with the theme of family conflict and the clash of generations —in this instance a virtual clash of cultures. The new periodicals also printed much propaganda about the need to reject the old family system.

Young Chinese men and women concentrated their attack on the family system and marriage customs because they suffered so directly from them. But underlying the family revolution was also the awareness, however vague, that the old family system could not exist in a modern, Western-type society of the kind necessary to create a national power capable of resisting imperialism. Modern society seemed to require impersonal, objective standards of achievement and capacities that were incompatible with the primacy of kinship criteria, symbolized by nepotism. Nationalism, as conceived in the context of warlord fragmentation, necessitated centralized control of a thoroughly integrated society; as a corollary of national power, nationalism was not consonant with localism, familism, and clannism. C. K. Yang, in his brilliant study of the Chinese family, notes that for half a century Chinese intellectuals consciously tried to detach "individuals from the firmest of traditional Chinese social ties, the kinship tie, in order to refit them into the mesh of new social relations based on the requirements of an industrial economy and a centralized political state."[30]

When the Kuomintang came to power in 1928, it took formal and official note of the fact that ideas about the family had changed, particularly as far as marriages were concerned. Laws were passed to forbid concubinage and other forms of polygamy, to permit divorce, and to allow for free choice in marriage if parents approved. But the Nanking government did little to intensify or accelerate the family revolution, and in the 1920s and 1930s family changes were still largely limited to urban intellectuals. In the 1930s and 1940s other urban groups, more especially the urban middle class, also began to participate in new family ways, though city intellectuals remained the major group affected by the revolution. The urban working class, and in particular the peasantry in the countryside, continued with essentially the same family system that had always dominated China.

That the rural areas were untouched by the family revolution was partly due to the fact that the new laws were communicated in writing, which effectively insured against their being known to the vast illiterate peasantry. Changing the law was obviously meaningless if communication was deficient, if those the law affected remained ignorant of its terms and its import. Significantly, the Chinese Communist government later demanded that peasants participate in some form in the discussion and promulgation of new laws; it recognized that participation in such circumstances is a form of communication.

More important than lack of communication about the new laws, however, was that the situation in the countryside had not changed in such a way as to demand or encourage new familial relations. The peasant family, tilling a tiny plot of land, retained the same economic functions that had always justified it. Further, in a time of civil strife and lawlessness, the family was the only source of psychological or material security. The movement from country to city or from one part of the country to another, forced upon many peasants by war and invasion strained and weakened some family ties, and fostered knowledge of the larger society and nation. But at the same time this turmoil increased the need for family cohesiveness, for mutual protection and survival. Even where circumstances tore families apart, they seemed to confirm the validity of long-held familial values.

In sum, from the New Culture Movement until 1949, the family revolution spread among urban intellectuals, whose familial relations and obligations became more similar to those in America and Western Europe, and increasingly compatible with economic developments in Chinese cities. This trend would ultimately, after 1949, be expanded by the Communist government, which would commit its power to extending the family revolution to other classes. The extension, however, did not occur during the period of the republic. Thus, families of urban intellectuals became more and more capable of being integrated into a new and modern economy and political order, but no such new order could be viable as long as millions upon millions of peasants had not heard of the family revolution, and would find it offensive if they had.

Reintegration During the Nanking Decade

Chiang Kai-shek's hope that the Kuomintang would be the integrating force that China needed was largely unrealized during the Nanking decade. Only limited progress was made in territorial integration, and social disintegration remained extreme.

After due allowance has been made for the substantial autonomy retained by many provincial leaders, there is no doubt that the national government exercised more control over China's provinces and localities in 1936 than it did when it came to power in 1928. Chiang's armies had defeated every provincial militarist who had challenged him on the field, and had forced even the traditionally independent provinces of the far south to acknowledge central government authority. By 1937 territorial integration was still weak—most important, it was produced only by the limited provincial acceptance of Chiang's political authority with but little national cohesiveness or even regional interdependence—but weak as it was, it was a great improvement over the national status of China at the beginning of the decade when territorial integration was virtually nonexistent.

The government was less successful in furthering social integration. The generally conservative, authoritarian rural elite—the local gentry—continued to dominate the countryside, and a modernizing urban elite emerged in the cities. The rural elite remained committed to local rather than national interests, and opposed social reforms that would have liberated the peasant from ancient bonds and integrated him into a modern nation; the urban elite wanted a strong nation and accepted the idea of Westernizing reforms, but had no contact with or understanding of rural China. Thus the Chinese elite was itself divided, and no portion of it tolerated by the Kuomintang had any functional relationship or rapport with the Chinese peasantry, the overwhelming mass of the Chinese people.

The phrase "local gentry" up to the Revolution of 1911, as noted in an earlier chapter, once denoted those who had passed the first civil-service examination. By the end of the Manchu era it designated a local elite based on wealth (from whatever source), political connections, control of armed force, professional and technical expertise—a designation still applicable throughout the republican period. The rural elite in the Nanking decade consisted of various local combinations of landlords, officials and their relatives, military officers if they were wealthy or had control of troops, successful bandits, and even some scholars, though a poor scholar seldom had real influence. The urban elite was formed of those involved in Western-style economic and intellectual undertakings. It embraced industrialists, bankers, and businessmen of all kinds. Professional men and government bureaucrats were included, and so were intellectuals—writers, teachers, journalists, technical experts.

A complicated pattern of relationships, still poorly understood, existed between these two groups and between them and the Nanking government, the provincial governments, and the military. The central government supported the rural gentry's economic domination of the countryside, hoping it would serve as a barrier against Communism and a bulwark of rural stability. The gentry wanted a strong army for the same purpose: to maintain law and order—the political-economic status quo—in the countryside; it was, however, the provincial, not the central, army that was important to them for that purpose, even though the provincial army might be at odds with the national government. The gentry recognized the advantages it derived from Nanking policies, and many of its members had personal contacts with Kuomintang officials. As a contemporary observed in 1937, even in provinces where Nanking's authority was far from complete, it was not unusual to find that "families which are locally powerful and have a vested interest in evading the control of the Central Government are at the same time intimately bound up with families or individuals powerful at Nanking."[31] But those were personal relations, aimed at personal advantage, not rooted in common commitment to a particular national order. The gentry was by its nature primarily local.

The republican gentry, by and large, did not have the national cohesion of its predecessor, the gentry of Confucian China. In traditional China, the gentry constituted what one astute scholar called a "national minded minority," whereas the mass of the common people had little knowledge of national interest and no deep sense of moral obligation to it.[32] With the disintegration of that minority, and the elevation to local power of people who were occupationally and ideologically heterogeneous, united by local power interests only, the elite of the various localities had less in common, were less "national minded." Members of the rural elite who went to the city for schooling or business might acquire a national point of view, but more often than not they simply remained in the city. Those who stayed in the countryside "operated in the traditional decentralized political pattern and remained largely unintegrated into the modern system of national central authority."[33]

The modernization of China depended upon the Westernized urban elite. Like the rural gentry, that group consisted of diverse interests that were not always in harmony: intellectuals, for example, tended to take more radical stands than businessmen. However, in general terms, the urban elite displayed two major shortcomings: an inability to control the Kuomintang government and alienation from the peasantry.

The Kuomintang government dissatisfied the urban elite on several counts. Modern businessmen and intellectuals wanted the army under civilian control, and disapproved of the great political power held by militarists. Urban intellectuals criticized the government for its disregard of civil rights, its nonresistance policy toward Japan, and its refusal to introduce genuinely democratic political processes. The business and industrial components resented government control and exploitation. The central government derived about 85 percent of its tax revenues from the modernized sector of the economy and placed more and more of it under its control. For example, it seized majority control of modern Chinese banks, and the big entrepreneurs found that they could prosper only after bringing Nanking bureaucrats into their organizations. Neither the Westernized business community nor the modern intellectuals could do much about the encroachments of the central government because they had little political power. In the face of Kuomintang repression, the intellectuals were unable to function as serious critics of government policies.

A more important feature of the urban elite was its alienation from rural China. In a bloodless sort of way, intellectuals recognized that China was an agricultural country, and that agricultural policy was therefore important. But they had no genuine understanding of agrarian problems and no real interest in them. They thought in terms of urban issues, of international affairs, of modernizing China to emulate Western countries; many never seemed to recognize the inevitable influence that the countryside would have on the course of modernization. As early as 1919, Li Ta-chao noted the isolation of intellectuals from the Chinese masses, and was fully aware of the dangers it augured. If the peasants are not liberated, he wrote, "then our whole nation will not be liberated; their sufferings are the sufferings of our whole nation; their ignorance is the ignorance of our whole nation."[34] That ignorance, he said, and the peasants' inability to resist oppression from the local gentry, is due to the fact that young intellectuals from rural China run to the cities to seek a livelihood among the bureaucrats and never return to the countryside. Li was quite right, and the situation grew worse in the following three decades.

Other observers have noted this phenomenon, but none more systematically and perceptively than Y. C. Wang, who has studied the education of young Chinese abroad. Wang pointed out, for example, that university students, and particularly students returned from foreign study congregated in China's port cities. Even those who had come from villages stayed in the cities. The need for intellectuals in the countryside was enormous, but as a renowned Chinese anthropologist noted in 1946, virtually all college graduates who had come from the country elected to remain in the city even when they were unemployed and had to borrow money to live. Most astonishing was the fact that this unwillingness to return to farmland China was also true of agricultural students. In 1926 an American missionary educator connected with the University of Nanking remarked: "I do not know of a single graduate of a college of agriculture returned from the United States who has gone back to a strictly rural community. . . . I know of no graduate of agricultural colleges in China who has done it."[35]

Not many students studied agriculture. Between 1905 and 1954 agriculture was the least popular of all major fields studied by Chinese students in the United States, involving less than 3.5 per cent. After 1935 even theology and music attracted more students. This neglect of agriculture reflected old attitudes about the proper role and function of an intellectual; it also reflected the attitude that if intellectuals did not study liberal arts they should at least study matters in which China was deficient: modern science, engineering, Western law. Too many took the subject of agriculture pretty much for granted. This neglect also reflected a curious myopia about the process of Westernization which saw China as Westernizing but not applying Western knowledge to Chinese conditions—a subtle, but terribly important, distinction.

Chinese intellectuals generally remained in the metropolitan areas because they sought high-paying jobs, especially in government or teaching, and these were available only in the cities. Moreover, having become accustomed to urban living either in Chinese cities, where all universities were located, or in Western countries, they were put off by the crudities and harshness of rural life. The same considerations accounted for the reluctance of agricultural students to go to the countryside, though their reluctance was augmented by the fact that their training had been in scientific procedures of foreign agriculture and was not always relevant to Chinese conditions.

Some may find the judgments offered above on Kuomintang achievements during the Nanking decade to be harsh and unfair, that they ignore the problems faced by China during those years. An American minister to China once remarked that the Nationalist Government never had a real chance to show what it could do because during most of the prewar decade it was faced by both war-lord and Communist subversion, by Japanese aggression in Manchuria and north China, and later by a massive invasion of the whole country. All that is true, but somewhat irrelevant. The test that history imposes upon any government is whether it met the problems it had, not the problems it would have had under other circumstances. The opportunity and necessity before the Kuomintang government was to show what it could do about warlords, Communists, invaders, and the need for national unification and modernization. In the final analysis, the Kuomintang failed that test. It failed not because it made no progress at all—on the contrary, the Kuomintang could boast of some achievements in every realm—but because its reintegrative effect was too slow. The process of reintegration was but little advanced when the Japanese invasion brought it all to an end. The Kuomintang's real achievements would be taken over by the Communists to facilitate their own form of national reintegration.

Imperialism in China

Anti-imperialism had triggered the beginnings of the transformation of China in the late nineteenth century, and had remained an important element in the Chinese revolution thereafter. Yet it had never loomed large in Kuomintang policies or propaganda until the reorganization of the party under Russian auspices in 1924. When Chiang broke with the Communists in 1927, the intensity of the party's anti-imperialism again subsided, but it did not disappear. Chinese nationalist intellectuals demanded the end of foreign privilege in China, and the Nanking government moved toward that goal immediately after the end of the Northern Expedition. In fact, the return of foreign concessions began when the left-wing government at Wuhan, with a combination of force and negotiation, repossessed two British concessions in 1927. The Nanking government subsequently obtained the return of three more concessions from Britain and one from Belgium, but the rest remained under foreign control. With the beginning of Japanese aggression in China in the early 1930s, the government felt that the existence of foreign enclaves in treaty ports might inhibit Japanese actions in some measure. It therefore decided that the matter of retrocession was not as urgent as the issues of tariff autonomy and extraterritoriality.

The Nanking government made swift progress in obtaining the restoration of tariff autonomy. The foreign powers had accepted the principle of tariff autonomy some years earlier, and had negotiated a new tariff with the warlord government in Peking in 1926. It was on the basis of that agreement that the Nanking government in 1928 arranged tariff autonomy with all powers except Japan. Agreement with Japan two years later eliminated the last vestige of foreign control over China's tariff.

The fight for elimination of extraterritoriality went more slowly. Germany had lost extraterritorial rights after World War I, and the Soviet Union had voluntarily relinquished them in 1924. The rest of the world powers accepted the end of extraterritoriality in principle, but the Chinese were expected first to create an efficient, modern legal system along Western lines. Negotiations were still going on when Japan took over Manchuria in 1931; the issue was then allowed to lie dormant for some years. Not until 1943 did the United States and England agree to the abolition of extraterritoriality and all the remaining elements of the unequal treaties; the other powers quickly followed suit.

While the Nanking government was making progress in removing the most onerous provisions of the unequal treaties, Japanese imperialism mounted a new offensive against China. Japan had pursued an aggressive policy in China early in the republic, exemplified by the Twenty-one Demands of 1915, and by the Japanese seizure of Shantung. During the 1920s, Japanese agents were active in China, and the Japanese were one of the chief targets of nationalist anti-imperialist agitation. It was only with the Manchurian invasion of 1931, however, that the full dimension of Japan's aims in China began to become clear.

On September 18, 1931, the Japanese military launched an attack against the Chinese in Manchuria. The Japanese Government, loath to reveal that it could not control its own military leaders, approved the action after the fact. The Japanese Army quickly gained control of China's vast northeastern territory, and in early 1932 organized it as the independent state of Manchukuo, under the ostensible rule of P'u Yi, the last Emperor of the Ch'ing Dynasty. After that conquest, the Japanese military continued to nibble away at north China. They took over the province of Jehol and organized separatist movements in the five northern provinces, an obvious first step to bringing them under Japanese authority.

The Nanking government under Chiang Kai-shek did not attempt to resist these Japanese encroachments by force. Chiang believed that national unity was a prerequisite to effective resistance, and that national unity required the destruction of the Chinese Communists. Chiang's preoccupation with domestic enemies in the face of foreign threats increasingly alienated Chinese intellectuals and a number of army officers, who pressured him to change his policy. By 1937 Chiang, apparently yielding to that pressure, was preparing to lead a united nation against Japan. The Japanese did not wait, however. They invaded all of China in the summer of 1937. The Sino-Japanese War had begun.

VIII

The Communist Victory

THE NANKING DECADE was followed by a decade of death and destruction. For eight years the Chinese fought stubbornly against the Japanese invaders. The old struggle between the Kuomintang and the Communists was more or less held in abeyance during this war of national resistance, but it flared up quickly after the defeat of Japan, and China was once again torn by civil war—four years of Chinese fighting Chinese. The end came in 1949, when Chiang Kai-shek and his followers fled to Taiwan, and Mao Tse-tung proclaimed the establishment of the People's Republic of China. This prolonged warfare was catastrophic for the Kuomintang. Weaknesses in the party, the army, and the government, which might have been tolerable under other circumstances, became fatal under the severe pressures of war. The pressures of warfare on the Communists, on the other hand, enabled them to develop a new national strength through social revolution, and they organized the peasant masses along new lines. In so doing, they created a sociopolitical basis on which to resist Japan and defeat the Kuomintang, and, in the process, they generated a high degree of integration in the regions they controlled.

Chinese Communism 1927–1937

The Kuomintang-Communist coalition came to an abrupt and bloody end in 1927, when Chiang Kai-shek set his troops to closing down left-wing organizations and to slaughtering Communists wherever they could be found. That attack decimated the Communist Party. The leadership was changed, party headquarters in Shanghai went underground, and many Communists—individuals, small groups, fragments of Communist-led military units—fled into the mountains and rugged areas along certain provincial borders. Here they reorganized their forces and recruited peasant soldiers. The Shanghai leadership, still following Russian directives, ordered these peasant troops to try to capture industrial and commercial centers, hoping that attacks from the outside would stimulate revolt within the urban areas. The attacks were futile however; the weakened party found little support in the cities, the strongholds of Chiang Kai-shek's power, and the Communists suffered one defeat after another. In 1930 they finally repudiated the fruitless policy of urban revolt and turned to the countryside, where elements of the Communist Party were already making a new beginning.

The key men in the rejuvenation of the Communist Party were Mao Tse-tung and Chu Teh. Late in 1927 Mao led a band of ragged followers to Chingkangshan, a mountain fastness on the Hunan-Kiangsi border, where he was joined early in 1928 by Chu Teh, a Communist military officer, and his small following. This meeting marked the beginning of what came to be known as the Mao-Chu leadership, with Mao the political leader, and Chu in charge of military affairs. It was also the beginning of a long period during which Mao and Chu developed political and military concepts and policies that were at odds with the central party leadership and the Comintern that stood behind it.

The Mao-Chu strategy was formed as a practical response to the conditions in which the Communists found themselves in 1927–1928. Earlier, while cooperating with the Kuomintang, the Communists had concentrated on the organization of the masses. Now, pursued by Chiang Kai-shek's armies, and in the total context of warlordism, the Communists recognized the need for a Red Army. The beginnings of the army already existed in the small units under Mao and Chu and under other Communist officers who had similarly fled to the hinterlands. But Mao envisaged the unification, development, and expansion of these various units into a Red Army, and he and Chu worked hard to improve and enlarge their own forces. By the end of 1929 they had developed the largest and best-disciplined Communist army in China.

Given the superiority of the Kuomintang and warlord armies in numbers and resources, Mao recommended that the Red Army rely primarily on guerrilla tactics. It would swiftly bring together numerically superior forces to destroy isolated enemy units, and just as swiftly disperse and avoid battle when it was outnumbered. Chu Teh summed up this credo of guerrilla war in 1928 in terms that became the classic statement of Red Army tactics:

> When the enemy advances, we retreat.
> When the enemy halts and encamps, we harass them.
> When the enemy seeks to avoid battle, we attack.
> When the enemy retreats, we pursue.

Guerrilla war requires the cooperation and assistance of the population among whom the guerrillas operate, so the Red Army had to develop links of intimate trust and mutual interest with the peasantry. Mao, therefore, insisted upon the most rigorous discipline and formulated rules of conduct for his army that were designed to cultivate good relations between the soldiers and the people. But Mao recognized that good troop behavior alone would not be sufficient for any kind of Communist success. A bedrock of peasant support had to be created by using the Red Army on behalf of peasant interests. He also recognized that the chief peasant interest was land. Mao proposed that the army help the peasant to revolt, to seize and redistribute the land, and to protect him afterward.

This program, of course, implied still another necessity: a territorial base. If the peasants were to receive benefits at the expense of landlords and others, the army would have to control the area to assure that the landlords, Kuomintang tax collectors, hostile soldiers, and others were kept out. Furthermore, a territorial base was essential in order to secure the revenues and material needed to maintain the army. In the context of warlordism and Kuomintang enmity, the territory should be as self-sufficient and as strategically located as possible. Finally, the base should form the core from which the Communists could expand their control into larger areas, thereby constituting an ever more formidable challenge to the government.

The urban proletariat had no role in this program; in the years after 1928, and especially after 1930, the Red Army was almost completely cut off from the cities. The absence of proletarians disturbed some Communists who, in orthodox Marxist terms, viewed the peasantry, with its strong sense of property, as essentially conservative. They feared that a Communist movement could not maintain its revolutionary integrity if cut off from a proletarian base. But Mao Tse-tung argued that the Chinese proletariat was small, concentrated in a few cities under the political control of the Kuomintang, and generally vulnerable to the power of imperialists. As for China's peasant millions, Mao had nothing but praise for their revolutionary potential. Mao's first notable expression of this view was in the spring of 1927, before the Kuomintang-Communist split, in a report evaluating the peasant movement in Hunan. Even that report was not a completely new departure in the Chinese Communist movement; Li Ta-chao, the pioneer Marxist, had also represented the peasantry as the chief force of the Chinese revolution. Despite his reliance on the peasantry and a peasant army, Mao never forgot Communist goals. He relied on a vigorously indoctrinated Communist Party to guide the peasant army in a fashion commensurate with proletarian and Communist objectives.

These, then, were the essential elements of the Mao-Chu strategy: a strong party at the head of a party army, a rural territorial base, rooted in peasant support gained by responding to the peasant's most deeply felt aspirations and needs. Though Mao and Chu formulated the chief elements of this strategy in 1928, it was elaborated and clarified in subsequent years, particularly after Mao came to power in the Communist Party. But the strategy bore its first significant fruit earlier, in the creation of rural soviet districts and the Chinese Soviet Republic.

Mao and Chu improved their army and expanded their territory during 1929 and 1930. Other commanders meanwhile organized armed forces and established political control in other territorial bases. These areas were called rural soviets, a name derived from the councils of workers, peasants, and soldiers set up in Russia during the 1905 revolution and later in 1917, although at the outset the term in China meant little more than an area controlled by the Communist Party. These bases frequently changed in number, in size, and in population according to the vicissitudes of attacks from government forces and the alterations in local circumstances, but by 1931 at least half a dozen major soviet areas had attained some permanence and stability as independent political entities. In December representatives of a number of soviets, and of Communist armies and organizations, met in Juichin, Kiangsi, and proclaimed the establishment of a new state embracing all the soviet areas. This state was the Chinese Soviet Republic. The representatives adopted the outline of a constitution, set up a central government, approved a political program, an agrarian policy, and certain basic social and economic policies.

Mao Tse-tung was elected Chairman of the Republic, and Chu Teh Chairman of the Military Council, which in effect meant commander in chief of the Red Armies. The Mao-Chu leadership, however, was much less firmly in charge than these positions would imply. Conflicts of program and personality divided the soviet leaders and the party leaders still in Shanghai. Although Mao was evidently able to control the organization—and hence the elections—of the congress that organized the new government, he did not control the party.

The Chinese Soviet Republic, which may finally have contained a population of as many as 9 million people, was designed to create a "democratic dictatorship of the workers and peasants in the soviet districts." Landlords, gentry, and others who were thought to live by exploitation were shorn of political rights and their land was expropriated. Supreme political authority was vested in a congress of deputies representing the soviets and various organizations, but between meetings real power was in the hands of a Central Executive Committee. Many shortcomings and failures ensued in organizing mass involvement in the functioning of the local soviets. Some progress, nevertheless, was made in that direction, at least in the chief soviet area.

The Soviet Republic promulgated a highly advanced labor code and, initially at least, an extremely radical land law. The labor law affected few people because there were few urban workers in soviet areas; far more relevant was the agrarian law, the culmination of a series of policy decisions taken by the party from the time it was forced into the countryside. The early radical land policy of Chingkangshan became more moderate as Mao increasingly recognized the importance of gaining the support of the middle peasants as well as of the poor and landless. Even so, the land law finally accepted by the Soviet Republic called for the confiscation of land belonging to landlords, gentry, and others who were said to live by exploitation. The seized land was to be redistributed to the poor and landless peasants, and to Red Army soldiers. It was left to the middle peasants to decide whether or not they wished to participate. The law was implemented with a good deal of local variation and flexibility, and in some areas landlords evidently retained much influence and some land. But large quantities of land were confiscated and redistributed to effect an important rural revolution.

The Shanghai leaders of the Communist Party still did not regard the actions and policies of the Mao-Chu faction with complete favor, but the clear fact that the dynamism of the Communist movement was all to be found in the countryside, and the increasing pressure of the Kuomintang police in Shanghai, ultimately drove the party center to leave Shanghai and go to Juichin, where the tug of war between pro- and anti-Mao elements continued. Scholars disagree about the date, but the move probably occurred in 1932. By that time, Chiang Kai-shek was again attacking the soviet areas in force.

In the fall of 1930, the warlord offensive waged by Feng Yü-hsiang and Yen Hsi-shan against the Kuomintang government finally collapsed, and Chiang Kai-shek had immediately turned his attention to the destruction of resurging Communist power. Late in the year, he had launched the first "annihilation campaign" against the soviet areas, and followed it up with a second campaign early in 1931, and then a third later in the same year that was called off when the Japanese invaded Manchuria. None of these campaigns had achieved its goal; on the contrary, the Communists had used swift, mobile tactics with great success against the Kuomintang armies, captured many weapons and prisoners, and gained much additional territory. It was with these successes behind them that they had formally established the Chinese Soviet Republic at the end of 1931.

Chiang started his fourth "annihilation campaign" in the summer of 1932, and operations went on until the spring of the following year. Chiang succeeded in liquidating some outlying soviet areas, but was badly defeated when he proceeded against the central soviet. However, his defeat was not a personal victory for Mao and Chu; their differences with the party center had resulted in a diminution of power for both men, and others had taken over leadership of the defense. Late in 1933, Chiang launched the fifth "annihilation campaign," but organized it in a fashion completely different from his earlier assaults. Following the suggestions of German advisers, Chiang surrounded the central area, established a tight blockade, and slowly and systematically tightened the noose by building constricting circles of fortifications. Finally, Chiang seemed about to realize his goal of "annihilating" the Communists. Faced with this prospect, the Communists had to abandon the soviet. In the fall of 1934, the Red Army and all the party's administrative and political personnel—perhaps 100,000 strong—broke through the ring of Kuomintang steel and started the extraordinary flight that is known as the Long March. It ended over a year later in the Shensi soviet in northwestern China.

The Long March has acquired such worldwide renown that historians feel a bit repetitive whenever they attempt to summarize its awesome features. Yet it is impossible—somehow unappreciative—to gloss over it without stressing its unique character. The vital statistics alone suggest the dimensions of the achievement: the marchers walked about 6,000 miles in a year and three days, or an average of more than 16 miles a day. They fought minor skirmishes virtually every day, with at least 15 days spent in major battles. They labored over snow-covered, freezing mountain passes, and traversed trackless swamplands where one could only rest standing up and where many comrades slipped into the bog forever. They starved and suffered and fought, but pushed steadily on to achieve "the most extraordinary march in human history."[1] It is difficult to be precise about the number of people who survived the Long

March. Some were left along the line of march for propaganda or other work. Still others were recruited during the march; should they be counted as survivors when they were not among the starters? Evidently only about 5,000—or less—survived the full length of the march. Finishing with this small group were several thousand people who joined the march somewhere on the route. The marchers, together with the party members already in the Shensi soviet, brought the total number of Communists there to about 20,000.[2]

Shensi was not the Communists' destination when the march began. On the way, party leaders held an important meeting in the town of Tsunyi, in Kweichow, in January, 1935. It has long been thought that at that conference Mao Tse-tung and his followers criticized the party leadership for policies that had led to the loss of the soviet bases, that they challenged the leadership's authority, and that Mao was then chosen party leader. A careful recent study maintains that Mao did not acquire dominance over the party until the early 1940s. However, party command was changed at the Tsunyi Conference and Mao became at least "first among equals in a collective leadership."[3] The new leaders gave the Long March a destination and purpose: "Go north to fight the Japanese!" By "north" was meant the Shensi soviet, the only soviet still in existence. Late in 1936, the year after the march ended, the small Shensi town of Yenan became the Communist capital, the center of a great effort to rebuild the Communist movement.

Chiang Kai-shek's armies pursued the Communists throughout the Long March. Once Mao and his followers had reached Shensi, Chiang was not about to permit them to reorganize and expand without interruption. On the contrary, Chiang promptly began to plan new annihilation campaigns to eliminate the weakened remnants of his hated enemy once and for all. Not all Chiang's armies shared this feeling, however. In 1936 the Manchurian Army of Chang Hsüeh-liang known as the Young Marshal, faced the Communists. Chang's army had been deprived of its homeland five years earlier when the Japanese seized Manchuria. It was more interested in fighting Japan than the Communists, and there were many other Chinese who held the same attitude as Japanese aggression in China mounted.

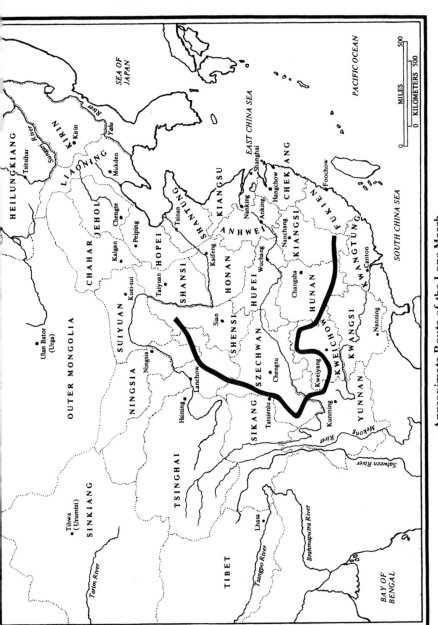

Approximate Route of the Long March

Ever since the conquest of Manchuria, the Japanese had been working to detach north China as well from the main body of the nation. They had created a string of regional administrations across north China with the fiction that each resulted from a local desire for regional autonomy. In the West, in Suiyuan, was the Autonomous Inner Mongolian Administration; east of it was the Hopei-Chahar Political Council, which administered those two provinces. This council maintained a link with Nanking, but all government troops and local agencies of the Kuomintang had to leave both provinces. Farther east, the East Hopei Autonomous Council was effectively controlled by Japan. With such a substantial beginning, the complete severance of north China by Japan seemed just a matter of time.

Chinese from every walk of life, but especially Chinese intellectuals, had been urging the government to resist Japanese encroachments by armed force. But Chiang Kai-shek had refused, arguing that the attainment of national unity through destruction of Communist power must precede war with Japan. Chiang had acquired German military advisers to help him create a powerful, modern, professional army, and he did not want conflict with Japan before such a force was trained and ready. On the face of it, this policy was not unreasonable; it was the policy of a prudent leader who wanted to acquire as much unity and strength as possible before facing a mortal challenge. However, with every passing year, opposition to his policy became more intense and vocal on the part of nationalistic Chinese, who included a number of military men. It certainly included the Manchurian officers and troops of Chang Hsüeh-liang's army, who responded sympathetically to the Communist appeal that Chinese should not fight Chinese, but should join together to fight Japan. By the winter of 1936 a virtual truce prevailed in the northwest, and Chang's headquarters in the Shensi capital of Sian was permeated with "United Front" thinking. In December Chiang Kai-shek flew to Sian to promote a more vigorous campaign against the Communists. Chang Hsüeh-liang and other Manchurian officers arrested the generalissimo in what has become known as the Sian Incident.

Chiang Kai-shek was held in custody for two weeks, and then released and returned to Nanking. The details of what transpired during those two weeks are still obscure, though it is known that the Communists, who had no part in the seizure of Chiang, immediately sent representatives to Sian to try to influence the outcome of the affair. Subsequent events made clear that during his incarceration Chiang came to some sort of understanding with the Communists to cooperate in resisting Japan. Probably Chiang became convinced that only by leading the nation against Japan could he continue to lead the nation at all. Urban intellectuals had been urging resistance for years; earlier, in 1936, the Kwangsi militarists had attracted much attention with their campaign to fight the Japanese; and now a non-Communist northern army had taken the most drastic action of all in order to press for the same policy. Such mounting pressure could not but impress Chiang. Moreover, the Communists apparently promised to accept his leadership in any anti-Japanese struggle.

The Communists, who many expected would work for the execution of their old enemy, advocated Chiang's release. There were several reasons for their doing so: Only by Chiang's release could they demonstrate the sincerity of their long-declared willingness to end the civil war in order to fight Japan; Chiang was not their prisoner to dispose of as they wished, and Chang Hsüeh-liang was determined to protect his personal safety; the Russians wanted Chiang released because they feared his death would lessen the chance of Chinese resistance to Japan, which the Russians wanted in order to keep the Japanese from Russian borders; pro-Japanese, anti-Communist elements in Nanking, whom only Chiang seemed able to restrain, were seizing the reins of power in Chiang's absence, and the Communists feared that their leadership would be less patriotic, and produce more disunity, than that of Chiang's.

The chief evidence about what was agreed upon at Sian is represented in the events that took place in the months following Chiang's release. The Communists declared their willingness to stop trying to overthrow the Kuomintang government, to redesignate Communist regions and armies as units under the national government, to stop confiscation of landlord lands, and to institute universal suffrage in their area. The Kuomintang did not respond formally to this proposal, but issued a set of four demands that closely paralleled the Communist offer. On the basis of these state-

ments, negotiations between the two parties continued and culminated in the United Front in 1937.

The Anti-Japanese War

Chinese disunity had always favored Japanese ambitions on the
mainland, for effective resistance was hardly possible on the part
of a China divided among warlords and torn by war between the
Kuomintang and Communists. But the apparent subordination of
Kwangtung and Kwangsi to the Nationalist Government in 1936,
and the unity augured by the Sian Incident and its aftermath,
helped some Japanese Army officers to decide to strike before
Chinese national unification became an even stronger reality. On
July 7, 1937, the Japanese initiated a local attack on Chinese near
Peiping. The Chinese fought back, and the Sino-Japanese War had
begun.

The Japanese offensive produced the most effective national
unity that China had known in a generation, at least temporarily.
Virtually all regional governments expressed support of the Kuomintang government in the national crisis. Most important, the Communists declared the Red Army to be part of the national armed
forces, under the ultimate command of Chiang Kai-shek, and the
Communist Party and the Kuomintang declared their intentions
to work together. Neither party publicly repudiated the United
Front until the end of the war in 1945, but actual cooperation between them was minimal and short-lived. Chiang's government
found it impossible to exercise effective command over the Communist armies. The government suppressed some Communist mass
associations, and the Communists denounced the refusal of the
government to arm its people in defense of the nation. Mutual denunciations led ultimately to clashes between government and
Communist troops. Thus, the two parties operated in different
regions, followed different policies, and generally functioned separately—particularly after troops of the two camps clashed in early
1941.

Given the disparate regional character of the armed forces, and their inferiority to the Japanese in technology and heavy armaments, the Chinese Government armies could not effectively employ positional warfare to resist the modern armies of Japan. Chiang Kai-shek, therefore, sought to trade space for time, all the while preserving his main forces. He reasoned that by retreating into China's vast hinterland, yielding territory to Japan, the invaders would soon reach the limit of their absorptive and administrative capacities; they did not have the men or resources to maintain firm control of a huge occupied territory, to keep their lines of communication secure, and still to exploit their conquest efficiently. While the Japanese struggled with those problems, the Chinese would have time to build up their strength and await the international assistance that Chiang expected would eventually come.

In accord with this strategy, the Kuomintang government and armies retreated first to Hankow, halfway up the Yangtze River, and then to Chungking, in the western province of Szechwan. Chungking became the capital of the government in late 1938, a status it held until the end of the war in 1945. Many urban Chinese from cities in Japanese-occupied territory streamed to the wartime capital. The Chinese dismantled more than 600 factories and carried them piece by piece to the interior, many to Chungking. Thousands of workers were also sent west. Students and teachers walked to Szechwan, taking precious books and equipment with them.

By the end of 1938 the Japanese had stopped their advance. They then controlled most of northern China and the eastern coastal regions extending inland as far as Hankow in the center of eastern China. To administer this enormous area, the Japanese developed puppet Chinese governments. They even succeeded in enticing Wang Ching-wei, the long-time Kuomintang leader, to defect to the Japanese side and head a puppet government in Nanking. After setting up their puppet administrations, the Japanese conducted limited troop operations, bombed Chungking and other cities, and waited for the Chinese Government to collapse.

The government did not collapse, but wartime conditions magnified some of its weaknesses. Until its move to the interior, the Kuomintang government found its primary support, and its chief sources of funds, in the cities of the eastern provinces, especially in the area of the lower Yangtze. Despite Chiang's attempt to re-

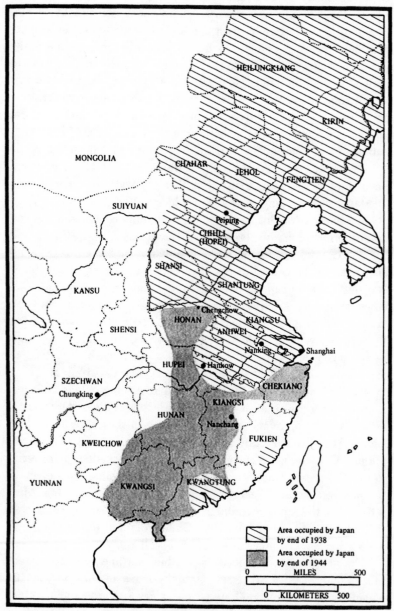

MONGOLIA

HEILUNGKIANG

KIRIN

CHAHAR

JEHOL

FENGTIEN

SUIYUAN

Peiping

CHIHLI
(HOPEI)

SHANSI

SHANTUNG

KANSU

Chengchow

HONAN

KIANGSU

SHENSI

ANHWEI

Nanking

Shanghai

HUPEI

Hankow

CHEKIANG

SZECHWAN

Chungking

KIANGSI

HUNAN

Nanchang

KWEICHOW

FUKIEN

YUNNAN

KWANGSI

KWANGTUNG

| | Area occupied by Japan by end of 1938 |
| | Area occupied by Japan by end of 1944 |

0 MILES 500

0 KILOMETERS 500

Japanese Invasion of China

invigorate Confucianism, and his reliance on the rural local gentry as the basis of national stability, the Kuomintang's urban base at least kept it exposed to various progressive influences. With the loss of these cities to Japan and the government's relocation in the western reaches of the country, it had to turn to the land tax for revenue; it therefore came to depend heavily on the landlords of interior China—particularly in Szechwan—a notoriously conservative group. This dependence strengthened the reactionary elements in the government and the Kuomintang. The government also felt threatened because it was in warlord territory, surrounded by militarists who felt but little loyalty to Chiang Kai-shek or his party. Partly for these reasons, the government became increasingly dictatorial and repressive.

A further weakness manifested itself in inflation. The government failed to develop revenues sufficient to meet wartime needs, and therefore "had no other recourse than inflation as a means of paying for the war."[4] Between 1937 and 1939, prices rose by 40 to 50 per cent a year, 160 per cent each of the following three years, and 300 per cent each year from 1942 to 1945. By 1943, the average salary of a civil bureaucrat was not more than 10 per cent of its 1937 value, and the salaries of other occupations had become similarly inadequate. The inflation impoverished the middle class, and encouraged corruption and speculation of all sorts.

In short, from 1938 to 1945 the Kuomintang government was in western China, substantially cut off from the rest of the country and the rest of the world, dominated by its most reactionary elements, and plagued by galloping inflation. Finally, Kuomintang military policies tended to weaken the armed forces. After 1941 the Chungking government increasingly counted on the United States to defeat Japan, and, in anticipation of a future war with the Communists, sought to conserve its own best forces. With regard to Japan, the government generally kept its armies on the defensive, but it also assigned large contingents of troops to enforce a blockade of the Communist territories in the northwest. These passive policies corroded morale in the government armies, already subverted by corruption of officers and neglect of the needs of the rank and file.

Despite these shortcomings, central government armies contributed to the anti-Japanese resistance. At the very beginning of the war, several crack units of the Nanking government put up a battle for Shanghai that attracted the attention and admiration of the world, though the Chinese suffered over a quarter of a million casualties in the process. When Shanghai was finally lost, Chinese fought with similar dogged courage to hold Nanking, but were again forced to retreat after heavy losses. The same process was repeated on a few later occasions; in each case the government's stance was defensive—it did not launch a single major offensive during the entire war—but the stubborn Chinese troops extracted a heavy price from the Japanese. Even during the years of relative quiet, the government armies kept large numbers of Japanese tied down; indeed, this drain on the Japanese resources was one great value of the China theater to the United States. In addition, some Kuomintang units participated in the Allied campaign in Southeast Asia.

As considerable as these achievements were, the Chiang government managed nonetheless to steadily alienate the Chinese people. Corruption, political repression, and inflation estranged the intellectuals and the urban middle class. More important from the standpoint of the government's military strength, the Kuomintang elite abused the peasants with incredible callousness. One of many possible illustrations of this abuse is the report of an American diplomat on his observations in southern Shensi in 1944, where he noted that the relations between the population and the Chinese military and civil authorities were bad because of the numerous and onerous taxes and because of the corruption and graft of government officials. "The poverty of the farming population, which is today very real, arises chiefly from the inordinate demands of the officials and the poor and oppressed farmers have been pressed almost to the point of desperation, and uprisings may result."[5]

It is even more astonishing that Kuomintang soldiers were treated with utter disregard for their health, their attitudes, and their lives. One of the many reasons for their low morale was that they could anticipate, if wounded, that their injuries might never be treated. American journalists in China at that time provided many moving descriptions of the famished, emaciated, hopeless men of the Chinese Army, but others, including American military

men, could also be eloquent on the subject. General Albert Wedemeyer, commander of American forces in China from late 1944 and
chief of staff to Chiang Kai-shek, sent Chiang a memorandum about
Chinese recruits which, he said, contained information that had
been carefully verified and would be of help to both of them in
their many intricate problems. Here are some excerpts from Wedemeyer's memorandum:

> Conscription comes to the Chinese peasant like famine or
> flood, only more regularly—every year twice—and claims more
> victims. Famine, flood, and drought compare with conscription
> like chicken pox with plague. Every disease has its stages. These
> are the stages of the most ravaging disease that sweeps China.
>
> First Stage
>
> Seasonal conscription occurs in spring and autumn. . . .
> There is first the press gang.
> For example, you are working in the field looking after your
> rice . . . [and] a number of uniformed men [come] who tie your
> hands behind your back and take you with them. . . . Hoe and
> plough rust in the field, the wife runs to the magistrate to cry and
> beg for her husband, the children starve. . . .
> Another way of being taken is arrest. If one man is wanted
> for conscription, the Hsienchang [county magistrate] arrests ten.
> Nine will be given a chance to buy their way out. The poorest
> stays in jail until the conscription officer takes him over.
>
> The conscription officers make their money in collaboration
> with the officials and through their press gangs. They extort big
> sums of money from conscripts which have been turned over to
> them by the officials and replace them with captives.
> Private dealers in conscripts have organized a trade. They are
> buying able bodied men from starved families who need rice
> more urgently than sons, or, they buy them from the Hsien-
> changs who have a surplus. . . .
>
> The Second Stage
>
> Having been segregated and herded together the conscripts
> are driven to the training camps. They are marched from Shensi
> to Szechuan and from Szechuan to Yun[n]an. Over endless roads
> they walk. . . . Many of those who run away run off during the

first few days. Later they are too weak to run away. Those who are caught are cruelly beaten. They will be carried along with broken limbs and with wounds in maimed flesh in which infection turns quickly into blood poisoning and blood poisoning into death.

As they march along they turn into skeletons; they develop signs of beriberi, their legs swell and their bellies protrude, their arms and thighs get thin. Scabies and ulcers turn their skin into a shabby cover of an emaciated body which has no other value than to turn rice into dung and to register the sharp pains of existence as a conscript in the Chinese army.[6]

Many recruits died before they reached training camp. Many of those who did manage to get to camp were sent to "hospitals," described in Wedemeyer's report as similar to German extermination camps at Buchenwald. And soldiers who survived training to reach the army at the front were still in a bad way, because the "Chinese army was starving to death in the field."[7]

It need hardly be added that such treatment did not produce strong fighting men, or ardent support for the Kuomintang government or its generals. Civilians, not surprisingly, were treated just as badly, and the result was at times militarily disastrous. In 1944, for example, Japanese forces launched an offensive in Honan. Thirty Chinese divisions were sent against the invaders, but some of the people of Honan helped the enemy; rarely did any of them help the Chinese troops, which proved to be a decisive factor in the Chinese defeat. The reason for the peasants' behavior was that Honan in 1944 was undergoing a terrible famine, and the Kuomintang government not only failed to render effective aid but pressed the starving people ruthlessly for taxes.

Completely different conditions prevailed in the "other China," the Communist regions. In the same way that many Chinese went to Chungking, the capital of "Free China," large numbers of young men and women made the long trek to Yenan, which for them was the chief symbol of resistance to Japan. During the anti-Japanese war, Communist organizations and territory expanded steadily—and membership in the Communist Party mushroomed. From approximately 40,000 members in 1937, the party grew to about 1.2 million by the end of the war in 1945. The Communist army also ballooned in size. Estimates of the number of Communist troops in 1937 vary from 45,000 to 90,000; estimates of Communist troop strength in 1945 also vary, ranging from about 500,000 to 900,000. Even if only the lower figures are valid, they represent a tenfold increase in the regular armed forces—and in absolute terms a large army in 1945. These figures relate only to the Communists' regular army, including trained guerrilla soldiers; they do not include a People's Militia of more than 2 million men.[8]

Communist territorial expansion took place behind Japanese lines as well as in Kuomintang areas. Historians of this period often say that the Japanese "conquered" the provinces of north China and those along the eastern coast, and in a sense that term is correct, though imprecise. In their swift thrust into China, the Japanese conquered the cities and the chief lines of communications between the cities. The conquest of the rural areas between the cities and the railroads was necessarily a much slower task because there were few roads or facilities for Japan's motorized army. It was in those rural areas, behind the Japanese-occupied urban centers, that the Communists gradually organized local and regional governments that exercised political authority, collected taxes, administered public services, and generally exercised all the normal prerogatives of government, including defense. These rural areas were called anti-Japanese bases. The first one emerged in the rugged border region between three provinces and was called the Shansi-Hopei-Chahar Border Region. Other border-region governments were also established, and the term "Border Region" is sometimes used loosely as a synonym for anti-Japanese base.

As the war progressed, anti-Japanese bases developed throughout north and east-central China. The juxtaposition of Japanese conquests and Communist bases was comparable to a checkerboard on which the Japanese controlled all the grid lines, with cities at the points of intersection, and the Communist-led resistance gradually expanded to fill all the squares between the lines. By the end of the war in 1945, a thick string of these bases stretched across all of north China, and south along the eastern coast to Shanghai and beyond. They contained a population estimated as high as 100 million —about one-fifth of the population of China. Although physically separated from one another by Japanese-controlled areas—the lines on the checkerboard—the anti-Japanese bases were united through the Communist Party, which provided leadership in all the areas.

The most significant reason for this extraordinary expansion was that the Communists gained the enthusiastic support of the mass of the Chinese peasants in north China. They achieved this backing by meeting the local, immediate needs of the peasants through reformist and radical social policies, and by providing leadership for the defense of peasant communities against the Japanese. In this fashion the Communists won peasant confidence and in the process began the transformation—the modernization—of rural China.

The Japanese invasion did not immediately provoke a great cry of rage, or an implacable determination to resist, on the part of the Chinese peasantry. Millions of peasants were but little touched by the currents of change that had long ago appeared in Chinese cities, and they did not share the intense anti-imperialist feelings so typical among Chinese intellectuals, especially from the time of the May Fourth Movement. Peasants harbored antiforeign feelings that derived from their traditional ethnocentrism and conservatism, occasionally spiced with specific resentments about such foreign innovations as railroads and churches. But these feelings would not normally have driven the peasantry to armed action against foreigners. Japanese brutality, on the other hand, virtually forced the peasantry to vigorous resistance.

At best, the Japanese invaders were a scourge on the Chinese land. They commonly seized chickens and provisions from the peasants, who had little enough to begin with. They sometimes simply shot Chinese soldiers rather then keep them prisoners, and they treated the civilian population cruelly. This harshness became ferocious brutality when there was a sign of opposition to the invaders. From 1938 to the end of the war, the Japanese army conducted "mopping up" campaigns in the countryside to extirpate resistance. Villages were razed, young men were selected from the population for public execution, women were maltreated. These campaigns subjected the peasants to such indiscriminate terror that they had little choice but to resist; nonresistance in no way assured security.

This terroristic policy was intensified in 1941 and 1942 when the Japanese initiated their "three-all" policy in north China: "kill all, burn all, destroy all." The Japanese would surround an area and destroy everything within it, including many, most, or all the inhabitants, in order to frighten Chinese generally and to produce such extensive desolation that guerrilla fighters would be denied substantive support. Such extreme terror was not used in all occupied areas. The three-all policy was employed in portions of north China, where Japanese policies were generally more ruthless than those used in the central part of the country. Where it was used, it transformed peasants from patient farmers to determined resistance fighters. They formed resistance groups to defend their local communities, and the Communists provided the weapons, training, general assistance, and leadership they needed. The Communists also linked one local group to another through party communications and organization into what gradually emerged as an anti-Japanese-war base.

In other areas, where resistance groups did not grow spontaneously, the Communists attempted to create them. They were aided in this task by the fact that officials of the Kuomintang government had, in many instances, fled from the occupied areas, leaving a governmental vacuum. Units of the Red Army tried to fill that vacuum where they found it by organizing new governments; in the process they also devised resistance measures. In this way, the Communists intensified the anti-Japanese struggle, provided regional government for peasants, and assumed the overall leadership in both government and resistance operations.

Anti-Japanese activity was only part of the Communists' appeal. The other part was their social policy and program. During the earlier period of the Chinese Soviet Republic, the Communists had confiscated and redistributed landlord holdings. The United Front with the Kuomintang necessitated moderating that policy, however, so during the war the official Communist policy called for a reduction of rent and a reduction of interest. At the same time, border-region governments were to guarantee the payment of rent and of interest to the landlord and the moneylender. The peasant, of course, was instantly much better off. The Communists also confiscated the land of rich families who fled to Japanese-controlled cities or in any way cooperated with the Japanese, and distributed it to poor peasants. Here, too, the peasant benefited. Many landlords fled to Kuomintang-controlled regions; the border-region gov-

ernments would then take over such land for "temporary" use, and
offer it to poor peasants and to immigrants coming from outside the
border region. The Communists introduced a new tax system that
favored the poor, but that was by no means confiscatory for the
rich. Nonetheless, it was designed to discriminate against income
from rents so as to encourage landlords to sell land to their tenants
and invest their surplus capital in industry instead of land.

The communists in the border regions restructured political relations to limit the power of the gentry and give the peasants a
voice and participatory role in government at all levels—a power
they had never before known. Local governments were in the hands
of groups of delegates elected by all adult villagers, and any dele-
gate could be recalled at any time he displeased his electors.
Elected "people's councils" were the chief organs of political power
at the district and regional levels. The peasants were also organized
into a host of mass associations, such as those for women, youth,
and workers. These mass associations had a voice in local and
regional government, and engaged in various public projects connected with the war or with economic and social improvement.
Furthermore, the Communists seized every opportunity to offer
rudimentary education to the peasants by formal and informal
means.

In short, in every way possible the Communists attempted to
help the mass of poor peasants, to persuade and educate them, and
in the process to gain their support. There is no doubt that they
succeeded. Communist Party members often constituted a minority
in local and regional governments—indeed, party policy was to
limit members to one-third of government positions—but the leadership abilities of that minority, and the widespread popular confidence in the integrity and purpose of the Communist Party,
assured that Communist programs and policies were invariably
approved by the people's governments.

The Communist wartime policies are usually labeled "moderate,"
but they were essentially far from that. Even ignoring the cases
where land was confiscated, the reduction of rent, taxes, and interest, when actually enforced, marked a radical change in rural
China. The shattering of the gentry's monopoly of local power and

the involvement of the poor peasantry in politically important community roles were profound changes that neither the gentry nor the peasantry considered merely "moderate." Such changes, indeed, signaled the beginning of a social revolution. In addition, as will be discussed in the next chapter, Communist wartime propaganda nurtured a *national* consciousness, and thus fostered national integration.

It is impossible to weigh precisely the contribution that each of these factors—leadership of the resistance and implementation of social reforms—made to the expansion and strength of the Communists during the anti-Japanese war. Some scholars stress one, and some the other. Yet it is rather curious that there should be disagreement over this question, because both the Communist social program and anti-Japanese activities were two aspects of a single policy.

The issue is confused by the fact that the anti-Japanese war bases were organized at different times, in different places, and inevitably under somewhat different circumstances. There were general basic similarities, of course, especially in the structure and functioning of the bases after they were established. But the nature of the initial Communist appeal depended upon local conditions. The anti-Japanese aspect was most influential in those regions that suffered most from Japanese abuse; it was the dominant factor in areas where peasant resistance groups came into existence spontaneously, and then accepted Communist offers of aid and leadership. Peasants who had not suffered Japanese cruelties were more likely to respond to Communist reform measures. For example, in the Shensi-Kansu-Ninghsia Border Region, which had little direct contact with the Japanese, the patriotic appeal to the peasants fell on deaf ears "when divorced from consideration of political, economic, and social reform."[9] We have already noted that in Honan Chinese peasants treated Chinese armies as hostile forces, and gave modest aid to the Japanese, because they felt the Chinese forces did not merit support on social grounds. In Shansi propagandists from Yen Hsi-shan tried to marshal support for the war effort but found the peasants cold and unresponsive. Yet these were the same peasants who responded with enthusiasm when Communists entered the province early in 1936 and provided 15,000 volunteers for the Red Army in less than two months. After the war began, those peasants participated effectively in the Communist guerrilla operations.

Despite such local variations, the link between social reform and resistance activity was in substantial measure dictated by the nature of guerrilla warfare. There had to be support from the people, identification of interests between the people and the resistance fighters for guerrilla warfare to be successful. Such unity could hardly exist where the people felt frustrated and resentful over economic or political abuses. Mao Tse-tung certainly had no doubt about the close relationship between the two factors. In 1937 he told a class graduating from the Red Military Academy in Yenan:

> Now our Party and our army must have these two guiding principles: first, to concentrate our army to fight the enemy in the most effective way; second, to disperse our political forces to work among the Chinese masses, and rouse them thoroughly to join the struggle for national liberation and the democratic revolution.
>
> In order to rouse the masses to support us, we must improve their own livelihood. We must abolish heavy taxes, and lighten the economic burden of the masses.[10]

It boiled down to this: in areas mobilized by Japanese brutality, anti-Japanese leadership was the chief Communist attraction, though effective resistance necessitated the kind of cooperation between government and people that social reforms could foster. In other areas, social reforms were the major appeal, and were used to involve the peasant in the anti-Japanese resistance movement, and the process of nation building.

It has often been said that the Communist program was a fraud, that Communists were not interested in fighting the Japanese, but only in expanding their power vis-à-vis the Kuomintang. To bolster this view, some allege that a once secret Communist document has revealed that Communist official policy was "70 per cent expansion, 20 per cent dealing with the Kuomintang and 10 per cent resisting Japan." A careful recent analysis concludes that this allegation is itself a fabrication.[11] It might be noted that expansion of Communist territorial control was by its nature anti-Japanese. The objective of the Chinese behind Japanese lines was not to seize railroads or cities, which they obviously could not hold against Japanese power, but to compel the Japanese to spend more and more energy and treasure to defend their holdings, and simultaneously to deprive the invaders as much as possible from profiting from their occupation. In gaining these ends, the Communists were superbly successful.

The Second World War ended abruptly in August, 1945. To Americans, it had been a long, grueling struggle. It occurred to few of them that it had been more than twice as long for the Chinese, and much more than twice as hard in terms of casualties, civilian suffering, and economic depletion. The Chinese had fought against Japan for four years and five months *before* the attack on Pearl Harbor involved other powers in the fight. Japanese surrender came only after nearly four additional years of fighting, a total of more than eight years of war. During that time the Chinese had made a substantial contribution to the Allied war effort. To give but one example: approximately one-quarter of the Japanese killed in all theaters were killed in China. But the cost was also enormous for the Chinese. It was enormous in lives and in national wealth, and when the war ended millions of ordinary Chinese looked for peace and order. But that was not to be; the defeat of Japan merely brought to a head the long-building confrontation between the Kuomintang government and the Chinese Communist Party.

Civil War 1945–1949

It is absurd to speak of an historical event as "inevitable," but the Communist–Kuomintang civil war almost demands that adjective. It is difficult in retrospect to see how it could have been avoided. An abyss of profound hostility and distrust, and the scars of brutal conflict, separated the two parties, to say nothing of their utterly different social philosophies. The instant the Japanese war ended, Communist and government troops raced to seize strategic areas from the Japanese occupiers. In the process, troop units of the two sides clashed with one another.

The two parties also started negotiations that were to sputter on and off for the following year and a half. Neither side wanted to seem responsible for again firing up the civil war, a posture dictated not only by the exhausted state of China, and the demands of politically articulate Chinese, but by the potential for American involvement. The American interest was expressed by the participation of Ambassador Patrick Hurley in the negotiations in the autumn of 1945, and by the arrival of General George C. Marshall in the closing days of the year. Marshall came as the personal envoy of President Harry Truman to help stop hostilities between the Communists and the Kuomintang, and to help bring about the political unification of the country. Marshall remained in China, mediating negotiations, until the beginning of 1947, but there was never really much chance that the talks could succeed. The Communists would not turn their army and territories over to governmental control until the government became something more than an extension of the Kuomintang, Chiang Kai-shek's personal party. They advocated the creation of a coalition government in which the Communists and other Chinese political parties would have a genuine share of national political power. Chiang Kai-shek, however, feared that a coalition government would simply put the Communist camel's nose in the Kuomintang's tent. He assured the Communists and the Americans that political liberalization would certainly come, but that the Communists should first give up their army. In the Communist view, surrender of their troops would leave them vulnerable to destruction as individuals and as a political party. This irreducible core of conflict could not be negotiated away. The American mediation, probably a mistake from the outset, was compromised by the fact that the United States continued to provide military aid to one party in the negotiations, the Kuomintang. By early 1947, the talks collapsed. Only a military solution was then possible.

Some Kuomintang leaders anticipated quick victory. Government armies outnumbered the Communist troops by four or five to one, and were far better supplied with weapons and military equipment. The Communists possessed no aircraft, and virtually no heavy armament, whereas the government had heavy guns and a small air force. At the time of the Japanese surrender, the government forces had been at something of a geographic disadvantage, for they were largely grouped in south and southwest China, while most of north China was controlled by Communists. But Americans had airlifted Kuomintang troops to northern cities, and government units also had entered eastern Manchuria. Despite warnings by American advisers that the move into Manchuria was a mistake, the prospects apparently seemed bright to Kuomintang strategists. During the two years following the cessation of negotiations, however, relative military strength shifted in favor of the Communists; Communist ranks grew while Kuomintang armies shrank, and the Communists acquired mountains of weapons and material from their defeated enemies. Russian troops in Manchuria gave them large stores of weapons seized from surrendered Japanese. The erosion of government strength, and the concurrent expansion of Communist power, reached the point in late 1947 where the Communists began to depart from their reliance on highly mobile, limited engagements, and increasingly they challenged government armies in positional battles. In 1948, the Communists completed the conquest of Manchuria, and were free to throw their full strength into central China. They moved from victory to victory. In April, 1949, they crossed the mighty barrier of the Yangtze with no effective opposition and advanced with incredible speed to the southern border. In the autumn of 1949, Mao Tse-tung formally proclaimed the establishment of the People's Republic of China, and during the following few months the last pockets of Kuomintang resistance were eliminated. In the meantime, Chiang Kai-shek and his closest followers, with some two million troops and frightened citizens, had fled to Taiwan.

What explains this stunning reversal? What accounts for the Communist victory in China?

In answering that question, as in comparing the Kuomintang and the Communists during the anti-Japanese war, there is the danger of picturing the Kuomintang as invariably corrupt, repressive, and ineffective, and the Communists as consistently principled, popular, and efficient—the good guys against the bad guys. Of course, neither side had a monopoly of honesty or ability, but when comparing the general patterns of the two sides' policies and practices the contrast is in fact extremely sharp.

The Communist achievement was first of all military; it is partly explicable in purely military terms. Communist leadership was excellent from top to bottom. Chu Teh and Mao Tse-tung carefully dealt with military realities, and gave no weight to considerations of prestige and face that often guided Chiang Kai-shek. Mao developed a clear and practicable long-range strategy that put into effect a fast, mobile warfare aimed at the destruction of Kuomintang armies rather than at the seizure of territory. Chiang Kai-shek, on the other hand, gave so little evidence of following a strategic plan that the chief American military adviser asked if one even existed. Chiang evidently did have a strategy, but it was a bad one; it envisaged the seizure and retention of cities, even where Communist control of the surrounding countryside left his troops dependent upon airlifted supplies. On occasion, Chiang tried to direct distant battles by telegraph, sometimes even neglecting to inform his staff what was going on. Communist field commanders were selected on merit, and given wide latitude to use their own judgment. They generally waged bold, aggressive, sometimes brilliant campaigns. Kuomintang generals, on the contrary, were commonly chosen on grounds of political loyalty to Chiang Kai-shek, and many who qualified on this basis demonstrated professional mediocrity or outright incompetence. Some of China's best strategists and most able commanders were denied critical posts, and those who finally were assigned commands found it difficult to obtain necessary supplies. Time after time, battles were lost because of the simple incompetence of government officers.

Leadership of government forces was further disrupted by frequent turnover of high officers and by the reluctance of generals to cooperate with one another, whereas the Communist armies were marked by continuity of command and a willingness to work together for the common goal. Some government commanders gave little attention to such matters as the regular distribution of supplies and weapons to their men, or the organization of adequate medical services. Not only incompetence but corruption too was rampant among Kuomintang generals, who stole and sold government property, sometimes to the Communists.

One particularly conspicuous instance of Kuomintang incompetence was the ineffective use of its air force. The Communists had no aircraft; hence, government planes dominated the skies and could have been used tellingly in various ways. But they were not; on a few occasions bombing strikes were attempted, but the planes flew so high and dropped so carelessly that the attacks had no value whatsoever.

With such leadership, morale in the government armies was understandably, at rock bottom. Nor did the deplorable conditions that still prevailed in the army after the anti-Japanese war help. The soldiers were inadequately paid and fed; training was poor to nonexistent; discipline was bad; the rank and file did not know what they were fighting for, and thus saw no reason to fight. The reluctance of the troops to engage the enemy was intensified by the defensive tactics that government commanders favored; to the disgust of American advisers, instead of moving out from the city walls to engage the enemy where there was room to maneuver, the government troops normally retired within the city to fire from behind its walls and await help which rarely came. But one reason for the government's inclination toward defensive tactics was precisely because they provided its troops with less opportunity to go over to the Communist side than when fighting in open country. As the war proceeded, the fear of such defections—which often occurred —became an important factor in every battle situation. The Communists encouraged defections by indoctrinating captured troops with Communist peasant and national policies and then allowing them to return to their units if they wished. Some remained with the Communists, but many who went back would never be implacable anti-Communist warriors.

Exactly opposite traits characterized the Communist forces. Soldiers were well cared for, well trained, thoroughly indoctrinated about the need and purpose of the struggle. The intelligent Communist strategy of fighting only when success seemed assured cultivated a feeling of victory among the Communist soldiers, and stimulated a spirit of boldness and offense that contrasted vividly with the defensive spirit of the government units. Morale in the Communist units was high.

Scholars in the West have disagreed about the extent to which the Communist conquest of China was a product of popular support. Some have claimed that the Communists rode to power on the crest of a peasant revolution not unlike those that led to the establishment of new dynasties in China since time immemorial. Others have argued that the conquest can be assessed only in military terms, that it was decided by military factors.

The desire of many Americans to view the civil war purely in military terms seems to derive partly from a post-1949 reluctance to acknowledge that Communists can have genuine popular support. Indeed, in the 1940s, especially during the anti-Japanese war, many Americans doubted that the Chinese Communists were genuine Communists. American diplomatic reports, for example, often referred to the "Communists," in quotation marks, and journalists were similarly skeptical despite the insistence of the best-informed writers—and the Communists themselves—that they were the real thing. The chief reason for Western skepticism was that the Communists did not collectivize the land or kill landlords, and they were thought to have established "democratic" governments and worked for peasant welfare and honest government, traits that many Americans could not bring themselves to attribute to Communists outside of quotation marks. At the time of the civil war, however, nobody doubted the "Communists' " extensive and enthusiastic popular support. After 1949, their wartime popularity was increasingly minimized as it was discovered that the "Communists" were in fact Communists, and discussion of their popular backing might be construed as approval of their government and policies. Yet without question the Communist armies enjoyed broad support among the peasantry.

Communist policies governing the anti-Japanese war bases has already been examined. To the peasants in those regions, the wartime Communist administration was the best government they had ever known. Their confidence was the unshakable base enjoyed by the Communists when the civil war began, and it was never seriously weakened throughout the years of struggle with the Kuomintang. Further, the Communists continued the practices during the civil war that had earlier elicited popular approval: soldiers did not abuse civilians; they paid for what they used; troops helped the peasantry when the opportunity or need arose. Wherever Communists acquired territorial power, they instituted honest government and a series of political and economic reforms that benefited the peasants.

In the course of the civil war, agrarian policies in the Communist base areas became increasingly radical. Shortly after the Japanese surrender, the Communist authorities reaffirmed the moderate wartime land policy of reduced rent and reduced interest— without confiscation of land. Even so, local authorities turned over landlord lands to the poor peasants in some communities. In 1946 the Communist Party approved these seizures, and a year later came out with a directive that formally launched a comprehensive social revolution in the countryside. On October 10, 1947, Mao promulgated a land law that was designed to realize the long-discussed goal of "land to the tillers." The law abolished the land-ownership rights of all landlords and organizations. It authorized village peasant associations to combine the confiscated land with the rest of the village acreage and distribute the total equally among all residents of the village, young and old, male and female. Moreover, the animals, tools, and other properties of landlords and "surplus" animals and implements of rich peasants were equally subject to confiscation and redistribution. Finally, the law canceled all debts incurred in the countryside to that time.

Without much question, this revolutionary program commanded the enthusiasm of the majority of peasants. They already supported the Communist government because of its eight or nine years of honesty in the resistance areas, a support manifested in their volunteering for Communist armies, helping in military transport and supply, and fighting as militia members. Mao's land reform, coming as it did *during* the civil war, added to the peasants' enthusiasm for the Communist cause.

In sum, Communist victory was built on the basis of the political and military organization of the anti-Japanese bases, and the legitimacy and moral authority derived from honest government and effective action against the invader. After 1945 that legitimacy and authority continued because of the memory of the Communists' wartime achievements and because of their accelerating program of social revolution on behalf of the poor peasants. Given the conditions that existed in China during the civil war, the question of military victory and of popular support are not separate issues, but two aspects of the same phenomenon. Certainly, American Government personnel in China at the time, as well as other American and foreign observers, had no doubt about the reasons for the Communists' successes. They sent forth a chorus of criticism of the government's refusal to take the only measures that offered any hope of survival: reform designed to regain some measure of popular approval of the Kuomintang.

The crucial and major element in popular support of the Communists was that rendered by the peasantry, for the peasants constituted the vast majority of China's population, filled the Communist armies, and provided the food, intelligence, and various forms of help needed if the Red Armies were to fight a guerrilla war. And it was to the peasants—especially the poor peasants—that the Communist program had its greatest appeal. Communist policies and ideology, however, were not without attraction to the other chief classes in Chinese society: the intellectuals, the students, and the middle class.

Aside from the peasants, the intellectuals constituted the most important other class in China. Intellectuals had been fiercely anti-imperialistic, at least from the time of the 1919 May Fourth Movement, and this attitude had become more intense as time brought repeated imperialistic outrages. The Chinese Communists were the most uncompromisingly anti-imperialist party in the country. They viewed imperialism as a product of capitalism, and thus Marxist-Leninist orthodoxy supplemented Chinese nationalist indignation. This stance naturally elicited a favorable response from intellectuals.

The unequal treaties were terminated in 1943, but the issue of imperialism remained very much alive during the civil-war period, with the United States considered the chief imperialist villain. In 1946 and 1947 students demonstrated against "the violent actions of American military personnel in China," which referred in particular to an alleged rape of a Peking student by two American servicemen. In the spring of 1948 another student movement agitated against American plans to rehabilitate the economy of Japan, China's erstwhile enemy. That the United States also supported the Kuomintang subtly linked that party with Japan and with imperialism generally. The sincerity and firmness of the Communist anti-imperialist attitude seemed confirmed in the spring of 1949, when a British naval frigate started up the Yangtze to take supplies to the British embassy at Nanking. The frigate clashed with Communist troops, and ultimately made its way back to Shanghai with many dead and wounded and severe damage to the ship. The incident demonstrated precisely the kind of implacable firmness vis-à-vis imperialist powers that Chinese intellectuals most wanted to see.

The Kuomintang's response to student movements and political agitation progressively alienated the students from the government. Students wanted an end to civil war, and the creation of a coalition government, but there is no evidence that they were enthusiastic about the prospects of a Communist government. The Kuomintang, however, responded to student political activities with such severity and arbitrary force that the young people became increasingly disenchanted with it, and thus increasingly willing to accept the Communist alternative.

Marxism-Leninism also had its attractions for Chinese intellectuals. Indeed, from the middle of the 1920s Marxist concepts and assumptions permeated the Chinese intellectual world, influencing the thinking of many who were not Communists in any direct political sense. Marxist class analysis, for example, had an appeal because it enabled nationalists to account for China's apparent backwardness in the nineteenth and twentieth centuries in terms of the shortcomings of the old Chinese ruling class, and thus avoided any implication that *national* deficiencies were involved. Thus nationalist intellectuals could take pride in the Chinese past—the people's past, the nation's past—even while denouncing much of the Chinese tradition—the gentry's tradition—as semifeudal, exploitative, backward. Conversely, Marxism-Leninism denounced not only contemporary China, but most contemporary Western countries. Acceptance of Communism seemed to imply that China was moving to the head of the march of history, jumping ahead of all those nations that had for years arrogantly asserted their own superiority and China's backwardness. It was a shortcut to self-respect for intellectuals who had so long been shamed by China's national power inferiority. Kuo Mo-jo, a prominent leftist intellectual, felt that by adhering to Marxism-Leninism he could "join forces with history and regain his sense of pride and responsibility as a participating member of an ancient culture with a badly bruised sense of self-esteem."[12]

Marxism purported to be scientific—"scientific socialism"—and that, too, was an attraction to those intellectuals who, from the beginning of the twentieth century, had been enamored of science and viewed it as the essence of modernity. In addition, the traditional anticommercial orientation of Chinese scholars was still a part of the outlook of twentieth-century intellectuals; they were predisposed to be anticapitalist, and to that extent inclined to sympathize with the Communists. This attitude was perhaps strengthened by the fact that the chief imperialist powers had always been capitalist powers.

Finally, after the May Fourth Movement many intellectuals had more or less come to accept the idea that China could never be a strong power until its peasants were liberated from tradition and ignorance. This view was held rather academically, and did not produce much practical action on the part of most non-Communist intellectuals; it did not alter the alienation from the countryside that characterized the elite. Nevertheless, it was there, and the Communists' demonstration that they could actually communicate with the peasant, and bring him into the national fold, was another persuasive argument for their cause among intellectuals.

Whereas Communism had these various appeals for Chinese intellectuals, the Kuomintang offered them little more than a return to a tradition that they had long ago rejected as sterile and irrelevant to the modern world. The most appealing aspects of the Kuomintang—its supposed commitment to constitutionalism, democracy, and Westernization—were so flagrantly violated in practice that they had little positive effect on intellectuals.

Little is known about the attitude of China's small proletariat toward Communism. Because it was small, politically repressed, and economically exploited, it generally maintained a discreet silence. But it seems reasonable to suppose that the workers saw many advantages in the ascendancy of a party that claimed to put the interests of the proletariat before all others.

The middle class in the cities—merchants, professionals, businessmen of all types, technicians—had ties with the student-intellectual class, and shared some of their views, although generally they assumed a fairly moderate stance. The corruption and incompetence of Kuomintang rule convinced many of them that

Chiang and his party were hopeless. The inflation of the anti-Japanese-war period had continued to accelerate during the years of the civil war, and salaried people simply could not support their families, although many businessmen made large profits from the inflation. Many in the middle class were aware that Communists had demonstrated their capacity to maintain economic stability and order on a regional level, and therefore might be expected to do it on the national level. Most businessmen, naturally supported the Kuomintang, fearing what might happen to them under a Communist regime. Yet even some of them felt that if a Communist regime should come to pass, a long period of development and preparation would have to take place before private enterprise was eliminated, or even drastically curtailed—an impression that Communist statements strengthened. More than any other group, the urban middle class probably held a variety of views about the Communists, not all of them unfavorable.

Communist rule, then, seemed to promise something for everyone, the best of the real available alternatives. But why should those who sought a democratic government have to choose between a moribund Kuomintang and a Communist Party that was vigorous but whose long range program involved political and economic changes unwelcome to many intellectuals and middle-class Chinese? Was there no other alternative? After a century of contact with the whole range of Western political thought and experience, and many decades during which Chinese studied in Western countries, were there no liberals in China?

The Liberal Alternative

When General George C. Marshall left China at the beginning of 1947, acknowledging that his efforts at mediation had failed, he remarked that the "salvation of the situation . . . would be the assumption of leadership by the liberals in the Government and in the minority parties, a splendid group of men. . . ."[13] The possibility of such a solution appealed to Americans who were alienated by the repugnant aspects of the Kuomintang, but could not view the ascendancy of the Communists with equanimity. But it was a futile hope: Chinese liberalism was much too weak for such a task.

From the very beginning of the republic, a few scattered individuals in China might reasonably be described as liberals. They advocated a popular-based government functioning in accord with the rule of law, they opposed narrow nationalism, and they thought most problems would yield to the disciplined use of man's rational faculties. The May Fourth Movement fostered several new isms, including liberalism; Hu Shih, then best known for his advocacy of the vernacular style in writing, became the most prominent liberal in later decades. By and large, the liberals remained in the intellectual and professional worlds rather than enter the realm of political activism. But some became members of the Kuomintang, several made brief forays into warlord politics, and a few became involved in the so-called minority parties.

Despite the Kuomintang's monopoly of power, it tolerated the existence of several small parties or groups during the 1930s and 1940s. The Youth Party, for example, was a reactionary organization centered among the landlords and politicians of Szechwan. The National Socialist Party—which became the Democratic Socialist Party in 1946—consisted of its leader, Carsun Chang, and a scattered following of academics and personal supporters. The Third Party claimed to follow the principles accepted by the Kuomintang in 1924 and 1926, before the split with the Communists, but it had only a skeletal organization and few adherents. There were other groups with even less political force. Obviously, these parties cannot all be described as liberal. But even the most conservative of them needed more freedom from Kuomintang control in order to seek their goals. Therefore in the fall of 1939 these parties came together in a loose association to coordinate their attempts to gain political concessions from the Kuomintang. They achieved very little, and two years later a similar attempt to create a federation of parties also foundered on the vigorous opposition of Chiang Kai-shek.

As the government showed itself unable to solve the problems of war and inflation, a wave of criticism arose inside as well as outside the party. In response, the Kuomintang eased its controls somewhat, and allowed the minority parties to resume activity. This led, in 1944 to the organization of the China Democratic League; it was created not as a federation of parties, as in the earlier organizational attempts, but as a party of individuals, although members of the minority parties joined the league. Not all members of the Democratic League were liberals, and not all liberals supported the league, but the party nevertheless was the closest thing to an organized political movement of Chinese liberalism. Its goals included democratic government through constitutional rule or coalition government, the prevention of the resurgence of the civil war, basic civil liberties, and the formation of a genuinely national army in place of the existing party armies.

When the civil conflict began to spread after the Japanese surrender, the Democratic League and other minor parties tried more vigorously than ever to become a third force in Chinese politics. The Kuomintang had been hostile to the league from the outset, but it still did not resort to official suppression, probably because of concern about the possible reaction of Americans. However, there were instances of harassment, intimidation, and brutality against league members. The homes of leaders were ransacked, and in 1946 two leading liberals were publicly assassinated.

The minor parties were allowed to participate in the discussions mediated by Americans in China, and, as noted above, some of their leaders impressed General Marshall. However, when the negotiations came to an end, and undisguised civil war broke out, the government's attitude became increasingly harsh, and culminated during the fall of 1947 in outlawing the Democratic League because of its association with "Communist bandits." Superficially, there was some truth to that accusation; in the preceding months some league members had come closer to the Communist Party because Kuomintang repression seemed to give them no other real alternative. In any event, the platform of the Communist Party at that time offered much that even the most conscientious independents could approve. With the dissolution of the league, the life of China's best-known "liberal" party came to an end, although it was resuscitated as one of the "democratic parties" in the People's Republic of China in 1949.

The chief causes of Chinese liberalism's political impotence are fairly evident. The basic reason is simply that liberalism assumes a stable context in which to function, and that did not exist in China. The Kuomintang government claimed to be in the tutelage stage, teaching the country how to operate constitutional government, but constitutionalism was still a plan for the future, not a reality. The rule of law generally did not prevail in China. Laws were bent, broken, and simply ignored by corrupt officials and arrogant militarists. The liberals' faith in reason and legal processes could not resist dictatorship and militarism.

To the extent that the minority parties, particularly the Democratic League, sought liberal goals, their weaknesses were weaknesses of Chinese liberalism. They were divided by personal and factional loyalties, opportunism, and complete lack of grass roots support. None of the parties had an army. Mao Tse-tung's often quoted and frequently denounced maxim that political power grows out of the barrel of a gun was no more than a simple statement of the truth, at least with respect to early twentieth century China: Warlord power was based on armed force. The Kuomintang government existed only because of Chiang Kai-shek's troops. The Communists were almost exterminated until they acquired their own army. In such a context, political groups that did not have armies survived largely on the sufferance of those that did.

The liberal movement as an intellectual movement was largely confined to Westernized intellectuals, especially academics, and the minority parties embraced only a slightly larger circle of bureaucrats, professional, and business people. These people had their own political weaknesses, which became the weaknesses of liberalism: they had individualistic political ideas; many were averse to the grubbiness of the political arena; they viewed themselves as specialists, experts in their own fields, who as citizens could criticize the political policies of others but who did not have the experience or expertise to develop their own; some businessmen did not yet command the capital, or were too tied up with foreign industry, to develop a great deal of independent political impact; their political ideas were in substantial measure drawn from alien circumstances that had limited relevance to Chinese realities.

For all these reasons, the liberals basically had very little political power. They had some influence which derived from the respect traditionally accorded intellectuals in China. They were admired by foreigners and had many foreign contacts, which could be translated into a certain amount of political influence in a government that relied heavily on foreign cooperation. Some members of the minority parties, not necessarily liberals, also had personal contacts with important individuals and cliques on the political scene, and could thus exert influence in that time-honored fashion. But in the final analysis, all these assets were peripheral. The liberals could not mount a genuinely serious challenge to the Kuomintang government or to the Communists. In those circumstances, the liberal alternative was no alternative at all.

It is clear that a host of factors went into the Communist success: Communist organizational abilities, the military talents of Communist generals, the attractions of Maoist ideology, the disastrous effect of inflation on the Kuomintang and its supporters, the assistance rendered by the Russians in aiding and arming the Communists in Manchuria, the political perspicacity of Mao Tsetung and his associates, the short-sightedness, arrogance, incompetence, and dishonesty of so many Kuomintang leaders. But the central factor was unquestionably the mobilization of vast numbers of Chinese, primarily peasants, into new political, social, economic, and military organizations, infused with a new purpose and a new spirit. This mobilization largely accounted for the Communist victory, but its significance went beyond that. It marked the beginning of the reintegration of China into a modern nation.

IX

National Reintegration

THE COMMUNIST POLICIES that proved so effective in the Sino-Japanese War, and in the civil war that followed, produced a high level of integration in Communist areas, and marked a significant step toward national reintegration. Communists extended their activities behind Japanese lines until they governed most of north China and about 20 per cent of China's population. By 1949 they had governed that territory for almost a decade. Despite the fact that these areas included stretches of relatively isolated regions around provincial borders, and were separated from one another by cities and lines of communication held first by the Japanese and later by the Kuomintang, the Communists succeeded in creating a far greater degree of genuine political unity than the Kuomintang had ever been able to do. As early as 1944, a knowledgeable American diplomat described the Communist areas as the most cohesive and disciplined in China.[1]

The most important aspect of this cohesion was the involvement of the masses in political affairs, precisely what we earlier noted to be one of the hallmarks of twentieth-century nationalist movements. Peasants voted to elect governing councils for the border-region government and for district government as well. They not only fought and worked in the army and militia, but had the right to criticize their officers, to discuss tactics, plans, and the execution of the plans both before and after battles. During land reform, the peasants were encouraged individually to speak out against landlords and local gentry and to take part actively in the revolutionary process, thereby making a personal commitment to the government's program. In addition, mass associations for youth, women, peasants, and other groups involved individuals in activities to serve group interests, but which were also directly or indirectly linked to the government and its programs. Through mass political participation, the Communists fostered a profound and wide sense of political community.

In the context of China in the 1940s, this extensive participation was, among other things, a form of mass communication. In China's environment of mass illiteracy, the printed word was limited as a vehicle for education and propaganda, and other means of mass communication were virtually nonexistent. The Communists recognized that under such circumstances one of the most effective means of communication was participation by the people in various organizations, because that entailed discussions, explanations, questions, and other activities that, in total effect, indoctrinated them in the goals and values of the government.

Widespread participation, furthermore, served to minimize the gap between the masses and the elite, between the directed and the directors. To some extent, this contraction of class distinctions was doubtless the natural consequence of continual personal contact and the close leader-follower relation inherent in rugged guerrilla war conditions. But in the Communist-controlled areas in the early 1940s it was intensified because the combination of Kuomintang blockade and Japanese attacks necessitated production increases if these areas were to be self-sufficient and survive. To achieve this objective, it was necessary for the Communist leaders to pay close attention to the peasants' needs and desires and to gain their cooperation without sacrificing the advantages of central leadership. And to meet that situation, a superb integrative device was employed: the mass line. Mao Tse-tung has described the mass line in brief and lucid fashion:

> In all practical work of our Party, correct leadership can only be developed in the principle of "from the masses, to the masses." This means summing up (i.e. coordinating and systematising after careful study) the views of the masses (i.e. views scattered and unsystematic), then taking the resulting ideas back to the masses, explaining and popularizing them until the masses embrace the

ideas as their own, stand up for them and translate them into action by way of testing their correctness. Then it is necessary once more to sum up the views of the masses, and once again take the resulting ideas back to the masses so that the masses give them their whole-hearted support. . . . And so on, over and over again, so that each time these ideas emerge with greater correctness and become more vital and meaningful.[2]

The mass line, in other words, is a dialectic process: from the masses to the party to the masses, and it is still a central feature of Chinese Communist thinking. Its integrative function is evident. Because the ideas that originate among the masses are defined in Marxist terms, and then selected, modified, and presented back to the masses in the form of party or government policy, they are certain to fit in neatly with overall government goals and strategy. At the same time, they are reasonably assured of popular support because they originated in the felt needs of the people, and the people believe they have participated in their formulation. If, in the process of systematizing them, they have been altered so that they do not meet popular needs, they can again be modified until both government goals and popular demands are reasonably reconciled in one policy. The mass line constitutes a powerful bond between the government and the population, the party elite and the people at large, and the implementation of the concept in the early 1940s did indeed produce heightened popular response to programs launched to gain self-sufficiency in the border regions.

A good example of the mass line in action involved the educational program in Communist areas. It is sometimes assumed that the illiterate Chinese peasants were panting · for learning, yet in fact they often felt neither the need for education nor that it was practicable to seek it. They particularly did not feel the need for education that was removed from the real conditions of their lives—the kind of irrelevant program that prevailed in the Kuomintang areas and that was initially offered by the Communists as well. The Communists recognized the problem, however, and analyzed it precisely in an article published in the border region. First of all, the article pointed out, the educational system being used.

is a product of countries at a high stage of capitalist development and not suited to Chinese demands; second, it is the product of a capitalist ruling class and not suited to the Chinese democratic base areas; third, it is a product of peaceful conditions and not suited to the demands of the war of resistance; fourth, it is the product of big cities and not suited to the demands of agricultural villages. . . . We are Chinese, who live in democratic base areas, in a time of war, in agricultural villages; to use this system and these courses and methods offers no way out.[3]

By applying mass-line techniques, the Communists completely transformed the educational system. Decision-making power was taken out of the hands of professional educators, and in substantial measure turned over to the communities; curriculum was changed to relate clearly and specifically to local needs and problems; and other changes were instituted to create a school system recognized as valuable by the people themselves while incorporating what the Communist Party considered important for the education of the border region population.

Effective use of the mass line technique required that the party members be clear about strategy, tactics, and goals, and united in seeking them; the elite itself had to be integrated. Yet by the early 1940s the party was threatened by several disunifying and debilitating factors. The Communist Party had expanded very rapidly since the beginning of the war with Japan, and had enlisted people of all classes, but especially peasants and intellectuals. Many of the peasants were poorly educated, and the intellectuals came from bourgeois homes. Like intellectuals in China generally, they had received a Western-style education, they had little first-hand knowledge of peasant China, and many were still seeking a firm set of personal and social values. People from such diverse and non-proletarian backgrounds had to be welded into a unified, disciplined group. In addition, the Communists had to contend with geographic disunity; the isolation of the war base areas from one another hampered communication and was a constant threat to consistency of policy.

In response to this situation, the party leadership in 1942 launched the Cheng Feng Movement, a period of intensive study, discussion, criticism, and self-criticism aimed at thoroughly indoctrinating party members with Marxist principles and work-style as conceived by the Maoist leadership. The movement stressed the need to avoid dogmatic imitation of Russian models. Marxist theory was basic, of course, but so was actual work and experience with specific Chinese problems, especially the problems of the peasantry. The major emphasis of the movement was the combination of Marxist thought with the concrete realities of the Chinese revolution. Underlying this main theme were others of importance: comradely cooperation, elimination of the gap between intellectuals and peasantry, subordination of individual desires to the needs of the party and the people. At the same time, the movement involved political changes in the party. Some members were purged as security risks, a few leaders associated with factions actually or potentially in competition with Mao were reduced in influence, and, most important, Mao Tse-tung consolidated his leading position in the party. Thus, as the Kuomintang became more hidebound in its views and less effective organizationally, the Communists tightened party organization and discipline under Mao Tse-tung, and undertook a crash program to cultivate informed party unity, to raise the party's ideological level, and to develop a realistic understanding of China's society and politics and their party's role in them.

Finally, the power of the Red Army was a crucial aspect of cohesion and control in the Communist areas. Here again, the relation of local interests to central needs was significant. The peasantry looked upon the Red Army as friend and protector, and therefore contributed to it and cooperated with it. Ultimately, it would be the army's task to achieve the essential prerequisite for national integration, the genuine conquest of all of China.

The unity to which all these elements contributed was, in one sense, regional; the Communist areas were mainly in north China. Their cohesion, however, was not an expression of regionalism but of nationalism. The Communists obtained popular support and legitimacy by meeting local needs, and they used that support and legitimacy to pursue national goals. As a consequence, the extension of Communist power was the extension of Chinese nationalism. The "rise" in Chinese nationalism in the 1940s was not just another periodic upturn in emotional anti-imperialism, but an increase in genuine awareness on the part of more and more Chinese that they were members of a nation, and as such were willing to devote their energies, talents, and even their lives to what they considered the interests of that nation. All the elements of unity and central control in the Communist areas therefore had a nationalistic dimension.

The Communist army, for example, exemplified a national army; indeed, it may have been the first real national armed force to have existed in China; the many provincial origins and dialects it contained emphasized that it was not a regional army, like so many Chinese forces of the time, but an army of the whole country. The army also differed from the prevailing military pattern in that it was not the personal army of any man, nor were its constituent elements the personal followings of their commanders. No matter in what region Communist forces operated, they did not display provincial or regional prejudices. The army was subordinate to the party, which spoke of its long-range goals in national terms. The political workers in all army units taught troops and civilians alike the same message.

The content of Communist propaganda and education dealt with national problems and goals, cultivated nationalistic ideas, especially during the anti-Japanese war, when much of it dealt with concepts such as national traitors, love of country, and unity of the Chinese people. Even the anti-Kuomintang aspects of the propaganda had nationalistic connotations. A striking illustration of such propaganda is a set of graded reading cards used in elementary reading instruction for adults; the following exercises are the first and last, the easiest and most difficult, of the cards:[4]

1. Men.
   Men and women.
   All are Chinese.
   All love China.

2. Reactionary elements.
   Reactionary elements specialize in making trouble for anti-Japanese armed forces.
   They kill young men and women who oppose Japan.
   They destroy anti-Japanese work.
   They secretly help the Japanese devils, and they secretly help Wang Ching-wei.

These cards illustrate another nationalistic dimension of the Communist approach: it was designed to reach Chinese of all classes. The reading cards were for illiterates, which included most of the peasantry. The Communists conceived of the nation in modern terms, as the mass of the people, and shaped their indoctrination efforts accordingly. And it worked. An American diplomat in the Communist regions reported that "political education and participation in the local, district and regional government units have made the people politically conscious."[5] Three days after the Allied landings in Normandy, an American journalist in the Communist area of China wrote that he and other journalists in his party were convinced "of the remarkably effective educational work that has led every soldier, farmer and workman with whom we spoke to know already of the opening of the Allied invasion of Western Europe and its direct bearing on the speeding up of the anti-Japanese offensive."[6]

Despite the absence of economic modernization, Communist regions were characterized by modern attitudes and values. Visitors invariably commented on the absence of claptrap, ritual, and empty formalities that made the Kuomintang areas so oppressive and irritating to Westerners. Communist leaders were informed, direct, competent. Work in the Communist districts at all levels was generally done with dispatch and efficiency, with no concern for "face." Women were treated as equals, and acted accordingly; indeed, one American diplomat in Yenan found that "their openness and complete lack of self-consciousness is at first almost disconcerting."[7] In government, army, and other organizations, authority was impersonal, not conditioned by kinship or personal relations. People in the Communist regions were becoming accustomed to functions and attitudes appropriate to a modern society. Not surprisingly, one correspondent with long experience in China expressed the prevailing view among foreigners when he said: "We have come to the mountains of north Shensi, to find the most modern place in China."[8]

Modern social scientists would agree. Manfred Halpern, a leading student of sociopolitical modernization, has proposed categorizing political systems in a way that well applies to China. He suggests that political systems might be defined as "traditional," "transitional," and "modernizing." Each category is based not on chronology, but on the capacity of the system for change. A traditional system in this scheme is a closed system limited by dogma; by low levels of technology, production, and income; by little political integration; by the autonomy of kinship groups; and, most important, by an inability to deal "with continuous systemic transformation." That definition describes traditional China fairly well.

Halpern's term "transitional" seems to fit warlord-Kuomintang China almost perfectly. According to him, the word

> applies to any political system in which the structural changes and demands set loose by the uncontrolled forces of transformation exceed the will or capacity of political authority to cope with them. . . .
>
> A transitional political system may be engaged in selective modernization without coming any closer to achieving a capacity for that systemic transformation which is characteristic of the modernizing political systems. . . . It may transform some of its institutions in a manner that is likely to inhibit further transformation. . . . A transitional political system may seek to fixate and ritualize the status quo it has achieved at any given moment, even though the unintended or uncontrolled forces of modernization continue to undermine the system in the long run. It may try to return to certain selected traditions. Any society is transitional which is no longer closed but not yet open, and whose destination remains uncertain.[9]

Halpern goes on to argue that "modernizing" applies to any political system that, by contrast with the transitional, has achieved the will and capacity to deal with social change.

Another student of modernization, David Apter, holds a similar view. He regards two conditions as the minimum attributes of modernity, and stresses that neither is limited to industrial societies. The first condition, says Apter, is

> a social system that can constantly innovate without falling apart, including in innovation beliefs about the acceptability of change and, as well, social structures so differentiated as not to be inflexible; and second, a social framework that can provide the skills and knowledge necessary for living in a technologically advanced world, including the ability to communicate in terms of the technology.[10]

According to Halpern's and Apter's definitions, the Communist regions of China were modern. But Apter's second attribute quite properly implies that a nonindustrialized modern society will see industrialization and economic-technological modernization generally as desirable. China was no exception.

Immediately after the defeat of the Kuomintang, and the establishment of the People's Republic of China, the government initiated wide-ranging programs to seek those goals. Thousands of miles of railroads were laid, the national network of roads was steadily improved and extended, and communications by waterway increased. In that fashion, hitherto isolated regions were brought into closer intellectual and economic touch with the rest of the nation. Industry was developed intensively, with all that industrialization implies regarding regional interdependence upon resources and products. Agriculture was collectivized, removing once and for all the possibility of reversion to the old landlord-tenant system that had inhibited the modernization of Chinese farming. A powerful central government was organized employing the same principles of participation and mass line used in the border regions. The population was organized by the tens of millions into associations of workers, women, youth, intellectuals, and numerous other categories to work for their own improvement and for the integration and advancement of the nation. School enrollment soared, and an intensive campaign for mass literacy was quickly developed. The state's propaganda system expanded, inculcating social attitudes and values as well as political goals that not only directly and indirectly subverted old loyalties to family, clan, and locality, but generated new allegiances to the party, state, and nation. In short, myriad links of national integration were forged.[11]

It was at that time that the modernizing achievements of the Kuomintang government, and even of its warlord predecessors, became significant. Though the Kuomintang did not integrate the nation—it remained, in Halpern's terminology, "transitional"—the changes wrought in Chinese society under the Kuomintang were part of the heritage received by the Chinese Communists when they took power. To the extent that those changes had integrative force, they facilitated integration under the Communists. In a sense, the decades from the middle of the nineteenth century up to 1949 constituted a kind of incubation period in which economic innovations occurred, attitudes were altered, and China was made ready for the accelerated, drastic, and decisive changes that took place under the People's Republic of China. The changes induced by the Kuomintang had never pushed China to the magic threshold of integration; those made by the Communists permitted China to step over it and beyond.

National integration certainly did not progress in a linear fashion after 1949. On the contrary, while the Communist government steadily strengthened territorial integration through economic modernization, the many changes involved in modernizing the country strained the high degree of social integration achieved earlier. For example, peasants who thought that the Communists served their real needs by redistributing the land in the late 1940s and early 1950s did not welcome collectivization of the land in the mid-1950s. Some who accepted Mao's thought as superbly appropriate for a guerrilla movement struggling in the hinterland found it irrelevant to the needs of a society engaged in industrialization. The increased reliance on professional expertise associated with greater technological sophistication again tended to increase the gap between intellectuals and masses, a tendency the Communists tried to counter by sending intellectuals to the countryside. These various strains on occasion became acute, and many of the most important phenomena of post-1949 China can be understood as crises of integration—the Cultural Revolution being a conspicuous example.

Yet despite the strains, social integration in China is still strong. Almost every visitor to China during the early 1970s has called attention, directly or indirectly, to the widespread sense of national purpose, to the people's general familiarity with national problems and aspirations, and to the participation in public processes·that marks the lives of millions upon millions of ordinary Chinese. Upheavals there have been, but they have occurred within the context of a fundamentally united nation. The era of disintegration in China is over.

Notes

Chapter I

1. Two examples of many such studies are: *Political Parties and National Integration in Tropical Africa*, ed. James S. Coleman and Carl G. Rosberg, Jr. (Berkeley and Los Angeles: University of California Press, 1964), the work from which I have drawn the notion that national integration has two aspects, although I altered their distinction somewhat; and R. William Liddle, *Ethnicity, Party and National Integration* (New Haven: Yale University Press, 1970). Liddle analyzes national integration in Indonesia in suggestive terms. George Dalton, "Peasantries in Anthropology and History," *Current Anthropology* 13, 3–4 (June–October, 1972): 1–31, also says many suggestive things about integration and modernization. There is a small body of theoretical literature on national integration.

2. The first quotation is from Hans Kohn, *Nationalism: Its Meaning and History* (Princeton: D. Van Nostrand, 1965), p. 9; Louis L. Snyder quotes Hayes' statement in *The Dynamics of Nationalism: Readings in Its Meaning and Development* (Princeton: D. Van Nostrand, 1964), p. 1; and the Shafer quotation is from his *Nationalism: Myth and Reality* (New York: Harcourt, Brace & World, 1955), p. 10.

3. E. H. Carr, *Nationalism and After* (London: Macmillan, 1968), p. 3.

4. Carr, *Nationalism*, pp. 18–19.

5. Philip E. Jacob and Henry Teune, "The Integrative Process: Guidelines for Analysis of the Bases of Political Community," *The Integration of Political Communities*, ed. Philip E. Jacob and James V. Toscano (Philadelphia: J. B. Lippincott, 1964), p. 8.

6. Claude Ake, *A Theory of Political Integration* (Homewood, Ill.: Dorsey Press, 1967), pp. 13–14, argues that "national integration" is a tautology.

7. Karl Deutsch, "Social Mobilization and Political Development," *American Political Science Review* 55, 3 (September, 1961): 494.

8. William Skinner, "Marketing and Social Structure in Rural China," *Journal of Asian Studies* 24, 1 (November, 1964): 32. This article is the first of three in which Skinner originated and developed the concept of "standard market area"; the other two were in succeeding issues of the *Journal of Asian Studies* (February, 1965): 195–228, and (May, 1965): 363–399.

9. Dwight H. Perkins, *Agricultural Development in China 1368–1968* (Chicago: Aldine, 1969), p. 169.

10. Perkins, *Agricultural Development*, p. 180.

Chapter II

1. Figures in this paragraph are from Shelley Cheng, *The T'ung-Meng-Hui: Its Organization, Leadership and Finances, 1905–1912* (Ann Arbor, Mich.: University Microfilms 62–6625, 1972), pp. 105–106.

2. Dwight H. Perkins, *Agricultural Development in China 1368–1968* (Chicago: Aldine, 1969), p. 174. On pp. 175–177, Perkins compares regional versus central military resources.

3. Shen Nai-cheng, "On the Powers of the Viceroys and Governors of the Provinces in the Last Years of the Ch'ing Dynasty," *She-hui k'e-hsüeh* [Social Sciences (Tsing Hua University)], 2, 2 (January, 1937), quoted in Ho Ping-ti, *Studies on the Population of China, 1368–1953* (Cambridge: Harvard University Press, 1959), p. 66. Jonathan Porter, *Tseng Kuo-fan's Private Bureaucracy* (Berkeley: University of California, 1972) China Research Monograph 9, Center for Chinese Studies, discusses Tseng's financial operations, and comments on the decentralization of the Ch'ing financial organization.

4. Letter from W. D. Straight to J. P. Morgan & Co., February 4, 1912, sent to the Secretary of State by J. P. Morgan & Co. State Department file relating to the internal affairs of China, file number 893.00/1191.

5. The assertions in this paragraph are based on the following: telegrams from Minister W. J. Calhoun to the Secretary of State, November 15, 1911, 893.00/670; November 17, 1911, 893.00/672; November 27, 1911, 893.00/700; December 6, 1911, 893.00/745; Decem-

ber 11, 1911, 893.00/759; January 8, 1912, 893.00/902; January 17, 1912, 893.00/934; August 31, 1912, 893.00/1435; and a dispatch from
⦁ E. T. Williams, chargé d'affaires, to the Secretary of State, July 18, 1911, 893.00/1811.

6. Reports received at the American legation from non-diplomatic personnel about conditions in Shensi and Shansi, forwarded to the Secretary of State by Minister W. J. Calhoun, December 23, 1911: 893.00/942.

7. Dispatch from the consul general at Canton to the Secretary of State, October 27, 1911: 893.00/709.

8. Memorandum from Commanding Officer, USS Monterey, To Commander-in-Chief, U.S. Asiatic Fleet, December 9, 1911: 893.00/976.

9. Dispatch from George E. Anderson, consul general at Hong Kong, to the Secretary of State, January 11, 1912: 893.00/1066.

10. Letter from Dr. C. D. Tenney, Chinese Secretary of the legation, to Minister W. J. Calhoun, quoted in Calhoun's letter to the Secretary of State, February 13, 1912: 893.00/1156.

11. Chuzo Ichiko, "The Role of the Gentry: An Hypothesis," in *China in Revolution: The First Phase 1900–1913* ed. Mary Clabaugh Wright (New Haven: Yale University Press, 1968), pp. 297–317.

Wright's volume is one of the most important works on the 1911 Revolution in any language. Wright not only edited the many excellent essays in the volume, but contributed a stimulating introductory discussion. In that, she disagrees with Ichiko's analysis, and says that the great changes taking place in China since the turn of the century could not have left the gentry unaffected. It is precisely the extent of those changes that, it seems to me, Wright overemphasizes. She argues that the years before the revolution were a time of extraordinary ferment and change. Yet in fact the ferment was only beginning to appear in the chief cities, and would not penetrate the countryside for decades. For example, to say that "footbinding was beginning to die out" is technically correct, but misleading because it took so long to die, despite the fact that it was one of the physical —as distinct from social or political—changes that were the first targets of modernizers, including the court. At that time, only a small number of progressive women stopped binding feet. Wright deprecates anti-Manchuism as the cause of the revolution, and points out that the Manchus were well treated and ignored after the revolution. Yet in fact many Manchus were killed during the revolution. In any event, passionate opposition to the Manchus as rulers does not necessarily imply persecution after they no longer held that status. Most important, Wright argues that nationalism was the moving force behind the revolution, and defines it in terms of anti-Manchuism, anti-imperialism, and a quest for a modern centralized nation-state. There are many ways to argue the point, but if we simply look to the situation that existed after the revolution we find that nationalism did not dominate the Chinese scene, even in the cities. What came after 1911 was the antithesis of a modern state, of centralization, of social reform, of anti-imperialism. It was warlordism, which expressed the chief currents that led up to 1911.

12. Dispatch from Consul General Bergholz at Canton to the Secretary of State, November 14, 1911: 893.00/779.

13. Enclosure in dispatch from W. J. Calhoun to the Secretary of State, April 5, 1912: 893.00/1296.

14. Dispatch from Paul Reinsch to the Secretary of State, March 16, 1914: 893.00/2101.

15. Dispatch from E. Carleton Baker, consul at Chungking, to Minister Calhoun, August 2, 1912: 893.00/1443.

Chapter III

1. I have drawn some of the material about Wu from the Ph.D. dissertation of Odoric Wou, "Militarism in Modern China as Exemplified in the Career of Wu P'ei-fu 1916–1928" (Columbia University, 1970).

2. E. T. C. Werner, "Chinese Ditties," *The New China Review* 3, 5 (October, 1921): 370. I have altered the translation slightly.

3. A personal informant in Taipei, Taiwan, who grew up in Peking, remembered this ditty from her childhood:
     Chang Tsung-ch'ang tiao-r lang-tang
     P'o hsieh, p'o wa-tzu, p'o chün-chuang.

4. For Li Tsung-jen's life, I have relied heavily on his own reminiscences, as told to Tong Te-kong for the Chinese Oral History Project at Columbia University, and on Diana Lary's Ph.D. dissertation, "The Kwangsi Clique in Kuomintang Politics, 1929–1936" (School of Oriental and African Studies, University of London, 1960), which Mrs. Lary kindly allowed me to read.

5. Donald Gillin, Warlord: *Yen Hsi-shan in Shansi Province 1911–1949* (Princeton: Princeton University Press, 1967), p. 35.

6. "The Reminiscences of Chang Fa-k'uei, as told to Julie Lien-ying How" (The Chinese Oral History Project, Columbia University), p. 110. This material was not in final typed form when I used it, and the pagination of the final copy may be different.

7. This paradox was emphasized in one of the two chapters that Chi Hsi-sheng kindly permitted me to read from a book manuscript he is preparing on warlord organization.

8. Anthropologist Fei Hsiao-tung, cited by Morton Fried, "Military Status in Chinese Society," *American Journal of Sociology* 57, 4 (January, 1952): 351.

9. "Reminiscences of Chang Fa-k'uei," p. 49; see note 6 regarding pagination.

10. "Reminiscences of Chang Fa-k'uei," p. 38; see note 6 above regarding pagination.

11. "Reminiscences of Chang Fa-k'uei," p. 112; see note 6 above regarding pagination.

12. "The Reminiscences of Li Tsung-jen, as told to Tong Te-kong," (The Chinese Oral History Project, Columbia University), pp. 10–11 of chapter 5. Like the "Reminiscences of Chang Fa-k'uei," this material was not in final typed form when I used it, and the pagination may have differed from the finished version.

13. Odoric Wou, in an unpublished manuscript, has studied the Chihli Clique in detail and worked out a comparison between its structure and the structure of a Chinese lineage group. His early ideas along these lines were published in "A Chinese 'Warlord' Faction: The Chihli Clique, 1918–1924," in *Columbia Essays in International Affairs*, vol. 3, ed. Andrew W. Cordier (New York: Columbia University Press, 1968), pp. 249–274. Chi Hsi-sheng, also in an unpublished work, discusses Wou's conception, and points out that elders in lineage organizations had real power, whereas they did not in clique arrangements unless they also happened to have a personal army.

14. Dispatch from W. Meyrick Hewlett, British consul general in Chengtu, April 27, 1917, in Great Britain Foreign Office Records Relating to China, file number FO 371–2907: 153–159. Hewlett was in the midst of fighting and of the negotiations that followed, so presumably his figures are accurate.

15. "Reminiscences of Chang Fa-k'uei," pp. 43–44; see note 6 above regarding pagination.

16. Dispatch from the British Consulate, Chungking, to the British Legation, August 19, 1924: FO 228–3140–7067/24/123.

17. "Reminiscences of Chang Fa-k'uei," p. 63; see note 6 above regarding pagination.

18. Report from Mr. Rose to British Minister Sir Beilby Alston, Yochow, Hunan, mid-June, 1920: FO 228–2980.

19. The report of the British consul in Mukden is in Mukden Intelligence Report, June Quarter, 1920: FO 228–3290. The quotation re-

garding Newchwang is in the Intelligence Report for September Quarter, 1919, from the British Consulate, Newchwang, Manchuria, October 11, 1919: FO 228-3289 12031/19/1.

20. This conclusion was also drawn by Odoric Wou, who has studied Wu's career most thoroughly.

21. Cited in R. F. Johnston, "Chinese Cult of Military Heroes," *The New China Review* 3, 1 (February, 1921): 59-61. Wen Cheng-ming was the poet.

22. F. W. Mote, *The Poet Kao Ch'i, 1336-1375* (Princeton: Princeton University Press, 1962), pp. 90-91.

23. Jerome Ch'en, "Historical Background," in *Modern China's Search for a Political Form,* ed. Jack Gray (London: Oxford University Press, 1969), p. 32.

24. Wou, "Militarism in Modern China," p. 177.

Chapter IV

1. The quoted phrases come from the following works, listed in the order the quotations appear: Lloyd Eastman, *Throne and Mandarins* (Cambridge: Harvard University Press, 1967), p. 165; George Yu, *Party Politics in Republican China: The Kuomintang 1912-1924* (Berkeley and Los Angeles: University of California Press, 1966), p. 140; Huang Sung-k'ang, *Lu Hsün and the New Culture Movement* (Amsterdam: Djambatan, 1957), p. 20; Jerome Grieder, *Hu Shih and the Chinese Renaissance: Liberalism in the Chinese Revolution 1917-1937* (Cambridge: Harvard University Press, 1970), p. 127; Cyrus H. Peake, *Nationalism and Education in Modern China* (New York: Columbia University Press, 1932), p. 89; Dison Hsueh-feng Poe, "Political Reconstruction, 1927-1937," in *The Strenuous Decade: China's Nation Building Efforts, 1927-1937* ed. Paul K. T. Sih (Jamaica, N.Y.: St. Johns University Press, 1970), p. 44.

2. Olga Lang, *Pa Chin and His Writings: Chinese Youth Between Two Revolutions* (Cambridge: Harvard University Press, 1967), p. 46.

3. Martin Bernal, "Chinese Socialism Before 1913," in *Modern China's Search for Political Form,* ed. Jack Gray (London: Oxford University Press, 1969), pp. 66-95.

4. Chow Tse-tsung, *The May Fourth Movement: Intellectual Revolution in Modern China* (Cambridge: Harvard University Press, 1960), pp. 25, 64-65.

5. The exact figure is 162,490. The figures in this and the following paragraph are from Chow Tse-tung's *May Fourth Movement*, p. 380; I have drawn from Chow's book for the specific events of the May Fourth period.

6. Some scholars denounce the "fallacy of an inert peasantry." Mary Wright, for example, in the introduction to *China in Revolution: The First Phase 1900–1913* (New Haven: Yale University Press, 1968) pp. 42–44 implies that the peasant was nationalistic, and, by extension, changing the pattern of his life. It is doubtless true that many peasants were nationalistic to the extent of resenting foreign influence in China, although this attitude was often combined with anti-modernism. Moreover, in a country of so many millions of peasants, one can doubtless find examples of an enormous range of attitudes, states of knowledge, sophistication, intelligence, and so forth. But if we must generalize about the peasantry, we must try to ascertain the chief characteristics that remain socially effective when all the peripheral aberrations have been considered. There is a good deal of evidence that the bulk of the peasantry was largely untouched by the modernizing trends coursing into China at this time. Many descriptions of peasant life a decade or two or even three later show the peasant's life to be brutish and backward, steeped in ignorance, and little exposed to the winds of change.

7. *North China Herald,* July 12, 1919.

8. Intelligence Report from His Majesty's Consul in Nanking to His Majesty's charge d'affaires, July 3, 1920, in Great Britain, Foreign Office Records Relating to China, file number FO 228–3279 6529/20/21.

9. Ssu-yu Teng and John King Fairbank, *China's Response to the West: A Documentary Survey 1839–1923* (Cambridge: Harvard University Press, 1954), p. 255.

10. Grieder, *Hu Shih and the Chinese Renaissance,* p. 142.

11. Charlotte Furth, *Ting Wen-chiang: Science and China's New Culture* (Cambridge: Harvard University Press, 1970), p. 108.

12. Furth, *Ting Wen-chiang,* p. 133.

13. Huang, *Lu Hsün and the New Culture Movement,* p. 95.

14. Henri van Boven, *Histoire de la litterature chinoise moderne* (Peiping: Chihli Press, 1946), pp. 43–44.

15. Chao Chia-pi, ed. *Chung-kuo hsin wen-hsüeh ta hsi* [A corpus of China's new literature] ti-erh chi, ed. Cheng Chen-to (Shanghai: Liang yu t'u-shu kung-ssu, 1935), pp. 14–15.

16. Lyman P. Van Slyke, "Liang Sou-ming and the Rural Reconstruction Movement," *Journal of Asian Studies* 18, 4 (August, 1959): 462, n. 25.

17. Merle Goldman, "Left-Wing Criticism of the Pai-Hua Movement," in *Reflections on the May Fourth Movement: A Symposium* ed. Benjamin I. Schwartz (Cambridge: East Asian Research Center of Harvard University, 1972), p. 86.

18. Laurence A. Schneider, *Ku Chieh-kang and China's New History: Nationalism and the Quest for Alternative Traditions* (Berkeley and Los Angeles: University of California Press, 1971), p. 124.

19. Leo Ou-fan Lee, "The Romantic Temper of May Fourth Writers," in *Reflections on May Fourth Movement*, p. 81.

Chapter V

1. Pichon P. Y. Loh, *The Early Chiang Kai-shek: A Study of His Personality and Politics, 1887–1924* (New York: Columbia University Press, 1971), pp. 87–88.

2. F. F. Liu, *A Military History of Modern China 1924–1949* (Princeton: Princeton University Press, 1956), p. 8.

3. Harold Isaacs, *The Tragedy of the Chinese Revolution* (Stanford: Stanford University Press, 1951), p. 111.

4. T. C. Woo, *The Kuomintang and the Future of the Chinese Revolution* (London: George Allen & Unwin, 1928), pp. 218–219.

5. Chang Kuo-t'ao, *The Rise of the Chinese Communist Party 1921–1927: Volume One of the Autobiography of Chang Kuo-t'ao* (Lawrence: The University Press of Kansas, 1971), p. 603.

6. Chen Ta, "Fundamentals of the Chinese Labor Movement," *Annals of the American Academy of Political and Social Science* 152 (November, 1930): 201.

7. The figures on trade union growth are from Chang, *Rise of Chinese Communist Party*, p. 550 and 710, n. 5; Jean Chesneaux, *The Chinese Labor Movement 1919–1927* (Stanford: Stanford University Press, 1968), pp. 345, 359, 362; Chen Ta, "Fundamentals of Chinese Labor Movement," p. 201.

8. The quotation is from Robert C. North and Xenia J. Eudin, *M. N. Roy's Mission to China: The Communist-Kuomintang Split of 1927* (Berkeley and Los Angeles: University of California Press, 1963), p. 31. Other figures in the paragraph come from Chang, *Rise of Chinese Communist Party*, pp. 602–603, 609, and Isaacs, *Tragedy*, pp. 67–68, 91, 105–106, 113.

9. Chesneaux, *Chinese Labor Movement*, p. 338.

10. North and Eudin, *M. N. Roy's Mission to China,* pp. 138, 141.

11. Chesneaux, *Chinese Labor Movement,* p. 351.

12. Wu Hsiang-hsiang, "Ho Chien ti i-sheng," [Ho Chien's life], in *Chung-kuo hsien-tai shih tsung-k'an* [Selected Articles on Chinese Contemporary History], ed. Wu Hsiang-hsiang (Taipei: Book World Co., 1964), 6: 235.

13. Dun J. Li (ed.), *The Road to Communism: China Since 1912* (New York: Van Nostrand Reinhold Company, 1969), p. 94.

14. Wu, "Ho Chien ti i-sheng," pp. 236–239; North and Eudin, *M. N. Roy's Mission to China,* pp. 120–121.

15. Chang, *Rise of Chinese Communist Party,* p. 637; North and Eudin, *M. N. Roy's Mission to China,* pp. 106–107, has the text of Stalin's wire.

16. Li, *The Road to Communism,* p. 101; see also pp. 95–112.

17. Quoted by Dorothy Borg, *American Policy and the Chinese Revolution 1925–1928* (New York: Macmillan and American Institute of Pacific Relations, 1947), p. 201.

18. Quoted by Borg, *American Policy,* pp. 296–297.

19. Li, *The Road to Communism,* pp. 108, 110.

Chapter VI

1. Letter from Counselor of Legation Willys R. Peck to the Secretary of State, December 6, 1933 in *Foreign Relations of the United States 1933,* 5 vols. (Washington, D.C.: Government Printing Office, 1949) 3: 476–477.

2. Donald Gillin, *Warlord: Yen Hsi-shan in Shansi Province 1911–1949* (Princeton: Princeton University Press, 1967), p. 123. I have drawn freely from Gillin's book for my discussion of Yen Hsi-shan.

3. Gillin, *Warlord,* p. 199.

4. Memorandum by the consul and vice-consul at Tsinan, H. E. Stevens and R. P. Ludden, of a conversation with Han Fu-chü on January 22, 1934, in *Foreign Relations of the United States 1934,* 5 vols. (Washington, D.C.: Government Printing Office, 1950), 3: 13–15.

5. The description of the Fukien rebellion is based primarily on chap. 3 of Lloyd Eastman's unpublished book, "The Abortive Revolution: China Under the Kuomintang, 1927–1937," in which he analyzes the rebellion in detail.

6. For my discussion of Kwangsi reconstruction, I have drawn freely from Diana Lary, "The Kwangsi Clique in Kuomintang Politics, 1929–1936" (School of Oriental and African Studies, University of London, 1960), pp. 313–371.

7. "The Reminiscences of Li Tsung-jen, as told to Tong Te-kong" (The Chinese Oral History Project, Columbia), pp. 14–15 of Chapter 30; this material was not in final typed form when I used it, and the pagination may differ from the finished version.

8. Hu Shih, *Nan yu tsa i* [Recollections of a trip south] (Taipei: Ch'i-ming shu-chü, 1959), pp. 52–53.

9. Robert A. Kapp, "Provincial Independence versus National Rule: A Case Study of Szechwan in the 1920s and 1930s," *Journal of Asian Studies*, 30, 3 (May, 1971): 536. Much of my information regarding Szechwan is drawn from this article and from Kapp's book, *Szechwan and the Chinese Republic: Provincial Militarism and Central Power, 1911–1938* (New Haven: Yale University Press, 1973).

10. Allen S. Whiting and General Sheng Shih-ts'ai, *Sinkiang: Pawn or Pivot?* (East Lansing: Michigan State University Press, 1958), p. 11.

11. "The Reminiscences of Wu Kuo-chen for the years 1946–1953, as told to Nathaniel Peffer," (The Chinese Oral History Project, Columbia University), pp. 390–391.

12. Ch'in Te-ch'un, "Wo yü Chang Tzu-chung" [Chang Tzu-chung and I], *Chuan-chi wen-hsüeh* [Biographical literature], 1, 2 (July, 1962): p. 14.

13. "Reminiscences of Li Tsung-jen," pp. 3–4 of chap. 39; see note 7 regarding pagination.

14. "The Reminiscences of K'ung Hsiang-hsi, as told to Julie Lien-ying How," (The Chinese Oral History Project, Columbia University), p. 129.

15. The figures are from Jerome Ch'en, "Historical Background," in *Modern China's Search for a Political Form*, ed. Jack Gray (New York: Oxford University Press, 1969), pp. 31–32.

16. "The Reminiscences of Chang Fa-k'uei, as told to Julie Lien-ying How," (The Chinese Oral History Project, Columbia University), pp. 244–245; this material was not in final typed form when I used it, and the pagination may differ from the finished form.

17. Harold Hung-mao Tien, *Political Development in China, 1927–1937* (Ann Arbor, Mich.: University Microfilms 69–22–499, 1970), p. 240.

18. Morton Fried, "Military Status in Chinese Society," *American Journal of Sociology*, 57, 4 (January, 1952): 349.

19. "Reminiscences of Li Tsung-jen," chap. 27, p. 16; see note 7 above regarding pagination.

Chapter VII

1. James C. Thompson, Jr., *While China Faced West: American Reformers in Nationalist China, 1928–1937* (Cambridge: Harvard University Press, 1969), p. 165.

2. Herman W. Mast, III, "A Heavy Hand in the Examination Halls: The Earliest Attempts of the Kuomintang to Staff a Modern Civil Service, 1928–1937," in *Studies on Asia, 1967,* ed. Sidney Devere Brown (Lincoln: University of Nebraska Press, 1967), p. 105.

3. Harold Hung-mao Tien, *Political Development in China, 1927–1937* Ann Arbor, Mich.: University Microfilms 69–22–499, 1970), pp. 96–97.

4. C. K. Yang, "A Chinese Village in Early Communist Transition," in the combined reprint of two of Yang's earlier volumes, *Chinese Communist Society: The Family and the Village* (Cambridge: MIT Press, 1965), p. 106.

5. This paragraph is based on chap. 1 of Lloyd Eastman's unpublished book, "The Abortive Revolution: China Under Kuomintang Rule, 1927–1937."

6. Ch'ien Tuan-sheng, *The Government and Politics of China* (Cambridge: Harvard University Press, 1950), p. 124.

7. All data in this paragraph are taken from Tien, *Political Development in China,* chap. 1; the quoted phrase is from p. 27.

8. Eastman, "Abortive Revolution," chap. 1.

9. *China Year Book 1931,* ed. H. G. W. Woodhead (Shanghai: North-China Daily News & Herald, 1931), p. 541.

10. Both quotations are from Lloyd Eastman, "Fascism in Kuomintang China: The Blue Shirts," *China Quarterly* no. 49 (January–March, 1972), pp. 5–6.

11. Eastman, "Fascism in Kuomintang China," p. 20.

12. Thompson, *While China Faced West,* p. 165.

13. Chiang Kai-shek, *China's Destiny and Chinese Economic Theory,* with notes and commentary by Philip Jaffe (New York: Roy Publishers, 1947), p. 222.

14. Arthur N. Young, *China and the Helping Hand, 1937–1945* (Cambridge: Harvard University Press, 1963), p. 1 saw the transformation; Douglas S. Paauw, "The Kuomintang and Economic Stagnation, 1928–1937," in *Modern China,* ed. Albert Feuerwerker (Englewood Cliffs, N.J.: Prentice-Hall, 1964), p. 127, saw the stagnation.

15. Arthur N. Young, "China's Fiscal Transformation, 1927–1937," in *The Strenuous Decade: China's Nation-Building Efforts, 1927–1937*, ed. Paul K. T. Sih (Jamaica, N.Y.: St. John's University Press, 1970), p. 112.

16. Quoted in George E. Taylor, "The Reconstruction Movement in China," in *Problems of the Pacific, 1936: Aims and Results of Social and Economic Policies in Pacific Countries*, ed. W. L. Holland and Kate L. Mitchell (Chicago: University of Chicago Press, n.d.), p. 396.

17. John K. Chang, "Industrial Development of Mainland China, 1912–1949," *Journal of Economic History*, 27, no. 1 (March, 1967): 56–81; and John K. Chang, *Industrial Development in Pre-Communist China: A Quantitative Analysis* (Chicago: Aldine Publishing Co., 1969).

18. Albert Feuerwerker, *The Chinese Economy, 1912–1949* (Ann Arbor: Center for Chinese Studies of the University of Michigan, 1968), p. 19. Some of the data in this paragraph come from the same author's "Industrial Enterprise in Twentieth Century China: The Chee Hsin Cement Co.," in *Approaches to Modern Chinese History*, ed. Albert Feuerwerker et al. (Berkeley and Los Angeles: University of California Press, 1967).

19. Ramon H. Myers, *The Chinese Peasant Economy: Agricultural Development in Hopei and Shantung, 1890–1949* (Cambridge: Harvard University Press, 1970), p. 14.

20. The statistics were gathered by Franklin Ho, who is quoted in Thompson, *While China Faced West*, p. 202.

21. The data come from Franklin Ho, cited in Thompson, *While China Faced West*, p. 203.

22. George E. Taylor, "Reconstruction After Revolution: Kiangsi Province," *Pacific Affairs* 8, no. 3 (September, 1935): 310.

23. Arthur N. Young, *China's Nation-Building Effort, 1927–1937: The Financial and Economic Record* (Stanford: Hoover Institution Press, 1971), p. 306.

24. Thompson, *While China Faced West*, p. 31.

25. Thompson, *While China Faced West*, p. 64.

26. The figures are from Theodore Hsi-en Chen, "Education in China, 1927–1937," in *The Strenuous Decade: China's Nation Building Efforts, 1927–1937*, ed. Paul K. T. Sih (Jamaica, N.Y.: St. John's University Press, 1970), pp. 298–299.

27. League of Nations' Mission of Educational Experts: C. H. Becker et al., *The Reorganization of Education in China* (Paris: League of Nations' Institute of Intellectual Cooperation, 1932), p. 166.

28. Victor Purcell, *Problems in Chinese Education* (London: K. Paul, Trench, Trubner & Co., 1936), p. 226.

29. League of Nations' Mission, *The Reorganization of Education in China*, p. 21.

30. C. K. Yang, "The Chinese Family in the Communist Revolution," in the combined reprint of two of Yang's earlier volumes, *Chinese Communist Society: The Family and the Village* (Cambridge: MIT Press, 1965), pp. 218–219.

31. Norman D. Hanwell, "The Dragnet of Local Government in China," *Pacific Affairs* 10, no. 1 (March, 1937): 44.

32. Yang, "A Chinese Village in Early Communist Transition," p. 118.

33. Yang, "A Chinese Village in Early Communist Transition," p. 118.

34. Maurice Meisner, *Li Ta-chao and the Origins of Chinese Marxism* (New York: Atheneum, 1970), p. 81.

35. Quoted in Y. C. Wang, *Chinese Intellectuals and the West 1872–1949* (Chapel Hill: University of North Carolina Press, 1966), p. 369.

Chapter VIII

1. Dick Wilson, *The Long March: The Epic of Chinese Communism's Survival 1935* (New York: Viking Press, 1971), p. xiii.

2. Wilson, *The Long March*, pp. 226–227.

3. James Pinckney Harrison, *The Long March to Power: A History of the Chinese Communist Party, 1971–1972* (New York: Praeger, 1972), p. 246.

4. Jerome Ch'en, *Mao and the Chinese Revolution* (New York: Oxford University Press, 1967), p. 243. The figures in this paragraph also come from Ch'en, p. 245.

5. Letter from Ambassador C. E. Gauss to the Secretary of State enclosing copy of a dispatch from Everett F. Drumright, on detail in Shensi, March 27, 1944, in *Foreign Relations of the United States, Diplomatic Papers 1944*, 7 vols. (Washington, D.C.: Government Printing Office, 1967), 6 (China), p. 384.

6. Charles F. Romanus and Riley Sunderland, *United States in World War II, China-Burma-India Theatre: Time Runs Out in the CBI* (Washington, D.C.: Department of the Army, 1959), pp. 369–370.

7. Theodore White and Annalee Jacoby, *Thunder Out of China* (New York: William Sloane Associates, 1946), p. 133.

8. Chalmers Johnson, *Peasant Nationalism and Communist Power: The Emergence of Revolutionary China, 1937–1945* (Stanford: Stanford University Press, 1962), pp. 73–74 discusses the various estimates in detail.

9. Peter J. Seybolt, "The Yenan Revolution in Mass Education," *China Quarterly*, no. 48 (October–December, 1971): 649–650.

10. James Bertram, *Unconquered: Journal of a Year's Adventures Among the Fighting Peasants of North China* (New York: John Day Co., 1939), p. 105.

11. The quotation is from F. F. Liu, *A Military History of Modern China 1924–1949* (Princeton: Princeton University Press, 1956), p. 206. Lyman Van Slyke, *Enemies and Friends: The United Front in Chinese Communist History* (Stanford: Stanford University Press, 1967), pp. 157–159, concludes it is a fabrication. Arthur N. Young, *China and the Helping Hand 1937–1945* (Cambridge: Harvard University Press, 1963) p. 457, n. 12 expresses a widely held view when he argues that whether the statement is authentic or not it did reflect Communist policy.

12. David Roy, *Kuo Mo-jo: The Early Years* (Cambridge: Harvard University Press, 1971), p. 5.

13. U.S. Department of State, *United States Relations with China with Special Reference to the Period 1944–1949* (Washington, D.C.: Government Printing Office, 1949), p. 688.

Chapter IX

1. Memorandum to Secretary of State by Second Secretary of the Embassy, John Davies, January 15, 1944, in *Foreign Relations of the United States, Diplomatic Papers 1944,* 7 vols. (Washington, D.C.: Government Printing Office, 1967), 6 (China), pp. 307–308.

2. Mao Tse-tung, *Selected Works of Mao Tse-tung,* 4 vols. (London: Lawrence & Wishart, Ltd., 1954–1956), 4, p. 113.

3. Peter J. Seybolt, "The Yenan Revolution in Mass Education," *China Quarterly,* no. 48 (October–December, 1971): 657.

4. Chalmers Johnson, *Peasant Nationalism and Communist Power: The Emergence of Revolutionary China, 1937–1945* (Stanford: Stanford University Press, 1962), p. 151.

5. Letter from Ambassador C. E. Gauss to Secretary of State, Chungking, February 6, 1944, enclosing a dispatch from Everett F. Drumright, on detail in Sian, in *Foreign Relations of the United States, Diplomatic Papers 1944,* 6 (China), p. 338.

6. Lawrence Rosinger, *China's Crisis* (New York: Alfred Knopf, 1945), pp. 88–89.

7. Report by Second Secretary of Embassy in China, John S. Service, Yenan, July 28, 1944, in *Foreign Relations of the United States Diplomatic Papers 1944,* 6 (China), p. 518.

8. Report by Second Secretary Service, July 28, 1944, in *Foreign Relations of the United States Diplomatic Papers 1944,* 6 (China) p. 520.

9. Manfred Halpern, "The Revolution of Modernization in National and International Society," in *Revolution,* ed. Carl J. Friedrich (New York: Atherton Press, 1967), pp. 185–187.

10. David E. Apter, "Political Religion in the New Nations," in *Old Societies and New States: The Quest for Modernity in Asia and Africa,* ed. Clifford Geertz (New York: The Free Press, 1963), p. 62.

11. This process is reflected in much of the enormous literature on China since 1949, but C. K. Yang, "A Chinese Village in Early Communist Transition," in the combined reprint of two of Yang's volumes, *Chinese Society: The Family and the Village* (Cambridge: MIT Press, 1965), pp. 174–175, has a particularly relevant description of the ways in which a village in Kwangtung, where he did field work between 1949 and 1951, was integrated into the national political structure during that time.

Suggested Reading

WESTERNERS HAVE for many years been complaining about their "ignorance of China"—an ignorance that in no way can be predicated on a dearth of material. Even about the republican era, which has attracted less research interest than many other periods, innumerable books and articles are available in English. Every year diligent scholars cooperate with eager publishers to pour out more and more books on China. I have not attempted, therefore, to be comprehensive in the following list, but to include only a generous sampling of important and generally available works—mostly of recent date—relating to the major subjects and periods of the republican era. It is always difficult to categorize scholarly works. Does a study of industrial development in the 1930s, for example, go under "Nanking Decade" or "Economy"? Nevertheless, despite the inevitable ambiguity and overlap, I have organized my suggestions under a dozen rubrics, and I leave it to the reader's imagination to locate works of particular interest to him or her. Here are the twelve categories:

1. Reference Works, including bibliographies, biographical dictionaries, maps, translated materials
2. General and Miscellaneous Works, including surveys and studies of specialized aspects of Chinese history during the republican years
3. The Revolution of 1911
4. Warlordism

1. Reference

One of the most convenient bibliographies is by Charles Hucker, *China: A Critical Bibliography* (Tuscon: University of Arizona Press, 1962), because each work is described and appraised. However, many important publications have appeared since 1962, and Hucker's book needs updating, particularly for works relating to the republican period; only a portion of Hucker's list concerns that era. A much more comprehensive listing, also not limited to the republic, is Yuan Tung-li, *China in Western Literature: A Continuation of Cordier's Bibliotheca Sinica* (New Haven: Far Eastern Publications, 1958), which also includes works in German and French; of course, it also lacks works published since it appeared in 1958, a major shortcoming for republican materials. The most up-to-date bibliographical source is the annual bibliographic issue of the *Journal of Asian Studies,* which attempts to list all books and articles published during the preceding year.

The most comprehensive and readily available biographical dictionary is *Biographical Dictionary of Republican China* (New York: Columbia University Press, 1967–71), 4 vols., edited by Howard L. Boorman and Richard C. Howard.

A standard geography is George B. Cressey's *Land of the 500 Million* (New York: McGraw-Hill, 1955), and a convenient atlas, which includes maps for all periods of Chinese history, is Albert Herrmann's *An Historical and Commercial Atlas of China* (Cambridge: Harvard University Press, 1935), now in a new edition edited by Norton Ginsburg and titled *An Historical Atlas of China* (Chicago: Aldine Publishing Co., 1966).

A variety of translated documents, excerpts, and other materials have been published, such as the compilation by William Theodore De Bary and others entitled *Sources of Chinese Tradition* (New York: Columbia

University Press, 1960); it contains material translated from the Chinese relating to the full sweep of Chinese history, including the republic. John K. Fairbank and Ssu-yu Teng's, *China's Response to the West: A Documentary Survey, 1839–1923* (Cambridge: Harvard University Press, 1954) has material relevant to the first decade or so of the republic. Roger Pelissier, *The Awakening of China, 1793–1949* (London: Secker & Warburg, 1967) contains interesting excerpts from the writings of participants and observers of the modern Chinese transformation, many of which relate to republican China. Dun J. Li, *The Road to Communism: China Since 1912* (New York: Van Nostrand Reinhold Co., 1969) includes absorbing translations from Chinese sources. Milton J. T. Shieh, ed., *The Kuomintang: Selected Historical Documents, 1894–1969* (Jamaica, N.Y.: St. John's University Press, 1970) offers materials selected by a friend of the Kuomintang.

2. General and Miscellaneous Works

There are no survey political histories of the republican period specifically, but O. Edmund Clubb has covered it quite thoroughly in his larger survey, *Twentieth Century China* (New York: Columbia University Press, 1964). *Modern China's Search for a Political Form*, edited by Jack Gray (London: Oxford University Press, 1969) has several excellent essays about diverse aspects of the republic. A very stimulating and readable synthesis is Lucien Bianco's *Origins of the Chinese Revolution, 1915–1949* (Stanford: Stanford University Press, 1971). *Republican China: Nationalism, War, and the Rise of Communism, 1911–1949* (New York: Vintage Books, 1967), edited by Franz Schurmann and Orville Schell, is a collection of different kinds of material, mostly excerpted from larger works. Barbara W. Tuchman, *Stilwell and the American Experience in China, 1911–1945* (New York: Macmillan Co., 1970) looks at China during the republic period through the prism of American involvement. Ho Ping-ti and Tang Tsou have edited three excellent volumes of essays titled *China in Crisis;* the first book of volume one, *China's Heritage and the Communist Political System* (Chicago: University of Chicago Press, 1968) provides some enlightening essays about the republican period.

A number of studies of crucial aspects of modern Chinese history that relate largely, though not exclusively, to the republic are also on the market. Y. C. Wang's *Chinese Intellectuals and the West, 1872–1949* (Chapel Hill: University of North Carolina Press, 1966) examines the history of Chinese educated in foreign countries, but it also includes a

vast amount of documented and interesting information about many
facets of modern China; it is one of the most important single books on
the republican era. Chester C. Tan focuses on political thinkers in *Chinese Political Thought in the Twentieth Century* (Garden City, N.Y.:
Doubleday & Co., 1971). O. Briere, *Fifty Years of Chinese Philosophy,
1898–1948* (New York: (Praeger, 1965), translated from the 1949 French
edition, offers a brief sketch of major philosophers and trends. Chan
Wing-tsin provides still another emphasis in *Religious Trends in Modern
China* (New York: Columbia University Press, 1953). John De Francis,
in *Nationalism and Language Reform in China* (Princeton: Princeton
University Press, 1950), examines the history of attempts to alphabetize
the Chinese writing system, the technical problems involved, and the
relation of the attempts to nationalism. Ho Ping-ti has written an important study of a basic problem that affects all eras of modern Chinese
history: *Studies on the Population of China, 1368–1953* (Cambridge:
Harvard University Press, 1959).

3. The Revolution of 1911

Long neglected, this subject has recently been investigated by a new
generation of China scholars. The best single volume is *China in Revolution: The First Phase, 1900–1913* (New Haven: Yale University Press,
1968), edited by Mary Clabaugh Wright; it contains eleven well-re-
searched and perceptive essays on various aspects of the revolution. Two
informative studies on the intellectual dimensions of the revolutionary
movement are Mary Backus Rankin's *Early Chinese Revolutionaries:
Radical Intellectuals in Shanghai and Chekiang, 1902–1911* (Cambridge:
University Press, 1971), and Michael Gasster's *Chinese Intellectuals and
the Revolution of 1911: The Birth of Modern Chinese Radicalism*
(Seattle: University of Washington Press, 1969). Two studies of revolutionary leaders have recently appeared: Hsüeh Chün-tu's *Huang Hsing
and the Chinese Revolution* (Stanford: Stanford University Press, 1961),
a sympathetic and informative biography, and K. S. Liew's *Struggle for
Democracy: Sung Chiao-jen and the 1911 Chinese Revolution* (Berkeley
and Los Angeles: University of California Press, 1971), an enlightening
survey. A Chinese Communist official describes the revolution, and his
own participation in it, in *The Revolution of 1911: A Great Democratic
Revolution of China* (Peking: Foreign Languages Press, 1962), by Wu
Yu-chang. Ernest P. Young, "Nationalism, Reform, and Republican
Revolution: China in the Early Twentieth Century," in *Modern East
Asia: Essays in Interpretation*, edited by James B. Crowley, pp. 151–179
(New York: Harcourt, Brace & World, 1970), is a clear analysis of the

forces at work from the last years of the Ch'ing through Yuan Shih-k'ai's presidency.

4. Warlordism

Little work has been done in English on the warlords. Lucian Pye's pioneering Ph.D. dissertation, written some two decades ago, has recently been published: *Warlord Politics: Conflict and Coalition in the Modernization of Republican China* (New York: Praeger, 1971). C. Martin Wilbur offers a stimulating interpretation in "Military Separatism and the Process of Reunification under the Nationalist Regime, 1922–1937," in volume 1, book I of *China in Crisis: China's Heritage and the Communist Political System*, edited by Ho Ping-ti and Tang Tsou (Chicago: University of Chicago Press, 1968). Two biographies of warlords have appeared in book form: Donald G. Gillin, *Warlord: Yen Hsi-shan in Shansi Province, 1911–1949* (Princeton: Princeton University Press, 1967), and James E. Sheridan, *Chinese Warlord: The Career of Feng Yu-hsiang* (Stanford: Stanford University Press, 1966). Several unpublished dissertations concern the warlord era, and at least two books are now in preparation. Almost no research has been done on warlords during the Nanking decade. An exception is the work of Robert A. Kapp: *Szechwan and the Chinese Republic: Provincial Militarism and Central Power 1911–1938* (New Haven: Yale University Press, 1973). Franklin W. Houn examines central government institutions instead of warlords in *Central Government of China, 1912–1928* (Madison: University of Wisconsin Press, 1957).

5. The Intellectual Revolution

The most important single work in this category is the excellent and thorough study by Chow Tse-tsung, *The May Fourth Movement: Intellectual Revolution in Modern China* (Cambridge: Harvard University Press, 1960). *Reflections on the May Fourth Movement: A Symposium* (Cambridge: East Asian Research Center of Harvard University, 1972), edited by Benjamin I. Schwartz, contains a number of interesting essays about specific aspects of the movement. Some of the most enlightening work on this subject has been in the form of biographical studies. Jerome B. Grieder, *Hu Shih and the Chinese Renaissance: Liberalism in the Chinese Revolution, 1917–1937* (Cambridge: Harvard University Press, 1970) examines one of the giant figures of the Intellectual Revolution, and provides a stimulating discussion of the liberal movement in China. Charlotte Furth, *Ting Wen-chiang: Science and China's New Culture* (Cambridge: Harvard University Press, 1970) is an excellent intellectual biography. A more radical figure, the "first Marxist in China," is studied by Maurice Meisner, *Li Ta-chao and the Origins of Chinese Marxism* (Cambridge: Harvard University Press, 1967). An important literary figure of the time has been analyzed by David Tod Roy, *Kuo Mo-jo: The Early Years* (Cambridge: Harvard University Press, 1971). An exemplar of the new scholar class who emerged in the Intellectual Revolution has been studied by Laurence A. Schneider, *Ku Chieh-kang and China's New History: Nationalism and the Quest for Alternative Traditions* (Berkeley and Los Angeles: University of California Press, 1971). Huang Sung-k'ang's *Lu Hsün and the New Culture Movement of Modern China* (Amsterdam: Djambatan, 1957) deals with China's leading writer of that time.

John Dewey lectured in China for two years, and was an important force in the Intellectual Revolution. His lectures, which have never been published in English, have recently been translated from the Chinese and collected in *John Dewey Lectures in China, 1919–1920* (Honolulu: The University Press of Hawaii, 1973), translated and edited by Robert W. Clopton and Tsuin-chen Ou. D. W. Y. Kwok, *Scientism in Chinese Thought* (New Haven: Yale University Press, 1965) examines one of the chief themes of the New Thought in China. Liu Chun-jo's *Controversies in Modern Chinese Intellectual History: An Analytic Bibliography of Periodical Articles, Mainly of the May Fourth and Post-May Fourth Era* (Cambridge: East Asian Research Center of Harvard University, 1964) is useful not only as bibliography but as a source for trends in the intellectual history of China from about 1917 to the mid-1930s. Robert A. Scalapino and George T. Yu have studied an early stream of radicalism in China in *The Chinese Anarchist Movement* (Berkeley and Los Angeles: Center for Chinese Studies, University of California, 1961). A Chinese intellectual and official in the Nationalist Government, Chiang Mońliń, tells the story of his life in *Tides from the West: A Chinese Autobiography* (New Haven: Yale University Press, 1947).

Joseph R. Levenson brilliantly interpreted one of the earliest of the Westernized intellectuals in *Liang Ch'i-ch'ao and the Mind of Modern China* (Cambridge: Harvard University Press, 1959). Levenson has also written an extremely influential trilogy that deals with intellectual change in modern China generally, and it is as valuable for the republican era as for all other periods: *Confucian China and Its Modern Fate*, volume 1, *The Problem of Intellectual Continuity;* volume 2, *The Problem of Monarchical Decay;* volume 3, *The Problem of Historical Significance* (Berkeley and Los Angeles: University of California Press, 1958, 1964, 1965).

6. Coalition and Conflict in the 1920s

One of the great books to emerge from the revolution of the mid-1920s is Harold Isaacs's *The Tragedy of the Chinese Revolution*, originally published in England by Specker and Warburg in 1938, but since reissued in a 2nd revised edition (Stanford: Stanford University Press, 1961). A later version of the same years and subject is by Conrad Brandt, *Stalin's Failure in China, 1924–1927* (Cambridge: Harvard University Press, 1958). An indispensable collection of documents taken from the offices of the Russian military attaché in Peking, with enlightening introductory and explanatory remarks, is *Documents on Communism, Nationalism, and Soviet Advisers in China 1918–1927: Papers Seized in the 1927 Peking Raid* (New York: Columbia University Press, 1956), edited and with introductory essays by C. Martin Wilbur and Julie Lien-ying How. A Russian who worked as student interpreter in China during the mid-1920s recalls those eventful days in *Two Years in Revolutionary China, 1925–1927* (Cambridge: East Asian Research Center of Harvard University, 1971), by Vera Vladimirovna Vishnyakova-Akimova.

K. C. Yeh examines Communist peasant strategy during part of the twenties in *The Chinese Communist Revolutionary Strategy and the Land Problem, 1921–1927* (Santa Monica: The Rand Corp., 1970). Hsiao Tso-liang reviews the decisions and policies relating to urban and rural insurrection launched by the Communists during 1927 in *Chinese Communism in 1927: City vs Countryside* (Hong Kong: The Chinese University of Hong Kong, 1970). *M. N. Roy's Mission to China: The Communist-Kuomintang Split of 1927*, by Robert C. North and Xenia J. Eudin, with documents translated by Helen I. Powers, is a collection of documents and commentary relating to the critical events of 1927.

There is a high degree of overlap between the 1920s and other categories in these Suggested Readings. For example, under Economy, Jean Chesneaux's *The Chinese Labor Movement, 1919–1927* (Stanford: Stanford University Press, 1968) contains much information about non-economic aspects of those years. A number of the works listed under Warlordism, Chinese Communism, and The Intellectual Revolution also treat the 1920s in detail.

7. The Nanking Decade

The ten years from 1928 to 1937 have been the subject of more partisan debate than solid research, though more objective analyses are now beginning to appear. Lloyd Eastman has written an important study of the decade which will soon be published. Part of Eastman's work has appeared in the form of an article, "Fascism in Kuomintang China: The Blue Shirts," *China Quarterly*, No. 49 (January–March, 1972): 1–31. Tien Hung-mao, *Government and Politics in Kuomintang China, 1927–1937* (Stanford: Stanford University Press, 1972) offers a splendid analysis of Kuomintang administrative and political institutions. Arthur N. Young, former financial adviser to the Chinese Government, has written a study of economic matters during that decade: *China's Nation-Building Effort, 1927–1937: The Financial and Economic Record* (Stanford: Hoover Institution Press, 1971). A collection of essays, many written by ex-Nationalist officials, is in *The Strenuous Decade: China's Nation-Building Efforts, 1927–1937*, edited by Paul K. T. Sih (Jamaica, N.Y.: St. John's University Press, 1970). Ch'ien Tuan-sheng, *The Government and Politics of China* (Cambridge: Harvard University Press, 1950) analyzes the theory, practice, and structure of Kuomintang government. *Student Nationalism in China, 1927–1937* (Stanford: Stanford University Press, 1966) by John Israel traces student involvement in politics during the Nanking decade. James C. Thompson, Jr., *While China Faced West: American Reformers in Nationalist China, 1928–1937* (Cambridge: Harvard University Press, 1969) focuses on American reformers but includes much material about the Nanking government and its programs.

Sun Yat-sen died in 1925, but his ideas ostensibly guided the Kuomintang during the Nanking decade, when Chiang Kai-shek was the man in charge. Surprisingly, little reliable biographical material about either of these two men, especially Chiang is available. The standard biography of Sun Yat-sen has long been Lyon Sharman's *Sun Yat-sen, His Life and Its Meaning: A Critical Biography* (New York: John Day Co., 1934); but Harold Schiffrin is now producing a more comprehensive, multivolume work that will probably become the definitive biography of Sun for some time; the first volume has been published: *Sun Yat-sen and the Origins of the Chinese Revolution* (Berkeley and Los Angeles: University of California Press, 1968). The basic translation of Sun's most important doctrinal statements has been done by Frank W. Price, *San Min Chu I: The Three Principles of the People,* published by the China Committee, Institute of Pacific Relations, 1927. This book has been the basis for many later publications on Sun's statements, including drastically cut versions of them; those interested in the fullest expression of Sun's thinking should be sure to obtain an uncut translation. A very useful source on Sun's thinking is the volume of several translations of his key works by Leonard Shihlien Hsu, *Sun Yat-sen: His Political and Social Ideas, A Source Book* (Los Angeles: University of Southern California Press, 1933). Paul Myron Anthony Linebarger, *The Political Doctrines of Sun Yat-sen: An Exposition of San Min Chu I* (Baltimore: The Johns Hopkins Press, 1937) is informative and sympathetic. Marius B. Jansen has explored an important and revealing aspect of Sun's career in *The*

Japanese and Sun Yat-sen (Cambridge: Harvard University Press, 1954).

A number of hagiographies of Chiang Kai-shek exist, but virtually no attempts at scholarly biography. The chief exception is Pichon P. Y. Loh's *The Early Chiang Kai-shek: A Study of His Personality and Politics, 1887–1924* (New York: Columbia University Press, 1971). A very useful translation of some of Chiang's most important statements is in his *China's Destiny and China's Economic Theory* (New York: Roy Publishers, 1947), with notes and commentary by Philip Jaffe. See also Chiang's *Soviet Russia in China: A Summing Up at Seventy* (New York: Farrar, Straus and Cudahy, 1957).

8. Chinese Communism

There is an enormous mass of material on this subject, and I will list here only a very few titles that relate specifically to the period of the republic. One of the best surveys of the development of Communism in China to the end of World War II is *The Chinese Communist Movement: A Report of the United States War Department, July 1945*, edited by Lyman Van Slyke (Stanford: Stanford University Press, 1968); despite all the research that has been done since 1945, this book remains a lucid and thorough summary. A more recent survey, which offers much more detail, is Jacques Guillermaz, *A History of the Chinese Communist Party, 1921–1949* (London: Methuen & Co., 1972), a translation of a work that first appeared in French in 1968. Jerome Ch'en, *Mao and the Chinese Revolution* (New York: Oxford University Press, 1967) is a clear and useful history of the Communist revolution to 1949, and includes translations of 37 poems by Mao Tse-tung. *A Documentary History of Chinese Communism*, edited by Conrad Brandt, Benjamin Schwartz, and John K. Fairbank (Cambridge: Harvard University Press, 1952), contains 40 important documents spanning the years 1921–1950, and the introductory comments constitute a kind of mini-history of the Communist movement during that period.

Benjamin Schwartz's *Chinese Communism and the Rise of Mao* (Cambridge: Harvard University Press, 1951), is a pioneering study that is still very useful. Chang Kuo-t'ao, one of the founding members of the Communist Party who later broke with Mao, has published his detailed autobiography in two volumes: *The Rise of the Chinese Communist Party 1921–1927*, and *The Rise of the Chinese Communist Party 1928–1938* (Lawrence: The University Press of Kansas, 1971, 1972); these are important and revealing volumes. John E. Rue's *Mao Tse-tung in Opposition, 1927–1935* (Stanford: Stanford University Press, 1966) deals with the years when Mao was at odds with the party leadership. Derek J. Waller, *The Kiangsi Soviet Republic: Mao and the National Congresses of 1931 and 1934* (Berkeley and Los Angeles: Center for

Chinese Studies, University of California, 1973) offers many insights and much good information about the little-known period of the Soviet Republic. Dick Wilson, *The Long March, 1935: The Epic of Chinese Communism's Survival* (New York: Viking Press, 1971) summarizes all the important information available about the pride of Communist history, the Long March.

One of the most important books about Chinese Communism is by Chalmers A. Johnson, *Peasant Nationalism and Communist Power: The Emergence of Revolutionary China, 1937–1945* (Stanford: Stanford University Press, 1961), which examines the social mobilization of the Chinese peasantry during the anti-Japanese war. It should be read in conjunction with Donald Gillin's article " 'Peasant Nationalism' in the History of Chinese Communism," *Journal of Asian Studies* 23, no. 2 (February, 1964): 269–289; Gillin persuasively argues that Johnson underestimated the appeal of Communist social programs to Chinese peasants. Mark Selden, *The Yenan Way in Revolutionary China* (Cambridge: Harvard University Press, 1971) examines a Communist base area, and the significance of the evolution of the mass line. Boyd Compton's *Mao's China: Party Reform Documents, 1942–44* (Seattle: University of Washington Press, 1952) offers translations regarding, and a lucid introduction to, the first great rectification movement in Chinese Communism.

A fascinating and important source of information about the Communist movement is the great body of writing by foreign visitors who watched the Communists firsthand. The most valuable of these is certainly *Red Star over China* (New York: Random House, 1938), Edgar Snow's great and absorbing classic of the Chinese Revolution. The same author's *Random Notes on Red China* (1936–1945) (Cambridge: Chinese Economic and Political Studies at Harvard University, 1957) is informed and insightful. Kenneth E. Shewmaker, *Americans and Chinese Communists, 1927–1945: A Persuading Encounter* (Ithaca: Cornell University Press, 1971) concentrates on the writings of Americans about China, and in the process illuminates aspects of the Chinese Communist appeal. Two books based on personal experience provide fascinating detail about the Communist-led social revolution in the countryside during the 1940s: *Revolution in a Chinese Village Ten Mile Inn*, by Isabel and David Crook (London: Routledge and Kegan Paul, 1959); and *Fanshen: A Documentary of Revolution in a Chinese Village*, by William Hinton (New York: Monthly Review Press, 1966).

9. The United Front and Civil War

Lyman P. Van Slyke's authoritative study of the United Front, *Enemies and Friends: The United Front in Chinese Communist History* (Stanford: Stanford University Press, 1967) includes much material relevant to general political problems of the 1930s and 1940s T. A. Bisson, *Yenan in June 1937: Talks with Communist Leaders* (Berkeley and Los Angeles: Center for Chinese Studies, University of California, 1973) summarizes interview answers by Mao Tse-tung, Chou En-lai, and other Communist leaders at a time when the United Front was taking shape. Two books have recently appeared on the Sino-Japanese War and collaboration: Gerald E. Bunker, *The Peace Conspiracy: Wang Ching-wei and the China War, 1937–1941* (Cambridge: Harvard University Press, 1972), and John Hunter Boyle, *China and Japan at War, 1937–1945: The Politics of Collaboration* (Stanford: Stanford University Press, 1972). Journalist James Bertram, conscious of the integrative significance of the anti-Japanese war, reveals it in his report on travels through Shansi in 1937: *Unconquered: Journal of a Year's Adventures Among the Fighting Peasants of North China* (New York: John Day Co., 1939). David Barrett describes his observations and recollections as commander of a mission to Yenan in 1944 in *Dixie Mission: The United States Army Observer Group in Yenan, 1944* (Berkeley and Los Angeles: Center for Chinese Studies, University of California, 1970).

The failure of the Kuomintang is shown in a collection of essays, documents, and excerpts edited by Pichon P. Y. Loh, *The Kuomintang Debacle of 1949: Collapse or Conquest?* (Lexington, Mass.: D. C. Heath & Co., 1965). A dramatic and moving account of conditions in Kuomintang China is Theodore H. White and Annalee Jacoby's *Thunder out of China* (New York: William Sloane Associates, 1946). Two views of the disastrous Kuomintang inflation are: Chou Shun-hsin, *The Chinese Inflation, 1937–1949* (New York: Columbia University Press, 1963), which is a professional economist's view of the economic aspects of the inflation; and Arthur N. Young, *China's Wartime Finance and Inflation, 1937–1945* (Cambridge: Harvard University Press, 1965). Young, financial adviser to the Nanking government, also examines foreign aid in China during the war years in *China and the Helping Hand, 1937–1945* (Cambridge: Harvard University Press, 1963). Carsun Chang, *The Third Force in China* (New York: Bookman Associates, 1952) details the author's participation in Communist-Kuomintang negotiations before and after World War II.

A detailed account of the military aspects of the civil war is presented by Lionel Max Chassin in *The Communist Conquest of China: A History of the Civil War, 1945–1949* (Cambridge: Harvard University Press, 1965). F. F. Liu, *A Military History of Modern China: 1924–1949* (Princeton: Princeton University Press, 1956) is a good treatment of the subject, and reveals much about the political and social aspects of the last two decades of the republican era.

Jack Belden, *China Shakes the World* (New York: Monthly Review Press, 1970), originally published in 1949, is one of the classic descriptions of the last years of the civil war. The Superintendent of Documents published America's White Paper on China in 1949: *United States Relations with China, with Special Reference to the Period 1944–1949*, based on files of the Department of State. This enormously useful volume of text and documents relating to the civil war period was reprinted in 1967 in an indexed edition by Stanford University Press. Graham Peck, *Two Kinds of Time* (Boston: Houghton Mifflin Co., 1950) consists of the very readable and wide-ranging observations of a sensitive and sympathetic observer of the China scene. A. Doak Barnett, *China on the Eve of Communist Takeover* (New York: Frederick A. Praeger, 1963) contains more than 20 field reports that Barnett wrote from various parts of China during the last two or three years of the republican period. Derk Bodde was also in China in the last days of the Kuomintang, and has described that period, and the first months of Communist rule in Peking, in *Peking Diary: A Year of Revolution* (New York: Henry Schuman, 1950).

10. Society

Olga Lang examines the family, with particular emphasis on the republican period, in *Chinese Family and Society* (New Haven: Yale University Press, 1946). *Family and Kinship in Chinese Society*, edited by Maurice Freedman (Stanford: Stanford University Press, 1970), offers 10 essays on the family in late Ch'ing and republican China. In 1959, C. K. Yang published two volumes: *The Chinese Family in the Communist Revolution* and *A Chinese Village in Early Communist Transition;* both works are excellent on the disintegration of China during the republican period and have been republished by MIT Press, 1965, in a single volume: *Chinese Communist Society: The Family and the Village.* Fei Hsiao-tung, *China's Gentry: Essays in Rural-Urban Relations* (Chicago: University of Chicago Press, 1953) illuminates the nature of the gentry during the republic. Among other publications by the same author are two fine studies of the peasantry: *Peasant Life in China: A Field Study of Country Life in the Yangtze Valley* (London: Kegan Paul, Trench, Trubner & Co., 1939), and, together with Chang Chih-i, *Earthbound China: A Study of Rural Economy in Yunnan* (Chicago: University of Chicago Press, 1945). Francis L. K. Hsu has recently expanded his important 1948 study: *Under the Ancestor's Shadow: Kinship, Personality, and Social Mobility in Village China* (Garden City, N.Y.: Doubleday & Co., 1967).

11. Economy

Among other things, the paucity of data has inhibited economic research for the republican period, especially the early years. Nonetheless, some important work has been done for the Nanking decade and has been listed under that heading. Studies of broader scope also exist, and one of the most seminal of recent years is G. William Skinner's "Marketing and Social Structure in Rural China," which appeared in three successive issues of the *Journal of Asian Studies* 24, nos. 1, 2, 3 (November, 1964; February, 1965; May, 1965). John K. Chang, "Industrial Development of Mainland China, 1912–1949," *Journal of Economic History* 27, no. 1 (March, 1967): 56–81 summarizes findings about industrial growth on the basis of 15 selected commodities. Chang's later study, *Industrial Development in Pre-Communist China* (Chicago: Aldine Publishing Co., 1969) is more comprehensive and shows the surprising industrial growth that took place. A very good, readable, and brief survey is Albert Feuerwerker's *The Chinese Economy, 1912–1949* (Ann Arbor: Center for Chinese Studies, Michigan Papers in Chinese Studies, No. 1, 1968). A broad survey of agriculture in China before, during, and after the republic is the clear and useful study by Dwight H. Perkins, *Agricultural Development in China, 1368–1968* (Chicago: Aldine Publishing Co., 1969). Ramon H. Myers, *The Chinese Peasant Economy: Agricultural Development in Hopei and Shantung, 1890–1949* (Cambridge: Harvard University Press, 1970) is a thorough and path-breaking study. Jean Chesneaux's *The Chinese Labor Movement, 1919–1927* (Stanford: Stanford University Press, 1968) is also an important work on the Chinese economy. Two books that challenge old interpretations about the effects of Western imperialism on the Chinese economy are Jack M. Potter, *Capitalism and the Chinese Peasant: Social and Economic Change in a Hong Kong Village* (Berkeley and Los Angeles: University of California Press, 1968), and Hou Chi-ming, *Foreign Investment and Economic Development in China, 1840–1937* (Cambridge: Harvard University Press, 1965).

12. Literature

Literature offers a superb entrée into the life and problems of modern China. C. T. Hsia, *A History of Modern Chinese Fiction*, 2nd ed. (New Haven: Yale University Press, 1971) is a good introduction to the chief trends and writers. A. C. Scott, *Literature and the Arts in Twentieth Century China* (Garden City, N.Y.: Doubleday & Co., 1963) is a much briefer treatment of a broader subject. Hsia Tsi-an, *The Gate of Darkness: Studies on the Leftist Literary Movement in China* (Seattle: University of Washington Press, 1968) contains six extremely interesting essays on men and trends in modern Chinese literature.

There are many translations of Chinese literary work available and their quality varies. C. T. Hsia, with the assistance of Joseph S. M. Lau, has edited a good collection of fiction: *Twentieth-Century Chinese Stories* (New York: Columbia University Press, 1971). Wang Chi-chen translated stories by many of China's best writers between 1918 and 1937, but especially the last decade of that period, in *Contemporary Chinese Stories* (New York: Columbia University Press, 1944; reprinted Westport, Conn.: Greenwood Press, 1968). Wang translated another collection in *Stories of China at War* (New York: Columbia University Press, 1947), and still another by the acknowledged dean of twentieth-century Chinese writers, Lu Hsün: *Ah Q and Others: Selected Stories of Lusin* (New York: Columbia University Press, 1941). The Foreign Languages Press in Peking has put out three volumes of translated selections from Lu Hsün: *Selected Works of Lu Hsün* (1956–1959).

Lau Shaw's novel *Rickshaw Boy* (New York: Reynal & Hitchcock, 1945) has been popular in the West. *Spring Silkworms and Other Stories* by Mao Tun (Peking: Foreign Languages Press, 1956) is a collection of 13 stories, most of which deal with life in China during the Nanking decade. The same author's *Midnight* (Peking: Foreign Languages Press, 1957) is a novel written in the early 1930s about contemporary Shanghai bourgeoisie. Pa Chin's *The Family* (Peking: Foreign Languages Press, 1958), is an important book of the republican era, but the edition published by Anchor Books in 1972 includes portions omitted from the earlier translation. Olga Lang has studied Pa Chin and his work in *Pa Chin and His Writings Chinese Youth Between Two Revolutions* (Cambridge: Harvard University Press, 1967).

Two novels by foreigners are well worth reading. Pearl Buck's *The Good Earth* (New York: John Day Company, 1933) deserves its long popularity, and *The Sand Pebbles* (New York and Evanston: Harper & Row, 1962) by Richard McKenna is a revealing novel about U.S. Navy men in China in the mid-1920s.

Hsu Kai-yu, has translated and edited *Twentieth Century Chinese Poetry* (New York: Doubleday & Co., 1963).

INDEX

Printed in the United States
142295LV00002B/4/A